Economic Democracy

Workers' Participation in Chilean Industry

1970–1973

JUAN G. ESPINOSA

Development Programming Division
Organization of American States
Washington, D. C.

ANDREW S. ZIMBALIST

Department of Economics
Smith College
Northampton, Massachusetts

ACADEMIC PRESS New York San Francisco London

A Subsidiary of Harcourt Brace Jovanovich, Publishers

ACADEMIC PRESS, INC.
111 Fifth Avenue, New York, New York 10003

United Kingdom Edition published by
ACADEMIC PRESS, INC. (LONDON) LTD.
24/28 Oval Road, London NW1   7DX

Library of Congress Cataloging in Publication Data

Espinosa, Juan G.
    Economic democracy

    (Studies in social discontinuity)
    Bibliography: p.
    Includes index.
    1. Employees' representation in management--
Chile. I. Zimbalist, Andrew S., joint author.
II. Title. III. Series.
HD5660.C5E76   1978   658.31'52'0983 77-6594
ISBN 0-12-242750-5

PRINTED IN THE UNITED STATES OF AMERICA

To our fathers,

CARLOS ESPINOSA

SAMUEL ZIMBALIST

Contents

List of Tables   ix

List of Figures   xi

Foreword   xiii

Preface   xv

Glossary of Acronyms   xvii

1   Introduction   1

What Is Worker Participation?   1

The Purposes of the Study   7

Formulation of the Hypotheses   9

Plan of the Study   10

2   Worker Alienation and Worker Participation in Capitalist and Socialist Countries: An Overview   13

Introduction   13

Alienation, Scientific Management, and the Capitalist Work Process   14

Some Consequences of Alienated Labor   18

The Limits of Work Humanization and Worker Participation under Capitalism   20

Socialism and Workers' Control   24

3   The Chilean Context   29

Introduction   29

The Industrial Structure of Chile   33

The Chilean Labor Movement   34

Experience with Worker Participation prior to 1970   38

4   An Overview of the Reforms Concerning Worker Participation   45

Introduction   45
Formation of the Sector of Social Ownership (APSM)   46
The Basic Norms of Participation   50

5   An Index of Worker Participation: Methodology and Mechanics   57

The Construction of Our Index of Participation   57
The Resulting Values and the Reliability of the Index   63
The Structural Components of Participation—Behavioral Characteristics of Our Index   67

APPENDIX I   Brief Description of the Survey   70
APPENDIX II   The Weighting Procedure and the Point System of the Index of
Worker Participation   74
APPENDIX III   Alphabetical List of Enterprises Surveyed   82

6   Analysis of the Factors Affecting Participation   83

The Technostructure   85
The Labor Force   95
The Intermediate Variables   114
Factor Analysis and Emerging Causal Model   117

APPENDIX I   Correlation Matrixes of Tables 6.2, 6.3, 6.5, 6.7, 6.8, and 6.10   120
APPENDIX II   Factor Analysis Data   123

**7   The Influence of Worker Participation on Enterprise
     Performance   127**

Introduction   127
Social Changes   129
Changes in Economic Performance   141

8   Commentaries and General Conclusions   177

Some Preliminary Considerations   177
Specific Conclusions   180
More General Considerations and Conclusions   186

Postscript   191

References   195

Index   209

List of Tables

2.1	The Evolution of the United States Labor Force	17
3.1	Level of Unionization in Chile, by Economic Sector, 1968	31
3.2	Income Distribution by Quintiles for Total Industrial Sector, Chile	32
3.3	Distribution of Industrial Concentration, Chile, 1963	33
3.4	Number of Industrial Firms and Industrial Workers	36
3.5	Number of Strikes, per Year, 1911–1924	37
3.6	IANSA Labor Contract Negotiations, 1962–1969	40
4.1	Interventions and Requisitions	49
5.1	Summary of Point System: Maximum Final Score	62
5.2	Relative Levels of Worker Participation in Firms (P_F): Partial and Total Results According to Scores and Categories	64
5.3	Correlation Coefficients between Central Components of Index	66
5.4	Levels and Areas of Participation	68
5.5	Levels of Participation and Time	69
5.6	Universe and Sample Breakdown of Distributional Characteristics	72
5.7	Cross-Distribution Ratio of Percentage in Universe to Percentage in Final Sample	73
5.8	Index Construction: Structure of Participation	75
5.9	Instances of Participation: Characteristics of Measures	76
5.10	Characteristics of Structure and Content Measures	77
5.11	Index Construction: Content of Participation	78
6.1	Variables Used in the Analysis	84
6.2	Technology and Participation	93
6.3	Technology and Organizational Structure	94
6.4	Organizational Structure and Participation	95
6.5	Education and Participation with Control Variables	101
6.6	Labor Mobilization and Participation	104
6.7	Political Parties and Participation	107
6.8	Union Attitude, Ideology, and Participation	111
6.9	Technology, Political Variables, and Participation	113
6.10	Disposition of the Administration and Participation	115

6.11	Information and Exogenous Political Variables, plus *DISPAD*	116
6.12	Participation and Strongest Explanatory Variables	117
6.13	Factor Analysis of Worker Participation	120
6.14	Correlation Matrix of Table 6.2	120
6.15	Correlation Matrix of Table 6.3	121
6.16	Correlation Matrix of Table 6.5	122
6.17	Correlation Matrix of Table 6.7	122
6.18	Correlation Matrix of Table 6.8	122
6.19	Correlation Matrix of Table 6.10	122
6.20	Varimax Rotated Factor Matrix	123
6.21	Factor Score Matrix	123
6.22	Factors with Eigenvalues Greater Than 1	125
7.1	Percentage of Workers Taking Courses in 1970, by Level of Skill	133
7.2	Work Organization, Technology, and Participation	137
7.3	Production Quality and Participation	147
7.4	Innovation and Participation	151
7.5	Workers' Opinions Concerning the Effects of the Introduction of New Modern Machines	153
7.6	Chile: Sources of Investment in the Private Sector	154
7.7	Investment, Participation, and Other Variables	157
7.8	Productivity, Participation, and Other Variables	163
7.9	Productivity and Participation, Controlling for Factors of Production and Demand	164
7.10	Productivity, Participation, and Technology	166
7.11	Productivity, Participation, and Wage Structure	170
7.12	Intermediate Variables and Variables of Results	172

List of Figures

1.1   Model of interdependence and expected causality between the variables.   9
4.1   The participating individuals and groups according to the *normas básicas*.   53
5.1   Worker participation in connection with participatory councils.   59
5.2   Distribution of participation index by categories.   67
7.1   Change in absenteeism and the level of participation.   145
7.2   Schematic representation of the interaction of participation and productivity.   171

Foreword

For 200 years people have been trying to counteract the impersonal and often cruel forces of industrial society. One consistent theme has been people's yearning to organize democratically in a community of work. Besides the natural and ever-increasing ability of capitalism to defend itself against competing forms, and equally potent obstacles to the formation of self-managed enterprises and creation of economically democratic systems, has been the ignorance of social, economic and political forces which would be favorable to self-management and economic democracy.

The forms of democracy and self-determination in the economic sphere are extremely varied, whether we look at them from the point of view of historical experience or as theorists. Among them, only a limited number are sufficiently viable or strong to survive, and perhaps in the distant future to supersede the industrial systems of today.

The nature of work has been continually transformed through time. In pretrade and no surplus societies, work was not conceived as a separate activity but rather was embedded in other social relationships. In nascent capitalist societies work was primarily carried out by small producers working for their own account. The worker was the master of the production process. As capitalism evolved, however, the self-employed farmer or craft producer gave way to the wage laborer, and with the development of mass production technology the worker has gradually been separated from the exercise of craft skills and the decision-making process. The normal condition of the worker today in both the developed and the underdeveloped world is as a replaceable part in or as an appendage to the production process.

An activity absorbing at least half of an individual's waking hours cannot help but exert a strong formative influence on human development. An unfulfilled and nonparticipatory worker is also an unfulfilled and nonparticipatory citizen. The seemingly inexorable march of technology has brought human civilization close to both self-destruction and self-realization. If technological change were to be consciously harnessed by society to serve social priorities democratically rather

than motivated by callous profit maximization, many of the social specters haunting us today would disappear.

An appropriate place to initiate this change is at the point of production, at the workplace itself. A new conception of work is needed. The last 100 years has witnessed dozens of examples of workers struggling to control their own work lives—many abortive, many successful but short-lived, and a few successful lingering on in isolation. Each struggle, however, has contributed to a vision of a more egalitarian and democratic work life. One such struggle affected the working class and the peasantry of an entire country just a few years ago. The lessons to be gleaned from the Chilean experience with workers' control during the period 1970–1973 are particularly significant due to its widespread application, profound scope, and contemporary context.

Economic Democracy is a unique and comprehensive record of this experience. It is important reading for all concerned with the humane reorganization of economic life. Espinosa and Zimbalist portray, through an extensive first-hand study, the process of enterprise democratization in a thoroughness, depth, and complexity not attained in previous studies in the area of worker participation. The authors analyze the interaction of social, political, technological, and economic variables in a manner which clarifies the failures and successes of past experiments with worker participation and the prospects for its future implementation. The study at once appeals both to social scientists in offering a new, systematic methodology for future investigation and to practitioners and lay readers in presenting lively, interpretive accounts and quotations from the workers involved.

In *Economic Democracy* I see a monument, however modest, to the struggle of Chilean workers which no domestic or foreign power will be able to take away from them. It is also a document for the future which, in my view more than any other empirical study, identifies the most promising strains of a new species of socioeconomic organization.

Jaroslav Vanek

Preface

During the eighteenth century, the liberal democratic revolutions gave life to the aspirations of freedom, equality, and citizen participation in the political sphere. In the nineteenth century, a natural extension of these concepts appeared in the demand that individuals be free to participate actively in decision making relating to the social and economic affairs of the society as well. This demand, adopted by the international socialist movement during the last century, has emerged spontaneously in all workers' uprisings and revolutions in this century.

In recent years, there has been a notable shift in the priorities of the labor movements in Western Europe, away from higher wages and the simple modification of working conditions, toward more worker participation and control. On January 26, 1977, the Bullock Committee, an official British government body, delivered a report recommending equal stockholder and worker representation on the boards of directors of major corporations in the United Kingdom. The majority report stated that labor representation in the boardroom was the wave of the present. A week and a half later something approaching a general strike swept the Netherlands where one of the major worker demands was increased participation in decision making. And in 1976 new legislation was passed in West Germany and Sweden extending worker participation.

What factors account for this surge of interest in industrial democracy? Are the United States, the Third World, and socialist nations affected by the same factors? How significant are these recent changes and where will they lead? If meaningful worker participation is implemented, what will the economic, political, and social effects be?

This book is about the 1970–1973 Chilean experience with worker participation at the enterprise level. One of the major and most interesting reforms of the Allende government in Chile, the first elected socialist government in the western hemisphere, was the creation of a large socialized sector of the economy. Into this sector, a system of worker participation was introduced. We endeavor to locate the Chilean case within the context of other experiments with worker participation and to explore in depth the background, the process—its limitations

and successes—and the implications of the Chilean experience.

The basic motivation of our study is twofold. First, the process of sociopolitical change in Chile and elsewhere has been all too typically analyzed with an exclusively global focus—concentrating on forces operating at the national and international level and paying little attention to the role of and effect on the common citizen or the producer. Undoubtedly, the struggle for individual emancipation and social change will not be realized at the level of the enterprise until there exists a political vision and organization which embraces the entire society. Yet at the same time a movement for broader democracy in the society cannot produce more than technical and empty structural reforms if it is not accompanied by an active involvement from the base.

Second, we feel that previous studies of experiences with industrial democracy have been primarily journalistic in character, usually referring to isolated experiments in individual enterprises. In this study, we develop and apply a concrete methodology for empirical investigation of this subject, taking as a whole the process of worker participation which affected the major factories of the industrial sector of the Chilean economy.

The reader will find that our presentation contains some technical material in Chapters 5 through 7. However, this material is at the same time verbally described in a manner we hope will be accessible to the reader without a sophisticated technical background.

We were fortunate to be living in Chile during the years 1970–1973 and to be able to observe the functioning of the socialized enterprises first hand. As the reader will appreciate, the circumstances and dimensions of our study required the cooperation and encouragement of many individuals. We wish to thank the following individuals for the invaluable stimulation, critical commentary, and support they provided during the various stages of elaboration of the present work: Sergio Bitar, Sam Bowles, Tom Davis, Valeria F. Espinosa, Ramón Fernández, Pedro Guglielmetti, Albert Hirschman, Hilda McArthur, Fernanda Navarro, Lydia Nettler, James Petras, Moira Tierney, Joaquín Undurraga, Luis Valencia, and Jaroslav Vanek. The authors accept full responsibility for the material presented herein; it does not represent the opinions of our affiliated institutions.

Glossary of Acronyms

Terms and Organizations

APSM—*Area de Propiedad Social y Mixta* or the *social area*

CORFO—*Corporación de Fomento de la Producción,* state development agency

CUT—*Central Unica de Trabajadores,* national labor confederation during Allende

FOCH—*Federación Obrera de Chile,* first national labor confederation in Chile

I.L.O. (O.I.T., in Spanish)—International Labor Organization

INACAP—*Instituto de Capacitación,* national training institute

MAPU—*Movimiento de Acción Popular Unitaria* (Movement of Unified Popular Action), political party in UP coalition

ODEPLAN—*Oficina de Planificcación,* state planning agency

UP—*Unidad Popular* (Popular Unity), Allende's governing coalition

Variables[1]

AP—Participation in administrative, social, and personnel problems

AUTOGOV—Autonomy in operation of enterprise from government

AUTOPL—Autonomy in operation of particular plant from overall enterprise

AVGR—Average remuneration

C—Content of participation

CE—Participation in control and evaluation

CH.DISCI.—Change in worker discipline

CH.P.R.S.—Change away from piece-rate system

CH.W.DISP.—Percentage change in differential between highest and lowest wage

COLL.BON.—Presence of collective bonuses

COMPMGR—Competence of management

COND—Change in work conditions by section

DCR.ABSENT.—Decrease in absenteeism

DEF.PROD.—Inverse of percentage change in defective products and thefts

DIFFBW—Difference in white- and blue-collar worker appraisals of level of participation

DISPAD—Disposition of the administration toward participation

DISTC—Change in product distribution system

DM—Participation in decision making

EFP—Participation in economic and financial problems

[1]Unless otherwise specified, variables refer to the enterprise.

ELSUP—Elimination of supervisors by section
EMPLC—Percentage change in employment
EX—Participation in execution
FCOR—same as *INCR.EDUC.*
FINGD—Finished good
HDIF—Horizontal differentiation
INCR.EDUC.—Training or instruction of workers in factory sponsored courses since socialization
INFO—Information
INNOV—Innovations and improvements
INVEST—Investment
JENL—Job enlargement by section
JROT—Job rotation by section
L_1—Level 1 of participation
L_2—Level 2 of participation
L_3—Level 3 of participation
LIM.FAC.—Economic factors limiting production
LMOB—Labor mobilization
$LMOB_1$—Form of socialization
$LMOB_2$—Strike activity prior to socialization
LOPC—Line of product change
NO.SHIFTS—Number of shifts
ORIG.W.DISP—Highest to lowest wage differential before socialization
PARHOM—Percentage votes for largest party in factory
PARORD—Party ordering
PCPCD—Weighted sum of *PCTCD* and *PCTCP*
PCTAD—Percentage administrative workers in enterprise employment
PCTCD—Percentage votes for Christian Democratic party
PCTCP—Percentage votes for Communist party
PCTPTA—Percentage administrative, technical, and professional workers in enterprise employment
PCTSK—Percentage skilled workers in enterprise employment
P_F—Participation index for firm
PRDUM—Technological typology using dummy weights with respect to productivity
PROD—Percentage change in productivity (annual)
P_s—Participation index for section
RE.NO.W.G.—Reduction in number of wage grades
S—Structure of participation
SIZE—Size of firm (number of employees)
SLID—Section leader ideology
SOCSER—Increases in social services
SPANC—Span of control
STRIKE—Strike activity after socialization
TCOMP—Technological complexity (percentage maintenance workers)
TDUM—Technological typology using dummy weights with respect to P_F
TDUMS—Technological typology using dummy weights with respect to P_s.
TIME—Time in social area
TINT—Technological intensity (capital–labor ratio)
TP—Participation in technical and production problems
TPL_3—Participation in technical and production problems at Level 3
TTYP—Technological typology
TTYPS—Technological typology by section
UNAGE—Average age of unions in enterprise

UNATID—Weighted sum of *UNID* and *UNATT*
UNATT—Union attitude toward participation
UNID—Union leader ideology
UNNO—Number of unions in enterprise
VDIF—Vertical differentiation

Economic Democracy

Workers' Participation in Chilean Industry
1970–1973

1

Introduction

"Que suis-je, si je ne participe pas?"
—Antoine de Saint-Exupery

"Without work all life goes rotten. But when work is soulless, life stifles and dies."
—Albert Camus

"Moreover, moving in the direction set by our predecessors, we also feel that the aspiration to actively participate in the life of enterprises they form part of and work in is legitimate in workers .... the exercise of responsibility by workers in productive organizations, besides responding to the legitimate claims peculiar to human nature, is also in harmony with historical development in the economic, social and political fields."
—Pope John XXIII, Encyclical
"Mater et Magistra," 1961

WHAT IS WORKER PARTICIPATION?

Worker participation in the management of firms and in general economic planning is one of the most controversial issues to emerge in recent times. It encompasses at once ideological, political, and technico–economic elements and cannot be adequately approached within the framework of a single discipline. Although previous experiences with worker participation have generally been limited in their reach and have not been applied broadly as a fundamental principle of economic organization, the idea has gained increasing currency and importance in both academic and political circles. In this sense, a recent international comparative survey on the organization of work carried out by the International Labor Office of the United Nations concluded that "the drive for worker partici-

pation in decisions within undertakings is a worldwide phenomenon which, as a basic proposition, is no longer contested [1975, p. 35]."

The nature of worker participation in any society will naturally be affected by the objectives sought by those who organize production. As a first approximation, we may distinguish three basic approaches to this question: ethical–philosophical, sociopolitical, and technico–economic. The first approach relates to the worker's position in the society and is concerned with the process of human development and individual self-realization. The second approach views participation in terms of the desirable distribution of economic and political power among social classes in the society. The third looks to participation as a mechanism to increase worker productivity or efficiency in general. Within each approach, proponents may argue for an "optimal" level of participation, greatly restricted in some cases and highly developed in others, which will best promote their objective. As we maintain in subsequent chapters, an extensive and profound system of worker participation may produce results compatible with each of these three approaches or objectives. The objectives which come to govern an economy's system of labor relations will be established in relation to the society's political development and the level and character of the organization of its working class. Corresponding to these objectives will be different systems of labor relations, which, in turn, will imply varying degrees of worker participation in industrial management.

The phrases *worker participation, worker control, self-management,* or *industrial democracy* each take on several different meanings, depending on who is using them. For some, *control* is more complete and deeper than *participation.* Lenin and the Bolsheviks, however, seem to have used *control* to mean only *supervision* over production, not the actual making of decisions (Brinton 1972, pp. 11–20). For André Gorz, "workers' control" is a process by which the working class progressively limits the power options of capital and thereby advances the class struggle. *Industrial democracy* is yet a more versatile catchword. For Hugh Clegg, democracy is equated with the existence of a legal opposition. Thus trade unions ipso facto signify industrial democracy.[1] Others, of course, imply something much more profound by *industrial democracy.*

The prevailing imprecisions in the literature cannot be set straight here. Rather, we propose an operational definition: *Worker participation* at the firm level is the ability of workers to directly influence or form the management and work process in an enterprise. Inherent in this definition is the notion of power, i.e., worker participation necessarily entails the wresting of some prerogatives from management or capital by the workers. It follows that participation occurs

---

[1]Referring to management, Carole Pateman has commented on Clegg's notion: "It would be a most curious kind of 'democratic' theorist who would argue for a government permanently in office and completely irreplaceable [1970, p. 72]."

at many levels and in many forms. Our present purpose is to systematize the diverse manifestations of participation into a coherent and workable framework.

To begin with, we may distinguish several "forms" of participation: grievance; collective bargaining; information and consultation; veto; and participation through minority, parity, and majority representation on decision-making bodies. Perhaps the most rudimentary and least significant form is the grievance procedure. In its preunion stage, this procedure is sometimes formalized through shop stewards, sometimes exists informally, and apparently sometimes does not exist at all.

The most common, albeit very limited, form of participation takes place through contract negotiation or collective bargaining. Even in most industrialized nations, this system rarely includes more than 35 or 40% of the active labor force.[2]

Profit sharing, through stock ownership or contract stipulation, is another form of participation. In Latin America, profit sharing schemes have been implemented in Argentina (de Castro 1969), in the *comunidades industriales* in Peru (Anderson 1972; Knight 1975a and 1975b; Pásara and Santistevan 1973; Pearson 1973), in Mexico and in Chile. The French and Swedish governments have also introduced legislation to establish profit sharing on a nationwide basis.[3] However, organized labor in both France and Sweden has rejected this government initiative on the grounds that it would be co-optive (Garson 1975).

Information and consultation is the second most common form of worker participation, best examplified by the Western European works' councils (OIT 1969; Sturmthal 1964; Garson 1975; Bernstein 1973). Works' councils were first introduced in the 1890s in Prussia and presently exist in Austria, Belgium, Canada, Denmark, Finland, France, India, Iraq, the Low Countries, Norway, Spain, Sweden, Tanzania, Tunisia, West Germany, and Zaire (OIT 1969, pp. 45–77 and ILO 1975, pp. 9–15). The works' councils have a consultive character which generally covers personnel and organizational issues. Sometimes they also have the right to receive the information distributed to stockholders regarding the firm's economic and financial performance. In France, the works' councils (*comités d'entreprise*) receive money allocations from management with which they administer all social services of the firm.

---

[2]A striking exception to this rule can be found in Sweden where collective bargaining affects practically the entire labor force. It is also interesting to note that legislation in Sweden (June 1976) broadened the field of collective bargaining to include *all* issues affecting labor and stipulated that the employer must contact labor before taking decisions that affect a large number of employees (see *Business Week,* June 21, 1976 and the Swedish Ministry of Labor 1975). A useful up-to-date comparison of collective bargaining practices in various countries can be found in S. Barkin (1975).

[3]The 1974 tax cut in the United States provides for an extra 1% investment tax credit to those firms participating in employee stock ownership programs. Elaborate profit sharing schemes such as the Kelso Plan are now being applied in several U.S. firms (see Hyatt 1975).

Most of the evidence suggests that works' councils are no longer fulfilling their intended purpose, which was "to create good relations and friendship between workers and employers" and "to increase productivity [OIT 1969, p. 75]." Nor do they seem to provide a substantial degree of worker influence in enterprise management. In England, whereas a survey conducted late in the 1940s indicated that three-quarters of all manufacturing establishments had joint-consultation bodies, a study conducted nearly 30 years later shows them to be constituted in only one-third of manufacturing undertakings (Garson 1975, p. 12). In France, the number of works' councils declined from 21,000 in 1954 to about 10,000 in 1964 (Garson 1975, p. 17). In Sweden, studies conducted by the Swedish labor federation (LO) in 1968 and 1969 show unionists have increasingly less faith in their ability to influence management through works' councils (Garson 1975, p. 21).

In India, works' councils were to be formed in 1947 in all enterprises with more than 100 workers. In 1963, only 61% of industrial enterprises had joint-consultation bodies, but these bodies were operating in only half the cases. Moreover, all studies indicate they have not functioned effectively (Kannappan 1968, p. 158). An ILO study quotes a lower management representative:

> Since recommendations are not binding on management, the company representatives on the committee feel, why oppose worker suggestions among the people we have to deal with every day? So we agree to many worker proposals, knowing that management will turn them down—but we don't get the blame [Kannappan 1968, p. 159].

Summing up the experience of works' councils, another ILO study notes a tendency for conflictual issues to bypass joint consultation and enter the union–management collective bargaining arena (OIT 1969, p. 74). Works' councils, then, seem to have ceased to serve the interests of either labor or management.

A less pretentious variant of the works' councils has been introduced on a reduced scale in the United States. The Scanlon Plan allows for the reception of workers suggestions to increase productivity and the sharing of resulting benefits. It was first introduced in the LaPointe Machine Tool Company of Hudson, Massachusetts in 1947 where it had immediate success (Granick 1966, p. 185, Hampden-Turner 1970, pp.183–216). By 1958, the plan had succeeded in over 50 companies, and more have been added since. "It has been successful in large plants and small ones, with complex technologies and relatively simple ones, in unionized and nonunion plants [Lesieur 1958, p. 207]." More recently, several hundred U.S. firms are experimenting with work humanization programs which often entail the solicitation of workers' opinions (see Chapter 2).

An extension of the joint-consultation concept is found in provisions for workers' veto power. The veto is generally restricted to personnel-specific matters, e.g., the works' councils in West Germany have veto power over decisions

regarding work schedules, vocational training programs, fixing of piece-rates, and the like. In participation schemes which have gone beyond the works' councils, the veto power takes on broader significance. For example, in Yugoslavia the Workers' Councils (to be distinguished from works' councils) may veto decisions of the Management Board which it appoints or worker representatives on either the Workers' Council or Management Board may be removed from their positions.

The final category of participation occurs when worker representatives sit on decision-making bodies (either at the shop floor level, on special committees, or on the superior body). Worker representation can be either minority, parity, or majority. Minority representation can be found in several European countries: in Spain, where the workers have one representative out of seven on the administrative council (Rivero 1969); in Austria, where the workers have two representatives on the supervisory board (OIT 1969, p. 50; Garson 1975, p. 34); in France, public enterprises, where the workers have one-third representation on the management board (OIT, 1969); in West Germany, where in all enterprises with more than 500 workers—save coal, iron, and steel enterprises—the workers have one-third representation on the supervisory board[4]; in Denmark, where, since 1973, workers are allowed two representatives on boards of directors (ILO 1975, p. 7); in Sweden, where, since December 1972, companies employing at least 100 persons, except insurance companies and banks, are required to admit two employee representatives nominated by the trade union local to sit on their boards of directors (ILO 1975, p. 8). In many of these cases, the role of the worker representatives is limited to something less than full voting power. Several other countries have limited worker representation on the boards of directors of certain public enterprises (ILO 1975, p. 5).

In the United Arab Republic, the administrative council in public enterprises is composed of four worker representatives, four state representatives and a president appointed by the state. The worker representatives, however, must be nonmanual workers and must be members of the Socialist Arab Union. A similar arrangement, plus profit sharing, for public enterprises, exists in Syria (OIT 1969, pp. 53–56).

The case of parity representation is typified by the German coal, iron, and steel industries in firms with more than 1000 employees. In such cases, union nominated worker representatives occupy 50% of the seats on the supervisory boards. This system of codetermination was informally introduced in the iron, steel, and coal industries in 1947 and codified into law in 1951. Despite the widely recognized failure of German codetermination to generate significant worker participa-

---

[4]According to 1976 legislation, in West German enterprises with over 2000 employees the proportion of employee representation will increase to just short of 50% (Dreyer 1976). This legislation will affect some 650 enterprises, including 120 that are foreign owned (Ball 1976).

tion in enterprise decision making, it is now serving as a rallying point for the labor movements in many European countries.[5]

There seems to be widespread labor dissatisfaction with schemes providing less than parity representation (Garson, 1975). The ILO (OIT 1969) has summarized the experience with minority representation:

> In general, the workers are conceded a given number of positions in [participatory] organisms and the situation in the company or enterprise, public or private, does not essentially change. Above all, with respect to the firm's objectives or goals, [minority representation] leaves them fundamentally unmodified. . . . The organisms meetings are generally private and the opinions expressed or the facts upon which decisions are based are not made known [pp. 45–46].

Majority representation takes many forms: producer cooperatives, self-management and comanagement. Producer cooperatives are worker owned and run. In capitalist countries, there have historically been many cooperative movements, but through lack of financial and organizational support they have usually petered out (Boyer and Morais 1973, p. 35; Horvat 1975, p. 27). Nevertheless, worker cooperatives have been able to survive in isolated instances. In present-day United States, there are a handful of successful cooperatives: the 18 Puget Sound plywood cooperatives (Berman 1967; Bellas 1972; Bernstein 1974), the Ithaca Project Coops, the Vermont Asbestos Group (Zwerdling 1974; Albelda 1976), the *Boston Real Paper,* etc. Outside the United States there are many more: the growing industrial undertakings on Israeli kibbutzim (Fine 1973; Melman 1970; Rosner 1970); in England, the John Lewis Partnership (Flanders, Pomeranz, and Woodward 1968), the Triumph Motor Bike Coop (Carnoy and Levin 1976) and several others (Jones 1974); in Spain, the large industrial complex at Mondragon (Oakeshott 1975), to mention only a few.

Self-management usually designates a situation where the enterprise is not juridically the property of the workers but is nevertheless run solely by the workers. Prominent examples of this form are found in some 7000 Yugoslavian firms, 300 Algerian firms (OIT 1969, pp. 31–43) and a small number of enterprises in Peru's "area of social property [Knight 1975b; ILO 1975, p. 5]."

Comanagement, as we use the term, refers to a situation where joint decision-making authority is shared by worker and state representatives but either the former prevail or decision making is not conflictual. Many socialist theorists hold this form to be more democratic than self-management because it generates

---

[5]This failure can be traced to three factors: (*a*) The worker representatives are not directly elected; (*b*) the representatives cease to do production work and receive managerial salaries and perquisites while on the board, and (*c*) there is no parallel system of worker participation at the shop floor level to involve rank-and-file workers. Indeed, some observers have argued that codetermination actually strengthens management's control over labor (cf., Schauer 1973; Jenkins 1973).

objectives for the microproduction unit based on both local and national interests. Needless to say, comanagement is only more democratic in this respect if the generation of the economic plan is itself democratic. Self-management, on the other hand, usually coexists with a market economy which, according to many, is less likely to be democratic since it gives more votes in the marketplace to those with a greater income.

Comanagement was the proposed initial model for the 420-odd enterprises in Chile's "social property area" under Allende. It appears to be operative in post–Cultural Revolution Chinese enterprise and in Cuba since 1970. We discuss the socialist experience with worker participation briefly in the next chapter.

In summary, we have presented an outline of different kinds of worker participation in industrial settings ranging from the most inchoate and undeveloped forms to the most mature and developed. The foregoing discussion, of course, does not encompass all possible arrangements for worker participation. No useful taxonomy is ever exhaustive. Absent from this presentation, for example, is mention of the growing experimentation with self-managing work teams at the shop floor level in a number of different countries or reference to schemes for worker participation beyond the enterprise level (see Chapter 2). In Chapter 5, in the description of the construction of our index of worker participation, we further elaborate our taxonomy to include the different "levels" within an enterprise (e.g., shop floor, sectional, top management council) and the different "areas" or subject matter (e.g., labor relations, administrative, technical, overall economic policy) of worker participation.

Our present purpose is to give an overview of various forms of worker participation in practice. It seems clear that of the above forms only parity and majority worker representation on decision-making bodies provide the potential for true industrial democracy. This potential, however, is not always realized. It is one of our intentions in this study to understand what conditions govern the realization of this potential.

THE PURPOSES OF THE STUDY

This study aims at investigating worker participation in practice. We seek to provide an explanation of (a) the strategic factors which influence the degree of worker participation attained; and (b) the effects of different degrees of worker participation on the economic and social performance of industrial undertakings. The analysis is based on a random sample of 35 enterprises in Chile's "social area" between late 1970 and mid-1973.

The study elaborates a framework for analyzing the question of worker participation with empirical evidence. It contributes a concrete methodology for iden-

tifying and measuring relevant variables, which, to be sure, must be further improved and divested of subjective evaluations and other errors. It is hoped that our methodology will provide a basis for the development of a common analytical method to be used in future studies of this subject. Only through the application of a consistent method will the study of worker participation be able to overcome the stigma of impressionistic reporting and seriously enter the field of systematic, comparative analysis.

It is also our intention to better support and substantiate the existing theory of worker participation and, in particular, elucidate certain factors relevant to the implementation of participatory programs where economic and political conditions are permissive. Any generalizations drawn from our study, however, must be qualified with reference to its limitations. Above all, we are studying enterprises situated in a unique historical context.[6] Although the study does not attempt to analyze the overall behavior of the Chilean economy and polity during 1970–1973, references to this topic at times become necessary. Furthermore, the evidence gathered and analyzed is short term in nature. Yet, a factor that distinguishes this study from previous studies dealing with participation in small, isolated, or peripheral enterprises is that it investigates large, modern enterprises at the industrial core of the Chilean economy.

We must also mention that worker participation in Chile arose during an administration with a concrete ideological position. Given the political polarization in Chile at the time and in the world in general, a dispassionate analysis of the Chilean experience is made all the more difficult. Some will argue that nothing genuine can be created in a Marxist regime and that the participation system set in motion was no more than a myth drummed up by propaganda. Others will affirm that participation was nothing more than an irrelevant factor in the process, devised only as a strategic need during one of its stages. However, if a balance is objectively struck, the wealth and depth of the lessons to be learned from this brief experience unfailingly emerge. Still, this study is not addressed to whoever may have settled into a safe and permanent attitude and is unwilling to review or renew his or her truth on the basis of experience.

Finally, it should be made clear that this study is limited to worker participation at the level of the firm, because of problems of time and availability of data. This constraint should in no way be construed to imply that worker participation occurs only within the confines of a plant. On the contrary, worker participation

---

[6]As mentioned above, we are concerned in this study only with industrial enterprises. Popular participation also occurred in other areas of the Chilean economy during the Allende period, particularly in the countryside. For an excellent discussion of peasant participation in Chile, see Marchetti and Maffei (1972); see also Cantoni (1972); Castillo and Larraín (1971); *Revista Agraria of Chile Hoy* (January 1973, February 1973, April 1973, May 1973) and Barraclough and Fernandez (1974, Chapters 4–6).

in the management of firms was always interpreted as a part within an articulated whole, in which workers assume increasing control at all levels.

FORMULATION OF THE HYPOTHESES

A fundamental assumption of this study is that worker participation in enterprise management is a quantifiable process, at least in relative terms. To this end, we developed a cumulative index which permits interfirm comparisons regarding the level of worker participation attained in each firm.

The relative participation level thus determined serves as a critical element in the two main lines of our analysis. On the one hand, it is assumed that the relative level of participation reached in a firm results from the presence in varying degrees of characteristics peculiar to each factory—its managerial structure and technology and the human, political, and organizational characteristics of its labor force. On the other hand, it is hypothesized, on the basis of various theories and propositions, that the level of participation exerts some influence on the firm's operation and, hence, on the results observed. These results are not only economic but also social, cultural, and political.

The general model of interdependence and expected causality between the variables examined in this study is depicted schematically in Figure 1.1. The so-called *independent variables* correspond to the characteristics of the firm's physical structure (technology, capital intensity, size, etc.), managerial organization (vertical and horizontal differentiation, type of management, etc.), and labor force (its educational level, union structure and ideology, differences between blue- and white-collar workers, etc.). These variables affect not only the participation level of the firm's workers, P_F, but also the *intermediate variables* and *variables of result*.

Furthermore, it is assumed that the variables of result (e.g., productivity, product quality) are affected by the participation level, P_F, either directly or through another set of variables designated as intermediate variables (e.g.,

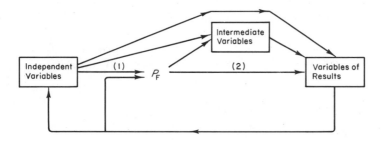

Figure 1.1. Model of interdependence and expected causality between the variables.

changes in the wage structure, in worker discipline, absenteeism, etc.). The latter have been included for three reasons: (a) their inherent interest; (b) the likely time lag between the emergence of participation and the appearance of variables of result; and (c) the desire for a correct specification of our model and consequently as strong an explanation for the variance of the result or performance variables as possible. For purposes of brevity and clarity of presentation, only the most significant relationships implied in Figure 1.1 are analyzed in the present study.

PLAN OF THE STUDY

The remainder of this book can be divided into four parts. The first (Chapters 2, 3, and 4) presents general background intended to locate and define the context of the Chilean experience with worker participation. In Chapter 2, we introduce the problem of worker alienation and provide an interpretation of recent experiences with changing work organization and worker participation in capitalist and socialist countries. Chapter 3 presents an overview of Chilean economic and political development up to 1970, including a sketch of the Chilean economy in 1970, a brief description of the Chilean working class and its historical development, and a review of Chile's experiences with worker participation prior to 1970. In Chapter 4, we discuss the structural economic reforms carried out by the Allende government, the creation of the "social property area," and the evolution and content of the basic guidelines concerning worker participation.

In the second part of the study (Chapter 5), we discuss (a) the design and implementation of our survey; (b) the construction of our index of worker participation; and (c) the structural components of participation and the behavioral characteristics of our index.

In the third part (Chapter 6), we seek to identify the principal independent variables which affect worker participation. We explain the choice and measurement of each variable with reference to earlier studies and consider the relative importance of each variable in explaining variations in the level of participation. In the first part of the chapter, we employ multiple regression analysis with linear functional form, and in the second part we use factor analysis to determine how the independent variables cluster and corroborate our earlier results.

The fourth part of the study (Chapter 7) refers specifically to the impact of worker participation on the economic and social performance of the 35 enterprises in our sample. We consider the relationship between worker participation and the intermediate variables, between worker participation and the variables of result, and between the intermediate variables and the variables of result. As in

Chapter 6, we draw on descriptive material and employ multiple linear regression analysis in deriving our analysis.[7]

Finally, in Chapter 8 and the postscript the chief results of the study are briefly recalled, and some commentaries and conclusions of a more general nature are made.

[7]Although path analysis is implicit in this approach, it was not applied explicitly as it is more appropriate in studies where the causal network is more complex. In the case of the multiple linear regression model with two independent variables, for instance, the path coefficients are identical to the ordinary partial regression coefficients. For more details, cf. H. M. Blalock (1971, Part II).

2

Worker Alienation and Worker Participation in Capitalist and Socialist Countries: An Overview

INTRODUCTION

In the first section of Chapter 1 we presented a somewhat static view of the different forms of worker participation.[1] Such a static view is useful for descriptive purposes to orient the researcher and the reader. Worker participation in practice, however, is a social process and must be treated as such for analytical purposes. In this chapter, then, we attempt to provide a dynamic perspective of worker participation in different political contexts. We discuss the origins of the concern with and the philosophical and political bases for distinct approaches to worker participation in enterprise decision making. In the next section we discuss alienation and the evolution of the capitalist work process. Following that, some of the social, political, and economic consequences of hierarchical work environments and alienated labor are considered. Then we offer an interpretation of the experiences with worker participation in capitalist and socialist economies respectively.[2] In general, considering these two basic models of economic or-

[1]The reader directly interested in the Chilean experience may skip to Chapter 3 without a loss of continuity.

[2]In choosing to classify economies as either capitalist or socialist we are, of course, obscuring certain ambiguities. Some countries defy clear-cut classification (e.g., Algeria or Tanzania), while other countries may fall into one category or another depending on one's analytical perspective (e.g., Yugoslavia or Chile under Allende). These ambiguities are often attributed to the transitional nature of the country in question. Ambiguities and omissions, however, are present whenever one abstracts for the purpose of analysis. Our abstraction seems to be the most useful and simple, given practices of common parlance and our own analytical predilections. Further refinements in our basic classification

ganization, one can observe that in capitalist economies, where experiences with worker participation have developed, they have done so in isolated enterprises or sectors and have usually been restricted to the shop floor; in contrast, in socialist economies, worker participation has been projected to the national level, yet, in many cases, it is participation by proxy through leaders and does not affect or involve workers at the base level.

ALIENATION, SCIENTIFIC MANAGEMENT, AND THE CAPITALIST WORK PROCESS

The alienating character of factory labor was clearly articulated 200 years ago by Adam Smith in *The Wealth of Nations:*

> The man whose life is spent in performing a few simple operations . . . has no occasion to exert his understanding or to exercise his invention in finding out expedients for removing difficulties . . . and generally becomes as stupid and ignorant as it is possible for a human creature to become, [and when factory work becomes widespread] all the nobler parts of the human character may be, in great measure, obliterated and extinguished in the great body of people [1937, p. 734–35].

Visiting the United States in 1831, Alexis de Tocqueville wrote:

> When a workman is increasingly and exclusively engaged in the fabrication of one thing . . . he loses the general faculty of applying his mind to the direction of work . . . in proportion as the workman improves, the man is degraded. . . . The science of manufacture lowers the class of workmen, it raises the class of masters. . . . The manufacturing aristocracy which is growing up under our eyes is one of the harshest that ever existed in the world [2:168–171].

In the *Economic and Philosophical Manuscripts of 1844,* Marx echoes and elaborates Smith's point.[3] Briefly, Marx distinguished between three main forms of alienation which he saw as a consequence of private property: alienation from product, since the worker neither owned the product produced nor identified with

---

(e.g., welfare capitalism, state capitalism, market socialism, and participatory or democratic socialism) could doubtlessly be made and would be appropriate, perhaps, in a study centered on the analysis of macroeconomic and political systems.

[3]Marx expounded at length upon the humanless conditions of industrial labor under capitalism in many of his writings. Another particularly good source of Marx's views on the effect of the technical division of labor in capitalist factories can be found in *Capital:* "The Capitalistic Character of Manufacture," (1967, pp. 359–371). In the prior section, Marx distinguishes between the social division of labor which exists in any society where exchange occurs and the technical division of labor or the division of labor in detail, as Marx calls it, which is unique to capitalism. The division of labor in detail or the division of labor between jobs within a workshop only occurs after (*a*) the capitalist has monopolized the instruments of labor; and (*b*) a market in labor exists. By this process, the worker becomes a detail laborer and as such is dependent upon the organizing function of the capitalist in the production process. Marglin (1974) elaborates on this point.

or decided upon its ultimate use; alienation from process, since the worker did not control the process of production; alienation from "species being," self and fellow worker which were seen as a consequence of private property and alienation from product and process and prevented the species from realizing its human potential. In the 1844 manuscripts Marx wrote that these forms of alienation would become more intense as capitalist accumulation advanced: "The wretchedness of the worker is in inverse proportion to the power and magnitude of his production [1971, p. 106]." This occurred because "Labour produced not only commodities; it produces itself and the worker as a commodity—and does so in the same general proportion in which it produces commodities [1971, p. 107]."

The advent of scientific management at the turn of this century seems to confirm Marx's expectation. Scientific management, in turn, can be regarded as a reaction to the joint process of capital accumulation and labor socialization that accelerated around the turn of the century (Stone 1974). Capital accumulation and the increasing socialization of the labor force meant that the working class was being brought together and homogenized by capital and as such presented a mounting threat to capitalist control. Scientific management advocated the deskilling and fragmentation (e.g., through individual piece-rates) of the labor force.[4] Here is how Frederick Winslow Taylor expounded his principles of scientific management:

> Under scientific management the "initiative" of the workmen (that is, their hard work, their good will and their ingenuity) is obtained by absolute uniformity and to a greater extent than is possible under the old system; and in addition to this improvement on the part of men, the managers assume new burdens, new duties and responsibilities never dreamed of in the past. The managers assume, for instance, the burden of gathering together all of the traditional knowledge which in the past has been possessed by the workmen and then of classifying, tabulating and reducing this knowledge to rules, laws and formulae which are immensely helpful to the workmen in doing their daily work.
>
> Thus, all of the planning which under the old system was done by the workmen, as a result of his personal experience, must of necessity under the new system be done by management in accordance with the laws of science.
>
> Without the element of stupidity the method would never work. A pig iron handler shall be so stupid and phlegmatic that he more resembles the ox than any other type. . . . The man who is mentally alert is entirely unsuited to what would, for him, be the grinding monotony of work of this character [*Scientific Management*. New York: Harper & Row, 1947. Pp. 36–38, 58–62].

H. J. Leavitt, an industrial psychologist, writes that "Taylorism continues to be . . . almost invariably present in American firms [1973, p. 339]."[5] The HEW task force on work in America, commissioned by Elliott Richardson in December

---

[4]For a more comprehensive discussion on the development of Taylorism, the deskilling of work and the labor process under capitalism, see Gordon, Reich, and Edwards (1973), Braverman (1974), Stone (1974).

[5]The discussion in the next two sections draws primarily on the U.S. experience. The United States is taken to be representative of most of the advanced world with respect to work organization.

1971, concludes its impressive report: "Industry is paying for its continued attachment to Tayloristic practices through low worker productivity and high rates of sabotage, absenteeism and turnover [1972, p. 186]."

Those who expected automation to eliminate difficult, tedious, and boring work have been sorely disappointed. Automation, and the concurrent process of accumulation, have led instead to the increasing proletarianization of the labor force and deskilling of jobs. The class of wage and salaried workers in the United States has grown steadily from 20% of the total labor force in 1780 to 83.6% in 1969. Within the class of wage and salaried workers, the share of blue-collar workers has remained more or less constant since 1910 at around 37%, while the share of white-collar workers (including service workers) has grown from around 25% in 1910 to around 48% in 1967 (Reich 1972, p. 178); see Table 2.1. The nature of white-collar work, however, has become increasingly routinized, impersonal, and uninteresting over time. The average clerical worker, the keypunch operator, the secretary in a corporate typing pool or word processing center, the telephone operator, or the check-out-counter worker in a supermarket are no better off than the blue-collar laborer. The HEW study reports growing signs of discontent among white-collar workers: "turnover rates as high as 30% annually and a 46% increase in white-collar union membership between 1958 and 1968 [1973, p. 39]."[6] Concurrently, craft blue-collar labor continues to be deskilled through the introduction of numerical control, continuous process techniques, and other new machinery (Braverman 1974: Chapters 9 and 10).

The American labor force has changed in other essential ways since the introduction of Taylorism. "From a workforce with an average educational attainment of less than junior high school, containing a large contingent of immigrants, . . . the workforce is now largely native-born, with more than a high school education on the average [HEW 1972, p. 18]." The labor force has more intellectual training, higher aspirations, and a new ethos. Judson Gooding quotes a foreman at Cadillac: "The old type tactics of being a supervisor don't work with these guys. In the past a man didn't need much motivation to do a job like this—the paycheck took care of that. But these guys they're different [1972, p. 119]."

Iver Berg (1970) presents evidence that higher educational attainment and deskilled jobs have produced a labor force of workers overqualified for their

---

Furthermore, managerial practices in the United States are generally applied in industry in the underdeveloped capitalist world. As is suggested in subsequent chapters, if anything, practices such as Taylorism exist in more oppressive form in Latin American industry. Technological changes, of course, also tend to be transferred over time to the underdeveloped countries.

[6]In a recent book, Judson Gooding (1972), an associate editor of *Fortune* magazine, presents an extended and convincing discussion of the "white-collar woes." The application of Taylorist methods to and the "manualization" of white-collar work is discussed in Braverman (1974, Chapters 15 and 16) and Aronowitz (1973, Chapter 6).

TABLE 2.1
The Evolution of the United States Labor Force

Year	Percentage wage and salaried employees	Percentage self-employed entrepreneurs	Percentage salaried managers and officials	Total
1780	20.0	80.0	—	100.0
1880	62.0	36.9	1.1	100.0
1930	76.8	20.3	2.9	100.0
1950	77.7	17.9	4.4	100.0
1960	80.6	14.1	5.3	100.0
1969	83.6	9.2[a]	7.2	100.0

Source: Michael Reich, "The Evolution of the United States Labor Force," in Edwards, Reich, and Weisskopf, The Capitalist System: A Radical Analysis of American Society, © 1972, pp. 175, 480. Reprinted by permission of Prentice-Hall, Inc., Englewood Cliffs, New Jersey.

[a] By 1973, this proportion had fallen to 8.5%, calculated from U.S., Department of Commerce, Statistical Abstract of the United States, 1974, p. 350.

work and finds that workers with more education tend to have higher turnover rates and poorer job performance. Jerome M. Rosow, a former assistant secretary of labor for policy, evaluation, and research, recently prepared a special report for the president on blue-collar life in which he observes that "millions of workers . . . are getting increasingly frustrated. . . . Their work is unsatisfactory but they see no way of breaking out . . . their total life pattern is discouraging [and] younger workers today much more than in past generations, expect to participate in the decision-making process in their job-world [quoted in Gooding 1972, p. 180]."

In a mid-1974 survey, 84.4% of 251 corporate presidents (of corporations with average sales of $138 million) perceived employee motivation to be of far greater concern than it was a decade earlier (Mills 1975, p. 128). Accordingly, in the last 3 years General Motors has expanded its staff of social psychologists by 2000% from 6 to 110, excluding its large Detroit headquarters.

A recent study, based on a representative sample of 1533 American workers, found workers first concern was that their jobs be interesting. Good pay ranked fifth (HEW 1972, p. 13). The HEW study, Work in America, observed: "Perhaps the most consistent complaint reported to our task force has been the failure of bosses to listen to workers who wish to propose better ways of doing their jobs [1972, p. 37]." The United Auto Workers conducted a survey of their rank and file and discovered the strongest desire was the chance to influence "the process of administering the plants [Jenkins 1974, p. 47]." A study by Smith and Tannenbaum (cited in Argyris 1973, p. 147) of 200 enterprises found that 99% of the rank-and-file groups wanted more control over their immediate work areas.

H. Holter (1965) reported that over half of the 5700 workers in heavy industry surveyed wanted more participation in decision making. It is not hard to replicate these findings in other countries. For instance, a survey conducted in Sweden during the 1960s revealed that 56% of blue-collar and 67% of white-collar workers wanted more control over their work (Jenkins 1973, p. 247). In Chile, a survey of 920 industrial workers in 1969 reported that 48% felt that production should be run by the workers and the state together or by the workers alone; an additional 15% felt that production should be run by the workers together with the managers (CORFO 1970, p. 150).[7]

SOME CONSEQUENCES OF ALIENATED LABOR

It is not surprising that an alienated and frustrated labor force should yield undesirable social, political, and economic effects.[8] The social problems created by tedious, unrewarding work are not difficult to identify. In one UAW local, 15% of the 3400 workers were reportedly addicted to heavy drugs (HEW 1972, p. 86). Gooding quotes the General Motors security chief as saying

> that drugs were responsible for much of the theft of tools, parts, and typewriters, and for some of the muggings in parking lots around the plants. Many, if not most of the workers whose shift ends at 2 a.m. at the Cadillac plant carry pistols because of fear of mugging by addicts [p. 77].

Drug addiction is not restricted to the auto workers. Many U.S. corporations have instituted urinalysis as part of the application procedure to screen out users.

In a system of production where workers are treated as a means to the end of capital accumulation, it is natural that their physical health is at best a secondary concern. In the United States in 1975:

[7]John Goldthorpe (1974) discusses the growing strength of rank-and-file union groups in Great Britain manifested in a sharp increase in wildcat strikes since the late 1950s and a challenge to typical management prerogatives in the areas of work practices, pay systems, discipline, and recruitment. The labor government has responded by attempting to institutionalize this pressure through vitiated joint management systems. In West Germany, under pressure from organized labor, new legislation in 1976 extended worker representation on boards of directors in firms with over 2000 employees. This worker representation, however, falls short of labor's goal of parity representation with management (Ball 1976; Dreyer 1976).

[8]Although these consequences are described in the context of our discussion of and with reference to capitalist economies, we, of course, do not mean to imply that alienation and its effects are not also present in socialist economies. Hierarchical workplaces exist in varying degrees in both socialist and capitalist economies. Taylorist principles of industrial organization were, in fact, embraced by Lenin in the spring of 1918 and have been applied in the Soviet Union in modified form ever since. A good discussion of the consequences of alienated labor in the Soviet Union (high labor turnover, wildcat strikes, etc.) can be found in Holubenko (1975).

The nation had 46,000 highway fatalities. In the same year, an estimated *minimum* of 112, 600 died from workplace accidents and diseases. There were about 2,200,000 accidents resulting in disabilities ranging from bed recuperation to permanent bodily impairment. A further three million accidents at work caused restricted activity for their victims. All told, almost nine million work accidents received medical attention. . . . Beyond this accumulation of disaster, however, stands an even more ugly statistic; an estimated *minimum* . . . of 22 million workers, one out of every four in the country, annually suffer health impairments of some nature from their work [Turner 1977, p. 7].

With regard to the political consequences of alienation, Arthur Kornhauser's study of 407 auto workers found that workers with low job satisfaction "were often escapist or passive in their non-work activities: They watched television; did not vote; and did not participate in community organizations [HEW 1972, p. 83; Hampden-Turner 1970]." Argyris (1973, pp. 154–155) cites a study by Meissner (1971) of 206 industrial workers and another by Torbert (1972) of 209 workers which support Kornhauser's conclusion. That is, workers alienated in their work lives are also alienated in their nonwork lives.

These results raise the question: How meaningful is political democracy without economic democracy? Carole Pateman, after reviewing the chief political theorists of democracy and studies conducted in Scandanavia and elsewhere, argues that experience with local democracy is necessary to teach people how to participate effectively at higher levels. For instance, Pateman quotes a conclusion of a cross-cultural study of political behavior covering five countries by Almond and Verba:

If in most social situations the individual finds himself subservient to some authority figure, it is likely that he will expect such an authority relationship in the political sphere. On the other hand, if outside the political sphere he has opportunities to participate in a wide range of social decisions, he will probably expect to be able to participate in political decisions as well. Furthermore, participation in non-political decision making may give one the skills needed to engage in political participation [1970, p. 47].

In this view, factory and community democracy are essential ingredients to an effective political democracy.

Alienated work also engenders economic costs. With the concurrent deskilling of jobs and the increasing level of educational attainment of the work force, the historically proven methods of Taylorism and workplace hierarchy seem to have exhausted their capacity to raise productivity. The economic costs of capitalist work organization manifest themselves in higher absenteeism, higher turnover, poor work motivation, production sabotage, slowdowns and stifled initiative.[9]

---

[9]For an excellent treatment of this phenomenon, see Whyte (1955); see also Aronowitz (1973, Chapter 1), Brecher (1972) and Mulcahy (1976).

The Bureau of Labor Statistics shows that absenteeism has risen by 35% since 1961 (Zwerdling 1973, p. 82).[10] The average quit rate in manufacturing rose from 1.35% during 1959–1962 to 2.25% during 1971–1974. That is, it rose by 66.7% over this 12-year period (*Monthly Labor Review*, January 1972 and October 1975).[11]

This grave situation has led many capitalists in recent years to experiment with new forms of work organization. Substantive changes in work organization seem to have a powerful influence in reducing these economic costs. After reviewing 34 cases where worker participation was introduced to some degree, the HEW task force concluded

> It is imperative, then, that employers be made aware of the fact that thorough efforts to redesign work—not simply "job enrichment" or "job rotation"—have resulted in increases in productivity from 5 to 40%. In no instance of which we have evidence has a major effort to increase employee participation resulted in a long-term decline in productivity . . . it appears that the size of increase in productivity is, in general, a function of the thoroughness of the effort [1972, p. 112].

THE LIMITS OF WORK HUMANIZATION AND WORKER PARTICIPATION UNDER CAPITALISM

The importance of organizational structures and motivational strategies in raising productivity has not gone unnoticed by the captains of industry. Experiments in humanizing the work environment in the United States date from the famous Hawthorne experiments in the late 1920s. The field of industrial psychology has since blossomed, and a significant body of literature has been produced attesting to the positive productivity and psychological effects of a humanized, participatory workplace (e.g., Argyris 1973; Herzberg 1968; Leavitt 1973; Lesieur 1958; Likert 1967; Maslow 1973; McGregor 1960; Vroom 1969, 1973). The first major experimentation in this area was introduced at the Lapointe Machine Tool Company (Hudson, Massachusetts) in 1947 under the guidance of Joseph Scanlon. By 1958, the Scanlon Plan had been successful in over 50 companies. More recently, the human resource development (HRD) or work humanization movement has been gaining momentum. A Western Euro-

[10]Absenteeism was actually higher in 1961 than in any year between 1957 and 1960. In 1974 it was 4.5% higher than in 1972 or 1973 (U.S., Department of Commerce, *Statistical Abstract of the United States*, various years). Absenteeism is defined as unscheduled absence from work caused by illness or other personal reasons.

[11]Since the quit rate demonstrates a strong inverse correlation with the rate of unemployment, it is of interest to note that the average rate of unemployment fell by only 5.2% between the two periods compared. The rate of absenteeism, on the other hand, does not seem to be significantly related to the rate of unemployment (*Monthly Labor Review*, July 1973, p. 26 and August 1975, p. 37).

pean variation of these experiments has appeared in the form of works' councils and minority worker representation on company boards (see Chapter 1). Two basic elements are common to the new job modification programs being implemented in various capitalist countries: (a) the expectation that they will raise worker productivity and minimize industrial conflict; and (b) the fact that in no instance has ultimate decision-making control been wrested from the managers or owners of industry.[12]

Ted Mills, former member of the National Commission on Productivity and Work, reports that there are currently in excess of 2000 firms in the United States involved in experiments with work humanization (Mills 1975). In 1974, two bills were introduced in the Senate for 1975 deliberation—each calling for a new National Center for Productivity and Work Quality and for the allocation of federal funds to encourage the private sector to experiment in work humanization.[13] Mills writes

> Until recently, [there] has been a surprising absence of organized labor in HRD advocacy, planning and implementation. Despite HRD's primary focus on work, workers and work conditions, available information indicates that until recently, most HRD activity in the U.S. has been in nonunion plants and offices and with a few notable exceptions has been without active union participation in the few organized workplaces where it has appeared.[14] It is probably correct to draw the conclusion . . . that many managements use HRD efforts either to weaken the strength or to keep unions out. In 1973, two well-known HRD practitioners even conducted a seminar called "Making Unions Unnecessary" [1975, p. 126].

From this account it appears that work humanization, far from threatening capitalist control over the production process, promotes labor's identification with capital and fortifies capitalist control. But this is true only as long as the initiative and direction of the programs remain with the capitalists. There's the rub.

There is ample evidence that, once given a taste of control over their work, workers go after more. If this occurs, the capitalists' control over the program is lost and their control over the entire production process becomes threatened. Whether or not the program gets out of hand, of course, will depend on several factors: the nature and extent of the program introduced; who introduced it; the prevailing technology and work organization in the plant; the character of the

[12]For an elaboration of these points, see Zimbalist (1975c). For a detailed description of some of these experiments in action, see Jenkins (1973) and Dickson (1975).

[13]In addition to promoting work humanization, the Congress has also passed four pieces of legislation since December 1973 that grant tax credits to corporations engaging in employee stock ownership plans. One such scheme, the Kelso Plan, is already being used experimentally in several corporations (see Hyatt 1975).

[14]Among the notable exceptions are I. W. Abel's latest 3-year "no-strike" contract of 1973 with the big 10 steel companies and the UAW's 1973 contract with GM, Chrysler, and Ford. The steel contract sets up "employment security and productivity committees" with labor–management participation. The UAW contract provides for "quality of work life committees."

union or other labor organizations; the political consciousness of the workers, and so on.

It is interesting that virtually all experiments in work humanization are being carried out under veils of strict secrecy. Mills reports that HRD activity is treated "as proprietary as new product R & D, and potentially as significant [1975, p. 127]." There are two apparent explanations for this secrecy: (a) Management wants to prevent their competitors from finding out about the productivity benefits associated with certain specific forms of work humanization; and (b) equally important, calling attention to their experiment could instigate worker initiative in the same or other factories and thereby threaten management control over the work humanization movement.[15]

Many of the most successful experiments in the United States with work humanization have been curbed or ended. In a recent article in *The Nation,* a liberal proponent of workers' participation, David Jenkins, made the following observations:

> The American Management Association found that job enrichment is surprisingly in vogue as a term but only lip service is paid to it. . . . The reluctance to act stems in part from the tendency of even so mild a measure as job enrichment to disturb established power patterns. Thus, many promising programs are killed off when they become too threatening. . . . For example, the only major work shake-up at Polaroid (more than ten years ago) was so remarkably successful that it upset all the orthodox power relationships and was swiftly liquidated [1974, p. 48].

It is instructive to follow the Polaroid experience a bit more deeply. Jenkins (1973) quotes Polaroid's training director, Ray Ferris, explaining why their program was terminated:

> It was too successful. What were we going to do with the supervisors—the managers. We didn't need them any more. Management decided it just didn't want operators that qual-

---

[15]An interesting anecdote which speaks to this point is provided by André Gorz (1972). He cites a study done by John Goldthorpe at the Vauxhall car factory in Luton, England in the early 1960s where Goldthorpe interviewed 80% of the factory's workers on an individual basis and concluded that class consciousness was practically nonexistent at the Vauxhall plant and that the workers were behaving according to middle-class patterns. Gorz writes:

> The Goldthorpe report was still at the printer's when a few militants got hold of a resume of [the] conclusions. They had the resume mimeographed and handed out a few hundred copies at the plant. A week or so later, the *Daily Mail* printed a report about the profits that had been made by Vauxhall . . . and sent back to General Motors in the United States. This piece of news also was circulated among the workers. The next day something happened which the *Times* reported as follows: "Wild rioting has broken out at the Vauxhall car factories in Luton. Thousands of workers streamed out of the shops and gathered on the factory yard. They besieged the management offices, calling for the managers to come out, singing the 'Red Flag' and shouting 'string them up.' Groups attempted to storm the offices and battled the police which had been called to protect them [1972, p. 480].

ified. . . . The employees' newly revealed ability to carry more responsibility was too great a threat to the established way of doing things and to established power patterns [pp. 314–315].

The March 28, 1977 issue of *Business Week* reports on the gradual dismantling of the showcase system of worker participation at the Topeka plant of the General Foods Corporation. This plant was perhaps the most heralded and extensive example of worker participation in the United States. Professor Richard Walton of the Harvard Business School estimates that it succeeded in reducing unit costs by 5% and produced an annual saving of $1 million for the company. The article quotes a former employee: "[The system] . . . was a mixed bag. Economically it was a success, but it became a power struggle. It was threatening too many people [p. 78]." The article goes on: "The problem has been not so much that the workers could not manage their own affairs as that some management and staff personnel saw their own position threatened because the workers performed almost too well." A former plant manager, who left Topeka to work for another company, adds the finishing touch: "The system went to hell."

The message here is clear. When workers begin to participate, their sense of isolation and ignorance begins to break down. A dynamic can be created which first attacks the lower levels of the executive hierarchy and then proceeds upward. Edwin Mills, the Director of the U.S. Productivity Commission's quality of work program, says that the democratization of work programs could "open a Pandora's box from which there's no return. Pretty soon you'll have the workers managing the managers. It's a first step toward encroaching on managements' prerogative of controlling and directing the means of production [Zwerdling 1973, p. 80]." A study of six U.S. firms where worker participation programs were terminated despite their economic success supports this argument (Kaus 1973) as does Stephen Marglin (1973) in his report to the Division of Human Rights of the United Nations.[16] For instance, Marglin quotes a shop steward referring to the initial success of an experiment at Imperial Chemicals Industries in Great Britain:

The social scientists are right to a certain extent—we are getting more out of our work. But it can't end here. You can't open up men's minds and let them stagnate. The amount of work in this plant that can still be taken over by the men is tremendous. Control by the worker is

[16]A similar argument is put forth in Bosquet (1972), in Gintis (1972), and in Bowles and Gintis (1975).

Recent deterioration in the far-reaching and economically successful experiment with worker participation at the Rushton mine in Pennsylvania is explained by Basil Massini, an older miner, in a like fashion: "They should have made their bosses learn it and go along with it before putting it into the mine. The president of the company [is] for it. But the rest of management and the foremen, most of them are against it . . . they want to keep their authority." See "The Rushton Experiment: Is There a Better Way to Run a Coal Mine?" *United Mine Workers Journal* 87 (December 16–31, 1976), pp. 3–13.

inevitable. We are capable of running and controlling this plant. Obviously, the next step is to
have more involvement in the broader decision making [p. 18].

There has been much discussion regarding recent experiments with worker
participation in Sweden.[17] However, a current study on worker participation
experiments in Scandanavia, by a member of the Swedish Government Commission on Industrial Democracy, suggests similar limitations to industrial democracy in those countries:[18]

> Both Norwegian and Swedish experience point to the fact that despite the proven superiority
> of workers management on the shop floor (both in productivity and work satisfaction) this form
> of organization seriously threatens the established organizational structure and managerial
> ethics. . . . The goals of preserving the existing differences in power, status and income by far
> are more important values than the overall efficiency of the firms [Karlsson 1973b, p. 51].

The preceding suggests an ultimate incompatibility between industrial democracy and private ownership of industry. The capitalist maximizes profits or
surplus, subject to one crucial consideration—the ability to control surplus appropriation. When control over the work process is recovered by the workers, a
major justification for private surplus appropriation is called into question. A
generalized movement toward workers' control cannot be absorbed by a
capitalist society. It must be resolved either by harsh repression and a return to
industrial autocracy within a capitalist or Soviet-type society or by transition to a
democratic socialist society.

SOCIALISM AND WORKERS' CONTROL

If private ownership necessitates hierarchical control over industry, public
ownership does not necessitate democratic control.[19] One need look no further

---

[17]See, for example, "Sweden Outdates Modern Times" (1974); Jenkins (1973); and Northrup
(1974). It should be pointed out, however, that there are some fundamental differences between
programs in the United States and those in Western Europe: First, work humanization and limited
worker participation have existed in Western Europe on a fairly wide scale for many years; second,
European unions and labor are much more directly involved in demanding changes in work organization than are American unions.

[18]Recently, an experiment in job enlargement was run in the engine assembly department of a Saab
car factory. The women workers involved began to push for greater control over inspection, production control, materials control, and control over recruitment of new workers. Professor Robert Guest
of the Dartmouth Business School provided this information in a recent communication. He also
reports secondhand knowledge of similar examples in Japan, Germany, and France.

[19]We refer here to socialist economies where public ownership predominates, not to the publicly
owned sectors of capitalist economies. Democratic control is certainly not evident in the latter (see
Chapter 1 for a fuller discussion of this point).

than the frustrated attempts at workers' control in the Soviet Union and Eastern Europe to be convinced of this (Brinton 1972; Carr 1966; Deutscher 1950; Narkiewicz 1970; Kollontai 1975; Prankratova 1972; Kovanda 1974; Horvat 1976; Babeau 1968; Pelikan 1973). Industrial management in these countries (excluding Yugoslavia) provides for worker consultation through the trade union committee and job security, but decision making is scarcely democratic beyond restricted labor relations issues at the plant level (Granick 1966; Schwarz 1951; Berliner 1957; Khitrov 1975).[20]

There is accumulating evidence, however, that decision making in Cuban and Chinese enterprises is increasingly democratic.[21] Management of Chinese industry, for instance, is in the hands of the Revolutionary Committee (and its standing committee) which is composed of elected representatives from three groups within each enterprise: the party cadres, the technicians, and the production workers. Problem solving of various kinds is carried out by three-in-one committees with members from each of these groups. The three-in-one committees help to break down the technical division of labor as does the Chinese practice of having cadres and technicians participate on a regular basis in manual labor. General policy guidelines within Chinese enterprises are set by the Party Committee in consultation with various worker groups and in accordance with the economic plan. The district, regional, provincial, and national economic plans are discussed and drawn up by the party committees, revolutionary committees and the planning boards at each and between different levels (Deleyne 1974; Lardy 1975; Robinson 1973).

The philosophy of economic management in China does not justify worker participation on the grounds that it is more productive or profitable; rather worker participation is seen as an essential element in constructing socialist social relationships. The purview of worker decision-making power within the enterprise is circumscribed by the priorities of the economic plan. But the Chinese see this circumscription as a deepening, not a vitiation, of workers' control. Without the coordination of an economic plan, enterprises behave in self-interested ways without regard to general social needs and become captives of the competitive market; workers within the enterprises are transformed into group capitalists;

[20]According to the International Labor Office (1975, pp. 17–20), however, the influence of the trade union committees in the USSR and elsewhere in Eastern Europe in various aspects of industrial management has been extended since 1971.

[21]On Cuba, see Karl (1975); D. Barkin (1975); Harnecker (1975); MacEwan (1974); Zimbalist (1975b). On China, see Deleyne (1974); Hoffmann (1975); Riskin (1974); Meissner (1972); Robinson (1973); Bettelheim (1974); Schurmann (1968); Goldwasser and Dowty (1975); Howe (1973); Brugger (1976); Andors (1977a, 1977b); Schell (1977). This assessment was made prior to the death of Mao and the purge of the gang of four. Although there are some indications that China is de-emphasizing worker participation, current information on management practices is still too incomplete and unclear to make a new judgment.

decision making becomes hierarchical in response to the vicissitudes and exigencies of the market; and inequality, concentration, and unemployment result.

The experience with workers' councils in Yugoslavia is instructive in this regard. There, a system of self-management was introduced in 1950 after a period of highly centralized management and planning. Since 1950, a number of reforms have been enacted which extend, deepen, and further decentralize economic management. Industrial production is theoretically controlled by democratically elected councils at the enterprise and production-unit levels. However, at least since the strengthening of market forces with the 1965 economic reforms, a trend away from democratic management and toward uneven, unequal development is perceptible.

In his comparison of two Yugoslavian textile firms, Adizes (1971) noted that the 1965 reforms created pressure on the firms to expand their middle management staffs. In one firm there was an immediate adaptation to the new market conditions. A new manager was hired, and the size of the marketing department expanded from less than a dozen to 39 people within a year. The need to make rapid responses to the unstable market and the attempt to influence actual market conditions meant that decision making was centered more and more in the hands of middle management.[22] Workers had less and less influence on decision making, and attendance at worker council meetings fell off. In the second firm, the management style, at least through 1966, did not change. Worker attendance and participation at council meetings were maintained, and by typical criteria of technical efficiency (productivity of capital and labor) this second firm was more efficient.[23] Nevertheless, the first firm, because of its further integration into the market, closer contact with the local bank, and greater willingness to take risks, experienced faster growth than the second. Adizes adds that on the basis of interviews with managers from several other enterprises there was a general trend toward managerialism in Yugoslavian firms after the 1965 economic reforms.

Other authors have pointed to the increasing concentration of capital and growing materialist consciousness in Yugoslavia in recent years (Obradovic 1972; Zapp 1973; Burt 1972; Hunnius 1973; Wachtel 1973; Jenkins 1973). It is likely that these tendencies are associated with the strengthening of the market and, in the long run, will contribute further to the weakening of industrial

[22]Lawrence and Lorsch (1967) have demonstrated a positive association between rapidly changing market conditions and horizontal differentiation (number and size of middle management departments) for successful American firms.

Andors finds in China during periods when worker participation in enterprise administration is emphasized that the size of the management staff is notably reduced (1977b, p. 216).

[23]Although Adizes does not make this argument directly, his evidence supports this conclusion. The first firm has 31.3% more productive capital per worker, yet its value of net product per worker is 22.7% below that of the second. The efficiency of working capital is also greater in the second firm. The ratio of "total sales" to "cost of production" (excludes wages) fell in the first firm from 203 in 1964 to 190 in 1966 and increased in the second from 216 in 1964 to 221 in 1966 (Adizes 1971, p. 74).

democracy. One expert on self-management in Yugoslavia puts the issue in the following way:

> Economization and particularization of interests of the employed is the result of the domination of the competitive system and the result of the domination of the ideology of development and consumption. All these factors have been reducing the need for participation in self-government and have been increasing the power of the leading groups in the enterprises [Obradovic 1972, p. 185].

On the other hand, it would be folly to assert that economic planning itself necessarily promotes workers' control. Here again we have the counterexample of the Soviet Union.[24] The planning mechanism must be democratic; workers must participate in decision making not only in their workplaces but also in the formulation of local, regional, and national economic plans. As indicated earlier, the Chinese have structured their planning process to allow for input from below through elected representatives.[25] In addition, the Chinese have emphasized regional self-sufficiency, balanced urban–rural development, and decentralization, all of which serve to minimize local dependence on the central state authority.

The evolution of the Chinese economic and political system since 1949 has not been incidental. The "mass-line," decentralization approach has its roots in the history of the Chinese revolutionary struggle against the Japanese, Kuomintang, and U.S. forces. The contrast with the making of the Soviet revolution in this regard is striking. The Chinese Communist Party (CCP) was based primarily in the peasantry, which constituted over 80% of the population. The leaders of the CCP were actively engaged in over 20 years of guerrilla warfare, fighting side by side with the peasantry. Tens of millions of peasants strategically supported or fought with the Red Army. Land redistribution and cultural upheavals were carried out, and village communes were set up in areas liberated by the Red Army beginning in the 1930s.[26]

The leaders of the Bolshevik Party were outside Russia or in Siberia for most of the period leading up to the October Revolution. The party based itself in the urban proletariat (around 10% of the labor force) and did not gain majority support within this group until two months before the revolution.[27] The Bolsheviks

[24]Some have argued, however, that the recent economic reforms in the Soviet Union, the introduction of profitability as a success criterion, the free labor market, and so on, make the Soviet economy not "planned," but "administered." See, for example, G.A.E. Smith (1975).

[25]In the last several years, and especially with the 1975 constitution, the Cubans have moved in this direction. See Zimbalist (1975b).

[26]See Selden (1971); Snow (1968); Hinton (1973); and Myrdal (1965) for interesting accounts of this period.

[27]This support was gained principally by default through the collaboration of the other left-wing parties in the bankrupt provisional government. Prior to October, the Bolsheviks supported the factory committees and the Soviets. After their victory, they turned against these bodies and brought them under party control imposed from above through the trade unions (see Brinton 1972).

had virtually no base in the peasantry, which, as in China, accounted for over 80% of the population.

The differences in the revolutionary ideology, in the relationship between the party leadership and the masses, and in the level of mass participation in the revolutionary struggle in the Chinese and Soviet cases would seem to contribute to an understanding of the different paths followed in the two countries. The point to be emphasized here is that worker control or economic democracy does not result from a simple policy action or concession from above: Rather, it is conditioned by historical forces relating to worker mobilization, consciousness and organization.

3

The Chilean Context

INTRODUCTION

Chile stands out among Latin American nations for having the longest history of stable political democracy. Although the early years of the Chilean Republic (1830–1871) were marked by a presidential authority with practically all-pervasive powers, the president was nonetheless elected, albeit by a small portion of the population.[1] In the twentieth century, presidential powers have been increasingly circumscribed by an elected bicameral legislature, and the proportion of the population registered to vote has increased sharply. In 1915, for instance, 5.2% of the population voted in the presidential elections. This proportion rose to 10.4% in 1938, to 18.4% in 1952, to 33.2% in the nationwide municipal elections of 1963, and to 38% in the municipal elections in 1971. In 1949, women were enfranchised. After 1958, electoral venality was reduced by the introduction of the secret ballot, and by 1970 suffrage had been extended to individuals over 18 years of age as well as to illiterates.[2] Chile's electoral democracy was blemished by only occasional and transitory periods of political instability or military rule (e.g., 1891, 1924–1925, 1927–1932). However, between 1932 and 1973 there was an uninterrupted period of over 40 years of electoral, civilian government.

Popular political participation was not restricted to the election of political representatives. Local union officials have been legally elected since 1924. During the Frei government (1964–1970) popular participation increased dramatically as the right to unionize was extended to rural workers and local, democratically controlled neighborhood boards, mothers' centers, health centers, and

[1]Federico Gil (1966) has termed these years an "autocratic republic." Property qualifications for voting were abolished by the constitution of 1833.
[2]Illiterates constituted 12% of the population in 1970.

29

consumer cooperatives were established. The electoral system also extended to other areas of the society, such as student associations and university governing boards. One revealing indicator of the upsurge in popular participation during the 1960s is the size of union membership which practically doubled from 276,346 in 1958 to 551,086 in 1970 (Stallings 1975, p. 103). The number of legal strikes increased sharply from 120 in 1958 (48,395 workers affected), to 723 in 1965 (182,359 workers affected), to 1819 in 1970 (656,170 workers affected; Zapata 1976, p. 86). In 1968, the level of unionization in different sectors of the Chilean economy had reached the proportions shown in Table 3.1.

The Chilean government has played a major role in the country's economic affairs since the 1930s. This role was forced upon the government following the collapse of the export sector of the economy during the Great Depression. In fact, Chile's economy was the hardest hit in Latin America between 1929 and 1932 when the value of its exports fell by 88%. Given the absence of a developed industrial entrepreneurial class and the failure of the export sector to provide a continuing basis for economic development, the government became the principal agent of industrial growth. Through the expansion of state credits and state-initiated industry, most of which was subsequently turned over to the private sector, Chile experienced the most rapid period of industrial growth in its history between 1931 and 1945. The cumulative annual growth rate of industrial output during these years was 7.9%.[3]

After World War II, the Chilean government continued to play an increasingly important role in the country's economic development. By 1970, 46.7% of total value added in the economy was induced by public sector expenditures (Ramos 1972, p. 78).[4] In 1969, direct public investment as a proportion of total fixed capital investment was 49.3%; if indirect public investment (government funds transferred to the private sector) is included, this ratio rises to 74.8% (Molina 1972, p. 82). The bulk of industrial capital, however, remained in private hands. In 1970, the state either owned or controlled 28% of the capital in the industrial sector (Stallings 1975, p. 422).

Despite the government's active intervention in economic affairs, the performance record of the Chilean economy has been poor. Davis and Ballesteros (1963) have estimated that the growth rate of real per capita income in Chile was less than 1% per year between 1915 and 1960. During the 1960s, the per capita growth rate of real income averaged 1.9%, led by the industrial sector. Within the industrial sector, most of the growth was attributable to the rapid growth rate

---

[3]Calculated from Mamalakis (1968, pp. A-50–A-67) in terms of constant 1950 *escudos*. Between 1946 and 1970 the annual industrial growth rate averaged around 4% (Mamalakis 1968; Stallings 1975).

[4]Government expenditures were financed primarily through indirect taxes and the expansion of public debt. For the period 1965–1970, an average of 58.6% of government revenues came from indirect taxes (Stallings 1975, p. 521).

TABLE 3.1
Level of Unionization in Chile, by Economic Sector, 1968

Sector	Percentage of workers unionized
Agriculture	14
Mining	62
Industry	40
Construction	27
Electric, gas, water	36
Commerce	22
Transportation, communication	48
Services	36
Overall	ca. 30

Source: Alan Angell, *Politics and the Labor Movement in Chile*, p. 46. Published by Oxford University Press (Oxford: At the University Press 1972) for the Royal Institute of International Affairs and reprinted here by permission.

of the durable consumer goods sector which averaged 10.2% per year during the decade (Stallings 1975, p. 410). This sector, of course, produced primarily for Chile's upper income groups. The production of capital goods lagged behind the rest of the industrial sector, and throughout the 1960s Chile imported between 80 and 90% of its capital goods.

Before World War II, Chile was a net exporter of food products, yet by 1970 it was importing over $300 million (around 30% of foreign exchange earnings) of foodstuffs per year. In 1965, 5% of agricultural properties controlled 86.8% of the land, and nearly 40% of arable land lay fallow (Thiesenhusen 1971, p. 115).[5] Between 1930 and 1970, food production per capita actually fell, and accompanying this poor production record was Chile's endemic inflation which averaged 26% per year during the 1960s.

Per capita income in Chile was estimated to be roughly $500 in 1970. However, this average disguises an underlying extreme inequality. A study done by ODEPLAN (government planning office) in 1964 estimated that the top 4.7% of income earners received 39.3% of personal income, while the bottom 29% received only 4.1% of personal income. Moreover, data available for the industrial sector alone suggest that the distribution of income was growing more unequal during the 1960s, as can be seen in Table 3.2.

It is not surprising that this unequal distribution of income combined with the

[5]Frei's agrarian reform, which redistributed 10.2% of agricultural land, altered this situation slightly by 1970. In that year, 5.3% of agricultural properties controlled 76.7% of the land (Thiesehusen 1971).

TABLE 3.2
Income Distribution by Quintiles for Total Industrial Sector,
Chile

	Percentage of income		
Percentage of population	1959	1964	1970
Bottom 20%	4.0	3.8	2.4
Second 20%	10.1	8.8	7.2
Third 20%	13.6	12.4	11.2
Fourth 20%	20.8	18.7	17.7
Top 20%	51.5	56.3	61.5

Source: Calculated from Barbara Stallings, "Economic Development and Class Conflict in Chile, 1958–73" (Ph.D. dissertation,
Stanford University, 1975), p. 490. In 1970, blue- and white-
collar income as a percentage of total industrial income was 36.9%;
this figure rose to 51.6% in 1972 (Stallings 1975, p. 496).

low level of per capita income was accompanied by severe social problems. For
instance, an article in the *New York Times* (Oct. 4, 1970) pointed out that:

> Half the children between birth and 15 years of age are undernourished and there are 600,000
> Chilean children who are mentally retarded because they have not had enough protein...
> 300,000 able men are out of work[6] and 43% of the population is badly nourished.

The general condition of Chilean society in 1970, then, was unstable. On the
one hand, the political system was characterized by an open democracy and
growing popular participation and militance. On the other hand, the economic
system was characterized by long-term stagnation and extreme and growing
inequality. These conditions were clearly incompatible. The society had either to
move in the direction of radical and progressive social change or in the direction
of severe political repression and dictatorship.

In the following sections of this chapter, we fill in remaining aspects of the
Chilean context that directly relate to our study of worker participation in the
industrial sector. The next section presents a more detailed picture of the organization and structure of Chilean industry in 1970, followed by an overview of

[6]This constituted approximately 11.5% of the labor force. Out of a total labor force in 1970 of 2.6
million, 3.2% were classified as employers, 19.6% as self-employed, 28.7% as white-collar workers,
42.6% as blue-collar workers (including 7% domestics) and the remaining 6% were undeclared
(Stallings 1975, p. 83). By sector, the labor force in 1970 broke down as follows: agriculture 20.3%;
mining 2.9%; industry 16.1%; utilities .8%; construction 5.8%; commerce 11.7%; transportation and
communications 6%; finance 1.6%; services 26%; other 8.7% (Chile, *Instituto Nacional de Estadísticas* 1971, p. 42).

Chilean labor history and legislation governing labor organization. The final section of the chapter provides a summary of the experience with worker participation in Chile prior to the Allende period.

THE INDUSTRIAL STRUCTURE OF CHILE

In 1970, the industrial sector in Chile accounted for 16.1% of total employment and 25.4% of gross domestic product (GDP) (Chile, ODEPLAN 1971a). Although industry's contribution to GDP was sizable, capital goods production was negligible. In 1967, the share of capital goods in total industrial production was only 7.7% (Aranda and Martínez 1970, p. 101).

In total, there were 36,220 industrial establishments in 1970. However, there were only 1386 industrial establishments employing more than 49 persons and 21,450 establishments had fewer than 5 employees (Bitar and MacKenna 1973, p. 37). If we consider only those establishments with 5 or more employees (14,770), we can develop the distributional picture of industrial concentration shown in Table 3.3.

This concentration throughout industry has been coupled with significant monopolization in capital ownership in each industrial sector. Considering a division into 47 different sectors in 1968–1969: In 25 sectors the largest three firms owned more than 75% of total assets of the sector; in 11 sectors the largest

TABLE 3.3
Distribution of Industrial Concentration, Chile, 1963

	Percentage of establishments	Percentage of employment	Percentage of assets	Percentage of value added
Large industry (more than 200 persons per establishment)	3	44	58	51
Medium industry (between 20 and 200 persons)	30	40	35	38
Small industry (between 5 and 20 persons)	67	16	7	11

Source: Chile, ODEPLAN, Antecedentes sobre el Desarrolo Chileno, 1960–1970. Plan de la economía nacional 1971–1976, Ser. 1, no. 1 (Santiago, 1971), p. 12. Concentration has increased considerably since then. Garreton and Cisternas (1970) found that in manufacturing industries in 1966, 144 establishments (equivalent to approximately 1% in this table) owned over 50% of total industrial assets.

three firms owned between 50 and 75% of total sector assets; in 10 sectors the top three firms owned between 25 and 50% of assets and in only one sector did the top three firms own less than 25% of total sector assets (Ramos 1972, p. 64).[7] The sectors with greater concentration were also the more modern and fastest expanding sectors.

The more modern and monopolistic sectors also showed higher levels of penetration by foreign capital. For example, in 1968, 32% of the assets in the chemical sector, 44% of those in rubber and 45% of those in equipment and electrical machinery were foreign owned (Bitar 1971, p. 3).[8] Foreign capital was present in 25.5% of the 833 existing Chilean industrial corporations (*sociedades anónimas*) in 1968. These 25.5% controlled 59.5% of total assets of Chilean industrial corporations (Ramos 1972, p. 50). If we consider only the 160 largest industrial corporations (by assets) in 1968, we find foreign capital present in 82 of them. In 54 of these, foreign capital owned more than 33% of assets, and in 37, more than 50% of assets (Bitar 1971, p. 4).

These features of the economic structure were sufficiently extreme to evoke a broad-based recognition of the need for substantive change. The 1970 campaign programs of both the Popular Unity Coalition, supporting Salvador Allende, and the Christian Democratic Party, supporting Radomiro Tomic, called for the gradual nationalization of the "commanding heights" of the Chilean economy, that is, the large, modern, foreign-penetrated corporations in industry, mining, and commerce. Together, Allende and Tomic received nearly two-thirds of the popular vote in the 1970 elections. In the next chapter, we describe the formation of the social ownership sector of the economy during Allende's presidency. It was in this sector that the Popular Unity government launched its program of worker participation.

THE CHILEAN LABOR MOVEMENT

The Chilean working class has a long history of militant action and organization. Initial worker protest began in the nitrate mining areas in the north and coal

[7]The ownership of corporate assets by individuals was also highly concentrated. In 59.4% of the largest 271 corporations, the 10 largest shareholders owned between 90% and 100% of total stock. Alternatively, in 84.9% of these 271 firms, the 10 largest shareholders owned over 50% of the stock (Ramos 1972, p. 73).

[8]Although foreign investment in Chilean manufacturing actually began in the last century and experienced a spurt in the 1920s and 1930s, it trebled in value between 1960 and 1968, from $22 million in the former year to $68 million in the latter. Most foreign investment in Chile was, of course, concentrated in mining. In 1968, the reported book value of foreign assets in Chilean mining was $586 million. In addition, foreign investment totalled $39 million in Chilean commerce in 1968 (Caputo and Pizarro 1972, p. 184).

mining area in the south.[9] The extremely harsh working conditions, the payment in tokens to use at company stores, and the very unstable employment conditions[10] are often held to account for the early radicalization of the Chilean labor movement. By the 1850s, worker strikes and revolt spread to the tailors, cobblers, and cigarette workers in the cities—soon to be followed by the typographical workers and longshoremen.

As spontaneous working-class actions spread, labor organizations began to emerge. During the last quarter of the nineteenth century, mutual benefit societies were formed. They concentrated, however, on providing social services outside the workplace by channeling worker and artisan savings. Doctrines of class conflict were absent in both the theory and practice of the mutualist societies. Their rapid demise after the first decade of this century has often been explained by the growth of the manufacturing sector and the concomitant decline in the importance of the artisan class.

Following a successful strike of dockworkers in Iquique, a new form of working-class organization was created in 1901—the *mancomunal*. The *mancomunales* were organized around class principles and demanded employment expansion, job stability, an end to blacklisting, and better salaries and working conditions. The *mancomunal* movement quickly spread to the nitrate workers in the north. Although the activities of the *mancomunales* were virtually extinguished by the massive repression of 1907,[11] the nitrate workers were eventually to become the chief force in the radicalization of the FOCH (*Federación Obrera de Chile*).

A parallel development to the *mancomunales* were the *sociedades de resistencia* (resistance societies). They had an anarchist orientation and were most important among the printers, bakers, and railroad workers in the center of the country. The resistance societies joined together in 1919 and entered the International Workers of the World (I.W.W.). Like the mutualist societies, anarchism lost importance as Chile industrialized.

The first national labor federation (FOCH) was formed in 1909. In 1912, the *Partido Obrero Socialista* (POS), headed by Luis Emilio Recabarren, was founded. In 1922, the POS changed its name to the Communist party, and the FOCH joined the Third International in 1919. A depression from 1910 to 1915, a short recovery at the beginning of World War I, and the ensuing nitrate crisis brought wild fluctuations to Chile's wage labor force. The instability, in turn,

---

[9]In both places, worker uprisings were recorded during the 1830s (see Barrera 1971a). Other interesting sources on Chilean working-class history are Barrera (1971b), Peppe (1971), Valenzuela (1973), Ramírez (1956), Castillo, Saez, and Rogers (1970), Noe (1971), Barría (1967; 1970), and Manns (1972).

[10]These were generated by the fact that mining production was principally directed at sharply fluctuating export markets and supplied with surplus, untied agricultural labor.

[11]Over 2500 nitrate workers and members of their families were killed during a strike in Iquique.

TABLE 3.4
Number of Industrial Firms and Industrial Workers

	1910	1915	1923
Firms	5,722	2,406	3,196
Workers	74,618	45,551	82,118

Source: Anibal Pinto Santa Cruz, *Chile: Un caso de desarrollo frustrado* (Santiago: Editorial Universitaria, 1962), p. 49.

provoked increasing worker militance and strike activity. See Tables 3.4 and 3.5.

The eruption of the workers' movement helped to bring liberal Arturo Alessandri to the presidency in 1920. In 1924, Chile had its first labor code, which legalized and institutionalized the already prevalent labor unions and strikes. Although the labor code created serious limitations to union strength and channeled working-class protest into the bourgeois democratic system, it also helped to preserve a certain effervescence, democracy, and political orientation within the labor movement.

The labor code created at least two separate unions in each company: one for white-collar workers and one for blue-collar workers. Unions were allowed to be formed only where there were more than 25 white-collar or blue-collar workers over the age of 18. Public employees were not allowed to unionize. Strike funds were barred, and all union funds were tightly controlled. Paid union staffs were prohibited and union officials were required to stay at their jobs. Officials were elected for 1 year. Collective bargaining took place at the plant level, and all labor federations were illegal. The latter three features served to impede union bureaucratization and to promote rank-and-file involvement and influence within their unions. According to a 1967 study of 920 industrial workers,

> Sixty per cent of *obreros* (blue-collar workers) said that the majority of the members had "much" influence over the decisions of the union, 27% said it had some . . . 82% thought the majority decided whether the union should go on strike. . . . 87% thought it was possible to remove leaders right away [Peppe 1971, Chapter 4].[12]

The labor code provisions for no federations and no strike funds led labor unions to seek tactical and financial support through the working-class oriented political parties. These provisions, which were intended to fragment labor organization, thus backfired and ended up politicizing and strengthening the defensive power of the labor movement.

[12]According to this study, 64.7% of the workers consulted said they always attend union meetings and an additional 12.6% said that they usually attend. Only 2.5% said they never attend (Barrera 1971b, p. 56).

TABLE 3.5
Number of Strikes per Year, 1911–1924

Year	Number of strikes
1911	8
1912	26
1913	27
1914	8
1915	7
1916	21
1917	18
1918	18
1919	71
1920	58
1921	59
1922	29
1923	58
1924	52

Source: Manuel Barrera, "Perspectiva histórica de la huelga obrera en Chile," *Cuadernos de la Realidad Nacional* (September 1971).

The offensive power, however, was never adequately cultivated. The popular front governments (1938–1952) brought short-term gains to the working class but ultimately led to its repression and the banning of the Communist party (1948–1958). When the Communist party (CP) was legalized again in 1958, it gained control of the new national labor federation (CUT),[13] formed in 1953. The part of the 1953 CUT program that called for the struggle for a socialist state was dropped by the CUT in 1959.[14]

The political leadership of the working class lagged behind its base. The 1967 survey cited previously revealed that 48% of the workers surveyed felt that industry should be run either by the workers or by the workers and the state. Nevertheless, the issue of worker control over production was never raised by the CUT prior to Allende's presidency, and union leaders gave very little priority to control issues (Barrera 1971b, pp. 30, 50; Valencia 1968).

The combination of rank-and-file involvement, political party leadership, and national coordination along with the institutionalization and economistic orientation of the trade union movement led to contradictory developments in the organization of the Chilean working class. These contradictions persisted

[13]CUT stands for the *Central Unica de Trabajadores*.
[14]The implication of the CP in this change was intended. Even by 1970 the CP line had not changed.

throughout the Allende period as the contrast between rank-and-file militance and inadequate worker leadership became more and more evident.[15]

EXPERIENCE WITH WORKER PARTICIPATION
PRIOR TO 1970

The earliest institutionalized form of worker participation in Chile came with the labor code in 1924. The code provided for 10% of profits to be set aside in each firm where there was a legally established blue-collar union (*sindicato industrial*). Five percent would be divided among the blue-collar workers as wage supplements. All blue-collar workers benefited, provided they had attended at least 70% of the working days during the year, but the bonus could not exceed 6% of the basic pay rate. The other 5% went to the union fund, and its disbursement was tightly controlled by a government agency. In all, this minimal profit-sharing scheme probably did more to discipline unionized labor than to stimulate broader worker participation (Núñez 1972).

No new forms of worker participation were introduced again until the late 1960s. Despite the rank-and-file interest in participation mentioned previously, trade union leadership concentrated their bargaining efforts on immediate economic gains. Management, of course, preferred to make concessions in the form of higher remuneration than in the form of greater worker involvement in administration. A 1966 study of 517 union petitions (Valencia 1968) illustrates the predominantly economistic character of union demands. He found that some type of worker participation was requested in only 27.8% (159 firms) of the petitions, the remaining 72.2% were concerned exclusively with economic issues.

Moreover, of the 27.8% of the petitions containing some kind of demand for greater participation, the great majority requested participation only in the structuring of wage and bonus policies. The limited nature of these petitions and the virtual absence of meaningful worker participation in Chilean firms during the late 1960s is described by Valencia:

> From the petitions honored with some participation content, a common aim can be observed—the formation of commissions in which the workers are represented on an equal footing with the entrepreneurs, although what attracts attention is the restricted nature of the range of action that the commissions have and that they do not have any influence on the running of the firm.
> If the participation that the workers asked for through their petition sheets was limited and

---

[15]The CUT was legalized in January 1971. By 1972 it was claiming to represent one million unionized workers, including those in the agricultural and public sectors. The total labor force was approximately three million at the time.

E 772

858.3

8224

324.493

4828

330.98

5835

647

31,1983
M874e
983.6646 3
D2
2 be u

the participation that the entrepreneurs were disposed to authorize or grant them was even less, in practice that limited participation disappears and is reduced to cases that can be treated as marginal [1968, pp. 113, 122; our translation].

During the 1960s, however, a series of factors brought the issue of worker participation to the fore: among others, the initiation of an agrarian reform that contemplated the administration of expropriated land by peasant cooperatives;[16] the growing militance of industrial workers; the failure of many small firms during the recession of 1968–1970; and the pressure from and ideological pronouncements of the more progressive sectors of the Christian Democratic party (CDP). With respect to this last factor, for example, at the CDP's second national congress, held in 1966, a program entitled "The Non-Capitalist Path of Development" was put forth by leading progressive members of the party. Among other proposals, the program called for the development of an area in the national economy where worker management would prevail.

After prolonged persistence and debate within the party, in 1967 a government agency, the Service of Technical Cooperation (SCT), was charged with preparing studies and a program to initiate worker-run enterprises, which it submitted to the government in July 1968.[17] However, the Frei government was reluctant to implement the report's proposals, and in the end, the funds for financing the recommended program were not appropriated. Between 1965 and 1970, the state assisted in the formation of only 22 worker-run enterprises, all with little capital and very little repercussion on the rest of the economy.

At the same time, the Frei government was confronted with numerous worker demands for participation in various public enterprises.[18] Among the most salient cases were IANSA (the state sugar refining company), ENAP (the national

[16]Related to this factor was the changing position of the church in the early sixties. Inside Chile, the church provided the basis for the first land redistributions during 1962–1963 as it relinquished its own holdings. Outside Chile, the papal encyclical of 1961, quoted in Chapter 1, emphasized the importance of worker participation in enterprise decision making as a basic human right.

Another external factor that may possibly have influenced the growing interest in worker participation is found in the reforms called for by the Alliance for Progress in the early 1960s which set in motion reform movements in many Latin American countries. In Chile, the reform movement assumed deeper proportions than it did elsewhere on the Continent, perhaps because of the more open and democratic nature of Chilean society. Thus, the Frei government's slogan of "Revolution in Liberty" and its programs for *promoción popular* ('popular participation') emerged in the wake of the reform impulse of the Alliance for Progress and, accordingly, raised popular expectations and brought to the surface previously latent aspirations of the workers.

[17]Servicio de Cooperación Técnica, "Proposiciones para la Creación y Fomento de Empresas de Trabajadores."

[18]During the Frei period, there were 43 state enterprises engaged in production. The state also held capital in some 70 enterprises.

petroleum enterprise), ENDESA (the state electric company), and LAN CHILE (the national airlines). Although in some instances, after protracted labor and political pressure, the workers eventually gained small minority participation on the enterprises' management boards, the procedure followed by government authorities was always evasive. They maintained a favorable public disposition to participation, but their concrete responses were uniformly discouraging—maintaining that the idea was good but premature, that other urgent problems had to be resolved first, that the idea must be subjected to further study.

The authorities' reluctance to grant real participation to workers in state enterprises is clearly exemplified by the history of labor contract negotiations at IANSA (see Table 3.6).

Similarly, as suggested above, worker pressure to gain control over production also began to emerge in small enterprises of the private sector during the late 1960s. One such instance occurred at the SABA electronics factory (Morris 1973, pp. 158–159). In July 1968, after 42 days of a legal strike, negotiations between management and labor broke down. Workers took over the factory but

TABLE 3.6
IANSA Labor Contract Negotiations, 1962–1969

Year	Worker demands	State response
1962–1963 [a]	Creation of a mixed commission to study remuneration and work schedules	Demand rejected
1964–1965	Worker participation in enterprise management	Demand rejected
1965–1966	Worker participation in enterprise management	Local management does not have the right to grant the workers participation
1966–1967	Worker participation in enterprise management	Two worker representatives given right to attend meetings of directorate when directorate believes the discussion pertains to worker interests. Local management "notifies CORFO of worker demand for participation" and CORFO responds "we have taken note of the workers' demand"
1968	Worker participation	Incentive commission formed. Two employee representatives allowed to attend without right to voice or vote
1969	White-collar union asks for one representative at meetings of directorate	Request denied

[a] During Alessandri government.

were quickly expelled. A media campaign vilifying the workers and sanctifying private property ensued (Arroyo 1974, p. 11).

The next worker takeover was preceded by active community work to gain popular support. By October 1968 the owner of Andrés Hidalgo metal works had accumulated large unpaid debts and begun to delay the payment of wages. When the owner attempted to dismantle his machinery, "vigilant community women watching the plant premises spread the alarm and within minutes neighbors stopped the operation [Morris 1973, p. 159]." The factory was taken over in December, but

> when the police did arrive, replete with tear gas pellets and masks, they found the plant surrounded by students, workers, families, and, in the front lines, several Congressmen and Congresswomen. Unwilling to accept the political consequences of action, the police withdrew, and the first battle of the workers was won [Morris 1973, p. 159].

Next the workers had to buy up the plant's machinery from Hidalgo's creditors. Neither the banks nor the Frei government would lend them any money, so the workers issued a "cooperation bond" which was subscribed to by workers and peasants throughout the country. The bonds were repaid and COOTRALACO (the company's new name) experienced considerable success. All jobs were rotated and everybody received equal pay, although the cooperative was small, containing only 175 members.

In 1969, a 40-year-old textile factory in Valparaiso, Sedamar, was about to be closed down by the owners, who claimed their business was no longer profitable. After 87 workers were fired, the workers asked the Frei government for permission to run the factory themselves. Authorities did not heed the workers' request and lent the owners 400,000 *escudos* instead. During Allende's first year, Sedamar was passed to the social ownership sector. Production rose 4.8 times, and Sedamar became the most profitable textile firm in the social sector (*Experiencias de Masas* 1972).

A similar example occurred in the metal-working factory, SOTRAMET. Through an agreement with its owner, SOTRAMET became a worker-run cooperative in 1968. In 1969, a special unit of the SCT, which was initially created to provide technical and financial assistance to promote worker cooperatives,[19] issued a report on the financial situation of SOTRAMET. The report said that SOTRAMET would be bankrupt in 3 months and the enterprise would be forced to close down unless it came under government tutelage (Arroyo 1974). The SCT offered three technical assistants and a small credit as part of the plan for government intervention. By unanimous agreement of the worker assembly at SOTRAMET, the government plan was rejected and the workers continued to

---

[19]By 1969, this unit had been almost entirely dismantled and politically reoriented.

manage alone without government loans or technicians. After 6 months, the
workers sent the SCT an economic report revealing production and profit gains.
One SOTRAMET worker commented on this experience: "Inventiveness, skill,
new ideas, responsibility, relations with the workers in other enterprises . . . were
things that the technical study of the SCT couldn't measure."

COOTRALACO and SOTRAMET were two of a total of some 30 production
cooperatives ("*empresas de trabajadores*") formed in the last 2 years of the Frei
government. The others all had fewer than 80 members, and each was formed in
a firm where the owner had abandoned the factory, the firm had gone bankrupt,
or there was a negotiation for sale of the company to the workers. The establishment of *empresas de trabajadores* accelerated under Allende: By September
1972, there were approximately 100, and a year later there were some 120. This
growth had prompted the formation of a national federation of producer cooperatives (*Federación de Brigadas y Empresas de Trabajadores*). The 120 producer
cooperatives employed a total of around 8000 workers. The federation had a
membership of 6000, or 75% of total employment in the cooperative sector.

Although the Christian Democrats did not promote the growth of *empresas de
trabajadores* in practice, they put them forth as the ideal form of economic
organization in their theory and rhetoric. When the Christian Democrats with-
drew their support for the development of the sector of social property during the
Allende government, the *Federación de Brigadas y Empresas de Trabajadores*
asked that its member cooperatives be incorporated into this sector. The head of
the federation, Victor Arroyo, who was not a member of any political party,
explained this decision on several different occasions:

> We understood that an isolated factory managed by its own workers had no meaning if there
> was not an interrelation with the rest of the working class. . . . We came to discover that
> self-management *per se* doesn't exist. It doesn't exist because we depended on one thing called
> the market and on another called the supply of raw materials, and on yet others, such as credits.
> We saw that it was essential to radically alter the whole socio-economic system to permit
> workers to have gradual access to the organisms of ultimate decision-making power . . . without
> central planning we run the risk of entering into ruthless competition with other worker
> collectives. We could say, then, that self-management requires central planning [*Panorama
> Económico*, September 1972].

> We don't want the enterprises to belong to the workers for a very simple reason: our history
> of more than 4 years has taught us that when we are owners we cease to be workers . . . we
> become a labor aristocracy. There's the example of SICH (a printing company) where the
> workers began to employ outside labor and gradually ceased to work themselves [*Chile Hoy*,
> June 23–29, 1972].

The Allende government, however, wanted to concentrate on the efficient operation of the larger enterprises already in the socialized sector of the economy and
therefore did not act on the federation's petition.

We have seen, then, that while worker participation had not experienced substantial growth in practice prior to 1970, it had been introduced as a major item on the political agenda. The 1970 campaigns of both Salvador Allende (Popular Unity) and Radomiro Tomic (Christian Democrat) emphasized the importance of worker participation and the need to form an area of social ownership in the economy.

4

An Overview of the Reforms
Concerning Worker Participation

INTRODUCTION

In Chapter 3 we discussed certain salient characteristics of the Chilean economy in 1970: sharp inequality, long-run stagnation, rapidly growing foreign debt, extensive penetration by foreign capital, dependence upon copper for over 80% of export earnings, and so on. The program of the Popular Unity contemplated a drastic restructuring of the country's economic institutions. More specifically, the program included proposals to sharply redistribute income and services to the poor; free the economy from control by foreign capital; nationalize large industry, finance, distribution, and mining; rapidly extend the agrarian reform initiated during the Frei government; and introduce popular participation at all levels.[1]

In the following sections of this chapter we concentrate on two areas of economic reform carried out by the Popular Unity government: the construction of the sector of social ownership in the economy and the introduction of worker participation in this sector.

[1]Although less extensive, similar reforms were proposed by Radomiro Tomic, the Christian Democratic candidate for president in 1970. For a comparison of the political programs of the Popular Unity and Christian Democrat parties in the 1970 campaign, see Joán Garcés (1971, pp. 101–107).

FORMATION OF THE SECTOR OF SOCIAL
OWNERSHIP (APSM)[2]

The Proposed Reforms

Since the creation of the state development corporation, CORFO, in 1939, the state has played an active role in establishing and maintaining certain enterprises. During the 1940s and 1950s, CORFO set up several dozen enterprises. Most of these were turned over to private capital when proven to be economically viable, but some continued to be owned and managed by the state. When Allende became president on November 4, 1970, there were 43 state enterprises, of which 30 were industrial. They included some enterprises owned fully by the state and some in which the state held majority ownership. The 30 industrial enterprises accounted for 11.8% of industrial production and 6.5% of industrial employment (Bitar and MacKenna 1973, p. 10).

The Popular Unity proposed to expand this state sector into a large area of social property which would include the "commanding heights" of the economy. The formation of this enlarged *social area* was justified on several grounds: One, it would be the basis of a new development model oriented toward serving the interests of the great majority of the population by ending the hegemonic control exercised by small groups of domestic and foreign capital; two, it would create the necessary conditions for launching a program of workers' control over decision making in the economy's most important enterprises; three, it would permit social control over a large portion of the total economic surplus which could be rechanneled to the production of essential consumer items and the further development of the country's basic mineral resources; four, it would enable a development strategy with priority to full employment and substantive income redistribution; five, it would reduce external dependence and promote an economic strategy geared to domestic development needs.

The area of social ownership would be made up of two subsectors: the APS (*area de propiedad social*), enterprises where state ownership would exceed 80%, which would include the large mining and major manufacturing, financial, and distribution enterprises of the economy; and the APM (*area de propiedad mixta*), enterprises where state ownership would be between 50% and 80%, which would include other key enterprises. The final bill sent by the Popular Unity to the Congress in January 1973 regarding the proposed composition of the area of social ownership would have, if enacted, brought an estimated 28.7% of

---

[2]APSM stands for the *Area de Propiedad Social y Mixta* ('Area of Social and Mixed Property'). It was often called simply the *area social*. For lack of a better term, we often refer to the process of a firm passing to the *social area* as *socialization*. As will become evident in this section, *socialization* encompasses several distinct juridical and organizational possibilities.

total industrial production into the APS and an additional 15.2% into the APM (Bitar and MacKenna 1973, p. 10). The remainder of industrial production would stay in the private sector (APP, *area de propiedad privada*) of the economy according to the Popular Unity proposal.

Implementation of the Reform

When Allende was overthrown on September 11, 1973, the Chilean state owned or managed some 420 enterprises which constituted the APSM or social area. In the following paragraphs, we describe the mechanisms used to expand the social area of the economy, the timetable and form of its expansion, and its ultimate importance in the Chilean economy.

There were five basic mechanisms available to expand the social area. One, the state could create new enterprises. During 1971 and 1972, eight such enterprises were created (*Instituto de Economía* 1973, p. 89). Two, a constitutional reform could give the chief executive nationalization powers. This was the case with Chile's natural resources. On July 11, 1971, a unanimous vote in Congress nationalized the Anaconda and Kennecott shares in Chilean copper mines, the Bethlehem Steel share in Chilean iron mines, and the Guggenheim share in the nitrate mines. Three, the government could enter into negotiations with any private company. Not surprisingly, many companies in Chile found the business atmosphere less than hospitable and were willing to negotiate the sale of their assets with the government. In all, the government negotiated to buy a controlling share in 58 companies—20 of which had been either "intervened" or "requisitioned" by the government.

The fourth and fifth mechanisms for expanding the social area were *intervention* and *requisition*. Unlike the first three mechanisms, *intervention* and *requisition* entailed a temporary condition of state management. The labor code (article 26) and the Law of Internal Security (article 38) provide for the Ministry of Labor to *intervene* in a firm where labor troubles are interfering with normal production. DFL (decree with force of law) 520 of 1932 and subsequent revisions permit the Ministry of Economics to *requisition* an enterprise where economic problems are causing production to fail. Intervention requires an extra bureaucratic step and is a longer process, but it gives the state appointed manager more financial powers than requisition. Intervention was usually preceded by some form of worker initiative: a slowdown, strike, or worker takeover. In many cases, the government was reluctant to intervene, but was forced to by the massive support and mobilization of workers from surrounding factories. Requisition at times occurred in response to worker initiative but more commonly followed an action by the owners, e.g., lockouts, layoffs, dismantling equipment, or trading on the black market. Many firms were both intervened and requisitioned. In total, out of the 420-odd enterprises in the state sector on

September 10, 1973, approximately 260 had been intervened or requisitioned. The great majority of these, however, were small firms with fewer than 300 workers.

Just as the government had legal recourse to expand the social area, the opposition had legal recourse to impede this expansion. First, because they had majority control in Congress, they could vote down government proposals to extend the state sector. Second, they had the unique institution, the *Contraloría,* whose purpose was to oversee the actions of the executive branch and pass judgment on their legal propriety. The head of this institution, the *contralor,* was appointed by Frei. Out of the list of 91 firms described later, the *Contraloría* judged in 15 cases that requisition or intervention was illegal. To override the decision of the *Contraloría,* the chief executive had to issue a *decreto de insistencia,* which had to be signed by all members of the president's cabinet. Third, the opposition could go to the judicial system to obtain a *decreto precautorio,* which made it practically impossible to administer the enterprise by imposing a set of restrictions: appointing a second administrator with greater powers than the one appointed by the government; freezing the bank account of the enterprise; prohibiting the hiring and firing of personnel; enjoining the deposit of all revenue in an outside account; requiring the endorsement of commercial documents by the owners and so on. In all, *decretos precautorios* were imposed in some 40 enterprises.

In December 1970, 11 firms passed to the social area. The next month, another 26 firms were socialized. This process continued apace during 1971, and the opposition began to demand that Allende set limits to expropriation. In October 1971, Allende sent the first bill to Congress delimiting three areas of the economy: social (APS), mixed (APM), and private (APP) and asking for executive powers to nationalize 253 enterprises, each with total assets exceeding 14 million *escudos* as of December 31, 1969. Enterprises with asset value below this level were to stay in the private sector. In the same month, the opposition put forth the Hamilton–Fuentealba constitutional reform proposal—its response to the government's bill—which would have made all interventions and requisitions after October 14, 1971 illegal and forced the return of the banks, large distribution firms, and other monopolies to the private sector. In addition, it stipulated that all future expropriations would require separate acts of Congress. During the discussions in Congress over these bills, Allende further delimited the proposed social area and presented a list of only 91 firms to enter the APSM,[3] but Congress did not grant him faculties to nationalize them.

In February 1972, Congress passed the Hamilton–Fuentealba constitutional reform, and Allende promptly vetoed the bill. Thereupon a debate ensued on whether or not a two-thirds vote was necessary to override the presidential veto.

[3]This list was later reduced to 90 and in January 1973 extended to 92.

TABLE 4.1
Interventions and Requisitions

Year	Procedure	Total	Returned to private area	Remained in social area
1971	Interventions	128	26	102
1971	Requisitions	39	1	38
1972	Interventions	65	27	38
1972	Requisitions	86	11	75
Totals		318	65	253 [a]

[a] It is important to remember that some firms were both requisitioned and intervened. Thus the totals are inflated because of double counting.

The opposition, which had a majority but not two-thirds, argued that although a two-thirds vote was needed to override an executive veto for ordinary bills, in the case of constitutional reform a simple majority sufficed. An ambiguity in the Constitution left the issue temporarily unresolved, and there was talk of a popular plebiscite. In June and July 1972, the UP (Popular Unity) and PDC (Christian Democrats) held extended negotiations in an effort to come to an understanding. The PDC wanted some 15 other firms (mostly textiles) to be removed from the list of 90 firms, and before they approved the passage to the APSM of the remaining 75 firms, they wanted the government to return 160 firms requisitioned or intervened prior to July 1972 to the private sector.[4] On the one side, the government, under pressure from the working class, could not accept these terms, and on the other, the Christian Democrats, considering that the negotiations were taking too long and concerned about the proximity of the next local congressional election in Coquimbo, decided to stop the search for agreement; and the talks broke down. With the question of socialization unresolved at the superstructural level, worker strikes and takeovers and owner sabotage continued at the base. Table 4.1 provides a summary of interventions and requisitions during 1971 and 1972.

During 1973, the government and the opposition initiated new attempts to overcome the constitutional impasse, but one after another they failed. Nevertheless, by Allende's last month in office, the social area had grown to be an important force in the Chilean economy. Fifty of the 74 manufacturing firms on the list of 91 had been incorporated into the APSM. Some 200 additional man-

[4]At this juncture, the government was prompted to send two new bills to Congress: One would give the status of law to the system of comanagement in social area enterprises which appeared on the list of 91 firms; and another would create a system of worker self-management in the remaining enterprises of the social area. See Chile, Popular Unity Government (1972a; 1972b). With the Christian Democrats and the National Party united in opposition to these bills, they never became law.

ufacturing firms not on the government list also passed to the social area. In total, the manufacturing enterprises of the social area accounted for over 40% of total industrial production (in sales) and employed around 140,000 workers, approximately 30% of the industrial labor force.[5] In addition, social area enterprises accounted for approximately 95% of total bank credit, 90% of total mining production, and 28% of food distribution.

THE BASIC NORMS OF PARTICIPATION

The Debate over Participation

The principle of communitarian or social ownership was officially adopted by the Christian Democrats during the Frei government. Although the Christian Democrats (CDP) presented no bills to Congress to institute social property and participation during the Frei period, the CDP developed an elaborate self-management system which was proposed to the Congress after Allende took office.

The basic elements of the CDP proposal were self-management, usufruct rights on capital to be rented from capitalists, workers' remuneration tied to the enterprises' income, market context and planning through fiscal controls, and a national finance fund for surplus transference. In contrast, the UP argued that the national interests should be represented on the administrative councils of all strategic firms, that it was implausible to expect capitalists not to demand an ultimate form of control under the usufruct arrangement, that workers' remuneration should not be tied to income which varied haphazardly with market conditions but instead should be linked to productivity gains, and that the market context would set up interenterprise rivalries and divide the working class. While the Christian Democrats said that state planning leads to bureaucratic control, the UP maintained that the market would lead to technocratic control.

On a theoretical level, the debate resembled the different Yugoslavian and Chinese approaches to the problem of socialist development. The actual PDC proposals to Congress, however, made it clear that the Christian Democrats were not out to create a Yugoslavian brand of socialism in Chile; on the contrary, the effect of their proposals would have been to preserve capitalist control over the

[5]These figures are our estimates based on data from Instituto de Economía, 1973; Chile, ODEPLAN (1972); Chile, CORFO (1970); and Bitar and MacKenna (1973). The 40% figure includes copper fabrication (bars, ingots, wires—division 3721), which is excluded from other estimates. The figure for total industrial employment is based on considering both industrial artisans and the industrial proletariat. In 1970, the industrial labor force in Chile broke down in the following way: 57.8% blue collar; 16.6% white collar; 3.1% employers and others; 22.5% self-employed workers (Instituto de Economía 1973, p. 150).

economy and the enterprises. The PDC bill that passed the House of Deputies stipulated that firms already in the social area on a permanent basis would become *empresas de trabajadores* if 60% of the workers in the firm so voted.[6] The PDC position on intervened and requisitioned enterprises was that they should be returned to their private owners according to the guidelines of the Hamilton–Fuentealba proposal. Although workers in state enterprises could choose to become self-managing, those in the private area, according to the House bill, could not do so unless 50% of the ownership agreed. This made it very unlikely that the sector of self-managed enterprises would expand. The House bill had another provision which vitiated the content of self-management: An *empresa de trabajadores* would be managed by a superior council of administration to be composed of an equal number of labor and owner representatives, but in the case of a tie, the deciding vote would be cast by the chief executive officer of the firm. Thus ultimate decision-making authority would be retained by the owners. Moreover, it is relevant here to recall that the Christian Democrats voted against the Popular Unity bill of July 1972 which would have converted all social area firms not on the list of the 91 strategic enterprises into worker self-managed enterprises.

The Proposed Reforms

In December 1970, the government and CUT agreed to set up a joint commission to consider the new participatory management system for social area firms. In February 1971, the joint commission delivered a provisional document to the ninth national conference of CUT. The document was discussed and amended by provincial and local bodies of CUT during March, April, and May (Chile, Comité Ejecutivo Nacional CUT—Gobierno de Participación 1972a). In June, the final text outlining the new worker-participation scheme was ready. The text provided general guidelines for the creation of participation organizations in the socialized firms and came to be called the *normas básicas de participación*. To stimulate and oversee the implementation of the *normas básicas,* a joint CUT–Government Executive Participation Committee was formed, composed of four representatives from the national CUT and five representatives from the government.[7]

---

[6]An *empresa de trabajadores* was the Christian Democratic vision of a worker-managed firm operating in a market context.

[7]The five government representatives included one from each of the following bodies: the Ministry of Economics, the Ministry of Labor, ODEPLAN (the National Planning Office), CORFO (The State Development Corporation) and INACAP (The National Institute of Training and Instruction). This executive committee was later to merge with the department of participation of CUT, which had been created with the express purpose of realizing studies and analyzing the modifications to the basic norms of participation suggested by the workers.

The basic content of the *normas básicas* may be summarized as follows. The superior decision-making body in an enterprise is the administrative council. The administrative council is composed of five worker representatives (three production workers, one administrative worker, and one professional or technical worker), five state representatives, and one administrator appointed by the state who presides over the administrative council. All members have the right to voice and vote. The administrative council generally meets biweekly.[8]

The worker representatives on the administrative council are elected in a general assembly. They are elected for 2-year terms and can be reelected once. They are also removable at any moment by a majority vote of the general assembly.

Calling the first general assembly and preparing for the election of representatives is the responsibility of the union commission.[9] Thereafter, the general assembly is to meet monthly and be presided over by the union commission. The essential task of the general assembly, beyond election and recall, is to oversee and control the activities of the other groups participating in the enterprise.

Also at the base level are the sectional assemblies, corresponding to the different production sections in the plant. Each sectional assembly meets monthly, elects and revokes representatives to the production committee, and oversees the activities of the latter body. The entire table of organization is shown in Figure 4.1.

Each production committee, which meets weekly, has between three and seven members, all workers from the section. The members, in turn, elect a president who attends the coordinating council. The production committees have no formal decision-making powers, since general policy is set by the administrative council. However, suggestions to increase production and quality or improve working conditions were generally accepted when feasible and consistent with overall policy.

Communication between the production committees and the administrative council is channeled through the coordinating committee. The coordinating committee meets biweekly, presided over by the head of the union commission, usually the president of the largest union in the enterprise.[10] Meetings of the coordinating committee are also attended by the five worker representatives on the administrative council and, as already mentioned, the presidents of the different production committees. The meetings of the coordinating committee, the production committees, the sectional assemblies, and the general assembly are

[8]It is stipulated that all bodies shall meet more frequently when necessary. It was not unusual, for instance, for an administrative council to meet several times per week during certain periods.

[9]This is simply a body of all the officers of all the unions in the factory.

[10]It will be recalled that Chilean firms typically had at least two unions due to the specifications of the 1924 Labor Code. However, during the Allende period there was a tendency for the white- and blue-collar unions to merge to form one "class-unified" union.

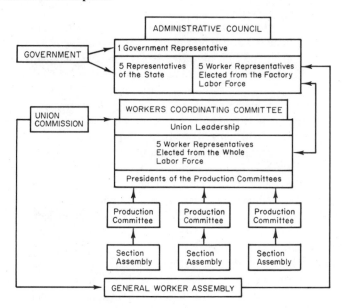

Figure 4.1 The participating individuals and groups according to the *normas básicas*. The number of production committees and section assemblies will vary depending on the scale of the enterprise.

all held after work hours. Elected worker representatives to these bodies receive no pay,[11] serve for periods of 2 years, can be reelected only once, and are immediately recallable.

The Implementation of the Reform

Although the *normas básicas* never had the force of law, they were applied flexibly and unevenly throughout Chile's social area. By June 1972, their application had begun in modified or complete form in 76% of the enterprises in the social area (Chile, Comité Ejecutivo Nacional CUT—Gobierno de Participación 1972b).[12] Although no aggregate statistics are available for the period after June

[11]This is also true of the representatives on the administrative council and of union officials.

[12]By this date, in 56% of the social area firms an administrative council was functioning, but the extent to which they functioned varied considerably among industries. In textiles, administrative councils were operating in 20 out of 22 enterprises; in metallurgy, it was operating in 21 out of 37; in large-scale mining, in 5 out of 5; in agroindustrial, in 8 out of 14; in fish processing and packaging, in 16 out of 17; in wood, furniture, and cellulose, in 15 out of 20; in medium-scale mining, in 9 out of 42; in chemicals, in 3 out of 7; in material for construction, in 9 out of 14; in electronics and communications, in 7 out of 13; in transport, in 3 out of 13; and in other services, in 5 out of 9. These statistics are based on the data presented in Chile, Comité Ejecutivo Nacional CUT—Gobierno de Participación (1972).

1972, it is very likely that the proportion of enterprises where the *normas básicas* were being implemented went up during the final 15 months of Allende's tenure.

The uneven application of the *normas básicas* can be explained by a variety of factors. Given the historically open and democratic nature of Chilean politics, it is natural that a transition period would be characterized by change more rapid in some economic sectors or geographical areas than in others. The heritage of a capitalist economy with its attendant decentralized features meant that each enterprise was on its own in carrying out the transformation to a participatory system at least until a state planning apparatus became operative.[13] The main institution in the existing central apparatus, CORFO, was relatively weak and without concrete powers to direct economic activity. During the Allende period, sectoral development committees were established within CORFO to oversee and coordinate the production of enterprises in various economic sectors. However, since CORFO had been created for purposes other than economic planning and there were other government agencies with parallel functions, a large number of deficiencies developed. Without adequate coordination within CORFO, the sectoral committees evolved different policies and maintained different relations with the enterprises under their jurisdictions. This explains, in part, the unevenness in the application of the *normas básicas* between distinct economic sectors. Finally, there were differences in the level of worker organization and consciousness among various enterprises in the social area that were produced by characteristics peculiar to each firm. This resulted not only in the flexible adaptation of the *normas básicas* in social area firms, but also in significant disparities among enterprises in the speed with which the new participatory system was introduced and how far it developed.[14]

A few brief comments on the content of the *normas básicas* are in order at this point. Union officers were to be in charge of setting up initial elections, calling meetings, and educating the workers about their rights and responsibilities under the new management system. They were also to preside over two basic participation bodies: the general assemblies and the coordinating councils. Thus, the activities and attitudes of the unions had a big influence on the development of worker participation.

Nevertheless, union officers were not eligible for election as worker representatives to either the administrative councils or the production committees. In this way, unions were not fully integrated into the new management structure and could maintain their independence in defending workers' interests. Although there was dissension within the UP over this issue, two additional points were often adduced to argue for union autonomy. First, as long as the class character

---

[13]Even the existing state enterprises in 1970 were managed in a largely autonomous fashion.

[14]This point is examined in detail in Chapter 6.

of the state was not clearly defined, independent unions were necessary to carry the class struggle forward. Second, and slightly contradictory to the first point, unions historically played a defensive role in looking after class interests, e.g., protect real wage levels or increase job security. Although the establishment of workers' control over production required an offensive leadership, the defensive posture of unions led them to paternalistic and at times bureaucratic behavioral modes. For this reason, the unions appeared less than optimal to direct the struggle for industrial democracy.

In fact, it was commonplace for Chilean unions to react jealously against the creation of new bodies to represent the workers because the unions thereby lost their hegemony over worker representation and, consequently, their power. A jealous union reaction would usually postpone the application of the *normas básicas;* or, in some cases, active party cadres undertaking this application would completely bypass the unions to stimulate discussion and call initial assemblies.[15]

Another fundamental feature of the *normas básicas* is their provision for six state representatives but only five worker representatives on the administrative councils. However, it was only in the very largest state enterprises that this ratio was actually observed. In over 90% of the social area enterprises and in all of the 35 randomly selected firms in our sample (see Chapter 5), the worker representatives had a working majority (and often over 75%) on the administrative councils. This came about for several different reasons. First, the state-appointed representatives were often chosen from among the workers in the factories. Second, the state representatives would frequently be unable to attend administrative council meetings because they were busy with other jobs.[16] Third, workers could increase their control over an administrative council by throwing out the government appointed administrator where the latter was found to be unresponsive, heavy handed, technocratic, or sectarian. In one factory we surveyed, there had been four different administrators over a 2-year period. A worker from another factory explained their experience with state-appointed administrators:

> Two years ago we took over the factory . . . and it was "intervened" by the government. . . . It didn't work out with the first administrator (*"interventor"*) so we exerted pressure and he was removed. The second administrator didn't please us either and again we exercised popular power—now we are waiting for the government to name one of our own comrades from the factory [*Chile Hoy,* August 3–9, 1973, p. 29].

[15]The role of the unions is treated more extensively in Chapter 6.

[16]It was usual for a single individual to be an appointed state representative on the administrative council of more than one factory. State representatives, when they were not workers, were typically employees of the pertinent sectoral planning office of CORFO, professionals in industry or government, or academics.

However, only in factories where the workers were well organized and militant did they succeed in replacing state administrators.

Finally, it is important to mention that the *normas básicas* set up no formal mechanism for worker participation beyond the factory level. Several ad hoc efforts were made to engage worker representatives in economic planning, but they never amounted to very much, partly, because economic planning in Chile itself did not amount to much. This was likely to be the case until the problem of political (state) power was resolved and the state's control extended further into the industrial and distribution sectors of the economy.

Despite the fact that the problem of planning was linked to the larger problem of state power, workers were constantly pressuring to be incorporated into the state planning apparatus through representation on CORFO's sectoral development committees. The first national assembly of workers from the textile sector (*Encuentro Textil*) of July 1972 called for "worker participation in planning production, commercialization, income, costs, hiring, supplies, profits, investment, among other things, in the textile sector." This call was echoed by subsequent *encuentros* in the metallurgy, forestry, and large-scale mining sectors.

During Allende's final year, the Department of Participation of CUT was preparing for a national workers' conference to discuss the establishment of new norms of participation inside and outside the factories. The *normas básicas* had essentially been implanted from above to lend some direction to the process. Now, after 2 years of experience, it was felt that the workers of the social area should meet to discuss, revise, and extend them. To this end, local assemblies in each factory were organized during May, June, and July of 1973. As a basis for discussion, CUT circulated a pamphlet with proposed changes. This pamphlet (*El Proyecto de Complementación de las Normas Básicas*) contemplated formalizing worker majorities on the administrative councils where they already existed and giving workers 50% representation on the sectoral and national planning agencies. The local assemblies were to nominate representatives to provincial CUT assemblies. Delegates from the provincial assemblies were to congregate for a national assembly on participation in October 1973. With the change of government in September 1973, these proposals, of course, were never brought to fruition.

5

An Index of Worker Participation: Methodology and Mechanics

In this chapter we provide (*a*) a general discussion of the construction of our index of worker participation;[1] (*b*) a review of the structural components and behavioral characteristics of our index; and (*c*) a description of the design and implementation of our survey, which is presented in Appendix I to this chapter.

THE CONSTRUCTION OF OUR INDEX OF PARTICIPATION

In Chapter 1 we discussed the various forms of worker participation: grievance; collective bargaining; information and consultation; veto; and minority, parity, and majority representation. For each form of participation there are several areas or sets of related issues in which the worker might participate.

A basic separation of areas between *technical issues* and *administrative and economic issues* has been made by Anderson. The former comprise issues related specifically to the organization of production on the shop floor. The latter deal with overall issues of economic and financial management (Anderson 1972).

Lars Karlsson has developed a more elaborate scheme (1973b, p. 4). He distinguishes five areas of basic issues:

Area 1: Work speed, work methods, choice of tools, ordering of tasks, etc.
Area 2: Hiring, firing, distribution of work tasks
Area 3: Technology, organization, planning, administrative routines, etc.

---

[1]A detailed discussion is presented in Appendix II to this chapter.

Area 4: Choice of products, quality of products, quantity of products
Area 5: Distribution of profits, investments, financing, budgeting.

As we move from Area 1 to Area 5, the decisions commit the firm more and more for the future and involve higher costs in any one decision. Thus it is hypothesized that worker participation tends to begin with Area 1 and work its way up.

The system we used to outline areas of participation is more closely related to the three-tier ILO scheme (OIT 1969a): personnel problems, technical problems, and economic and financial problems. We elaborated the ILO scheme in the following way:

Area 1: Social, administrative, and personnel problems
      a. Hiring and firing
      b. Work rules and system of internal discipline
      c. Creation and maintenance of social services
      d. Educational and vocational training
      e. Labor relations
      f. System of participation
      g. New wage scales, forms of remuneration, job evaluation, promotion, incentives, etc.

Area 2: Technical and production problems
      a. Improvement in work conditions, problems of industrial hygiene and safety
      b. Transfers, job rotation, and job enlargement
      c. Changes in work organization and administration
      d. Maintenance of machinery and equipment
      e. Quality control
      f. Raw materials supplies
      g. Sales and commercialization policy, inventories and stocks
      h. Research and development of new products
      i. Selection and modification of technology, specific and general (methods, movements, time, etc.)
      j. Information and communication system within the firm

Area 3: Problems of economic and financial management
      a. Investment and growth of the enterprise
      b. Production planning—lines of production and quantities
      c. Financial situation of the firm: assets–debits
      d. Profits–losses situation
      e. Pricing policy
      f. Wage and salary policy (level, not internal structure)
      g. Financing of investments

    h. Financing of operating expenses
    i. Budgeting and production costs

In this enumeration of issues, we hoped to isolate the most central matters pertaining to decision making in industrial enterprises. In Area 2, items a through f tend to relate to technical problems of the shop floor, while items g through i relate more generally to technical problems of the firm. Items i and j, however, may also relate specifically to the shop floor. Under a comanagement system, Area 3 is where the state can be expected to intervene: Most items in this area are affected by forces outside the firm in both planned and market economies.

Workers in Chile usually had previous experience with the issues in Area 1 through their unions. Although workers rarely influenced decisions in Area 2 in the past, they generally had a profound knowledge of the machinery and the organization of production in their sections. Items in Area 3 involve specialized knowledge to which workers had rarely been exposed in either the factory or the schools. We hypothesized, therefore, that participation would begin with Area 1, then move to Area 2, and finally to Area 3.

To this point, our scheme is summarized in Figure 5.1. According to this figure, worker participation may ordinarily be represented along three dimensions: the purpose of the workers' presence on decision-making bodies; the magnitude of workers' presence on these bodies; and the nature of the topics

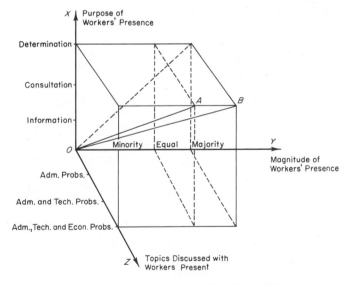

Figure 5.1. Worker participation in connection with participatory councils.

dealt with by these bodies. As we move away from the origin out along the $X, Y,$ and Z axes, it is presumed that participation increases.[2]

Finally, it must be noted that as each form of participation may cover different areas, each area of participation may, in turn, encompass different instances. We may distinguish three instances of participation:

1. Policy formulation or decision making
2. Decision execution or implementation
3. Evaluation and control of the making and execution of decisions

The *normas básicas,* as discussed in Chapter 4, provided a new structure for decision making within the firm. In a loose sense, the participating bodies of the *normas básicas* can be interpreted to replace the boards of directors and the decision-making options which inhere to the management of typical firms. The executive hierarchy or the organizational chart, on the other hand, is not altered by the *normas básicas*. If workers were to participate in execution, it would be on an ad hoc basis or through the creation of special commissions.

Control and evaluation is more nebulous. It can occur either in the participating bodies or outside them. Its essence is the expression of organized sentiment to change or reaffirm the way things have been going. The recall of an elected officer is an example of control and evaluation. We expected, therefore, that workers would participate more in decision making, less in control and evaluation, and still less in execution.

The basic model described above was followed in constructing our measure, although the case of APSM in Chile relates specifically to the majority representation form. Two additional elaborations were made on the model. First, a distinction was drawn between the *formal structure of participation* and the *content of participation* in the firm. *Formal structure* refers to the existence of participatory bodies, the frequency of their meetings, and the attendance at their meetings. *Content* was divided into matters covered in the various meetings of participation bodies and the influence that the labor representatives had in the final making of decisions.

Second, consistent with the structure of the *normas básicas,* we isolated three levels of participation: Level 1 corresponds to the administrative council; Level 2 to the coordinating committee; and Level 3 to the production committees, sectional or shop floor assemblies, and the general assembly, i.e., it relates most directly to the participation of the rank and file worker. For each item at the various levels we took the average of the respondents' answers.

---

[2]As may be seen in Figure 5.1, the forms of grievance, collective bargaining, and profit sharing have not been included. This is done because in this study worker participation is being analyzed in connection with participatory councils or other mechanisms explicitly created to institute worker involvement in the decision-making process. The comanagement mode proposed in the *normas básicas* would be represented by point A in Figure 5.1.

The weighting coefficient was selected to give us a certain proportionality between the various components of our measure. Here we considered both the importance of the component and the reliability of our estimate. The less reliable our estimate (i.e., the fewer respondents or the less precise the question), the less weight we gave the item. Table 5.1 presents the point system of the index considering the maximum final score for each of its component elements. The weighting procedure is presented in full detail in Appendix II to this chapter.

The general procedure and the basic assumptions employed in the construction of our index may be summarized as follows:

1. The index is formed by three complementary and separately measured elements: namely, the functioning of the participation structure, the topics or areas discussed in the participatory bodies and the effective influence exercised by the workers or their representatives.
2. Regarding the functioning of the structure of participation, a greater number of points were assigned
   a. The larger the number of participatory bodies (prescribed by the *normas básicas*) which were functioning in the enterprise;
   b. The more frequently the bodies met;
   c. The greater the attendance at their meetings;
   d. If the meetings were held outside of normal work hours.
3. Regarding the allocation of points in relation to the content of participation, the main points of consideration were
   a. That all questions (areas) of an administrative, technical, or economic–financial nature were equally necessary and important for the normal development of the firm and, hence, Areas 1, 2, and 3 were weighted equally;
   b. That the 26 items in Areas 1, 2, and 3 were assigned more points according to the frequency with which they were brought up;
   c. That the frequency of discussion was multiplied by a measure of the intensity of the verbal participation of workers or their representatives for each of the 26 items in determining the scores for content of participation in each of the three areas.
4. In forming the point system to determine the effective influence of the workers in the taking of decisions, the following features were considered:
   a. A greater number of points were assigned each time it was the workers or their representatives who decided upon or introduced the subject for discussion;
   b. A greater number of points were assigned where the administrative council regularly functioned with a majority of worker representatives, and the greater the majority, the greater the number of points;
   c. Additional points were also allocated to enterprises where the workers

TABLE 5.1
Summary of Point System: Maximum Final Score

	Level 1	Level 2		Level 3			
	Administrative council	Coordinating committee	Production committee	Sectional assembly	General assembly	Total	All levels
Structure of participation	20	10				20	50
Frequency of the meetings							
Existence of participatory bodies							
Attendance at the meetings							
Content of participation and worker influence	40	20				40	100
Policy formulation or decision making							
Content of participation (Areas 1, 2, and 3)							
Influence of workers or their representatives (Areas 1, 2, and 3)							
Control and evaluation							
Execution							
Total	60	30				60	150

themselves removed the state-appointed administrator or appointed the new administrator;

d. Where there was disagreement on the administrative council between state and worker representatives and the position of the latter prevailed or where there was no disagreement but the position adopted originated with the worker representatives, additional points were assigned to the measure of worker influence.[3]

e. Where there was disagreement and the position of the state representatives prevailed, it was scored negatively.

5. The measurement of the structure, content, and influence of worker participation was done separately at three different levels (with some modifications) within the enterprise:

a. The highest level (L_1), referring to the administrative council;

b. The intermediate level (L_2), referring to the workers' coordinating committee and the union;

c. The base level (L_3), referring to the production committees of the production units, the corresponding sectional assemblies, and the general assembly of the whole enterprise.

6. In addition to considering worker participation in decision making, two additional instances of worker participation were considered: policy execution and overall control and evaluation. All three instances were considered as part of the content of participation. The bases for evaluating execution and control and evaluation are elaborated in Appendix II to this chapter.

THE RESULTING VALUES AND THE RELIABILITY OF THE INDEX

As indicated in Table 5.1, the value of our index of worker participation (P_F) may theoretically vary between 0 and 150 points. In practice, for the 35 randomly selected manufacturing enterprises in our survey,[4] the index varied between 38.21 and 110.48 (see Table 5.2).

The basic question with respect to the reliability of the index is whether or not the weighting scheme distorts our results. As described in the preceding section, the weights were chosen in consideration of two central factors: (a) our opinion

---

[3]It could be argued that this consideration is unsound, since the state representatives could often be right, representing a more technical and rational view of the problem. However, it must not be forgotten that the worker representatives were elected from different strata of the work force, including technical, administrative, and blue-collar personnel.

[4]A discussion of the selection and representativeness of the 35 firms appears in Appendix I to this chapter.

TABLE 5.2
Relative Levels of Worker Participation in Firms (P_F): Partial and Total Results According to Scores and Categories

Firm	Structure (1)	Content (2)	P_F (1)+(2)=(3) (3)	P_F in categories (4)	Levels within firms (5)+(6)+(7)=(3)		
					L_1 (5)	L_2 (6)	L_3 (7)
1	45.9	64.6	110.48	8	43.5	22.8	44.2
2	42.2	67.3	109.69	8	49.5	19.8	40.4
3	43.3	62.9	106.17	8	45.6	20.4	40.1
4	40.2	64.4	104.53	8	45.6	20.6	38.3
5	41.9	52.3	94.24	7	45.1	13.8	35.4
6	37.1	56.8	93.90	7	41.5	16.4	36.1
7	39.9	53.8	93.67	7	37.0	17.9	38.7
8	36.6	48.1	84.73	6	41.1	7.1	36.6
9	36.5	49.9	84.40	6	39.7	15.2	29.6
10	42.1	41.9	84.02	6	41.0	15.9	27.1
11	42.0	42.1	84.01	6	33.8	16.8	33.4
12	38.9	44.0	83.07	5	33.4	16.6	33.0
13	32.3	50.7	82.99	5	33.6	17.6	31.8
14	40.5	40.4	80.90	5	40.0	10.6	30.3
15	37.9	42.3	80.55	5	33.3	15.6	31.7
16	41.2	34.1	75.20	5	35.7	8.9	30.5
17	38.0	35.8	73.76	4	31.5	15.2	27.1
18	42.8	29.0	71.77	4	29.3	13.5	29.0
19	35.5	36.1	71.58	4	33.1	11.0	27.5
20	30.4	40.0	70.41	4	35.7	4.6	30.1
21	31.7	38.7	70.40	4	30.4	14.6	25.4
22	31.7	35.4	67.11	4	30.6	14.0	22.6
23	32.1	33.0	65.13	4	28.8	14.8	20.6
24	24.6	37.6	62.26	3	30.7	12.3	19.3
25	31.0	30.7	61.67	3	24.9	14.3	22.5
26	30.0	29.7	59.72	3	24.0	12.9	22.9
27	23.0	34.5	57.43	3	20.1	6.2	21.1
28	22.1	34.0	56.09	3	38.3	6.6	11.2
29	27.9	26.7	54.51	2	25.4	5.7	23.5
30	19.1	34.6	53.67	2	28.8	4.9	20.0
31	33.0	20.3	53.22	2	20.8	9.5	23.0
32	25.9	25.0	50.90	2	32.4	2.7	15.8
33	29.8	20.1	49.90	2	26.1	2.1	21.7
34	18.9	22.8	41.64	1	16.7	2.0	23.0
35	21.3	16.9	38.21	1	12.5	8.4	17.3

Note: Rounding errors account for some small discrepancies in column 3.

of how important each component was to the participation system; (b) how precise our measure of each component was, which in turn was a function of the number of respondents, the number of questions, and the clarity of the questions relating to each component.

For instance, it is noted that we assigned a total of 30 possible points (structure plus content) to Level 2, while Levels 1 and 3 were assigned 60 points each. Our reasoning here entailed two considerations: On the one hand, fewer decisions were taken at Level 2 than at Levels 1 and 3; on the other, we had fewer questions and fewer respondents for Level 2.

A more important value judgment, perhaps, was our decision to weight Areas 1, 2, and 3 equally. That is, we assumed that administrative, social, and personnel related issues are just as important to the effective running of the firm as are technical and financial matters. Our weights reflect this assumption.

Another ostensibly arbitrary designation is weighting content (100 points) twice as heavily as structure (50 points). Clearly, this 2:1 ratio involves nothing sacred. Assuming, in fact, that reasonable arguments could be made for a ratio anywhere between 1:1 and 4:1, we examined the impact of these new weights on our participation index. In the most unfavorable case, only three firms were moved from one category to another.

It should be pointed out that all the central components of our measure are strongly and positively related to each other within the appropriate breakdowns (see Table 5.3). In fact, with the exception of Control and evaluation and Execution ($r = .472$), all the correlation coefficients are above .540. The more closely related components are correlated, the less possible distortion can be produced through the weighting system.[5]

No external measures of participation were available for use in either weighting our components or checking our final ranking. However, we were able to compare the scored answers for the first questionnaire of the professional or technical workers and the production workers as a measure of internal consistency. The correlation coefficient between these two scores is .712. When we consider that the professional and production workers are viewing worker participation from different perspectives and on the basis of different experiences, this appears to be a significant correlation.

With the above limitations and caveats in mind, then, we can go on to look at the resulting characteristics of our index. The index had a possible range of 0 to 150. The observed index (P_F) varied from a low of 38.21 to a high of 110.48. The average value for P_F was 73.77 and the standard deviation equaled 18.79.

It is difficult to make any inferences about the absolute extent of participation in the sampled firms from our index. For instance, it would be virtually impossi-

[5]The same conditions make a principal components analysis of the index less interesting. Simple correlation coefficients are significant at the 5% level for values above .35 given our sample size.

TABLE 5.3

Correlation Coefficients between Central Components of Index

	S	C			L_1	L_2	L_3
S	—	.6589		L_1	—	.546	.696
C		—		L_2		—	.699
				L_3			—
	DM	CE	EX		APL_1	TPL_1	$EFPL_1$
DM	—	.657	.544	APL_1	—	.839	.803
CE		—	.472	TPL_1		—	.826
EX			—	$EFPL_1$			—
	APL_2	TPL_2	$EFPL_2$		APL_3	TPL_3	$EFPL_3$
APL_2	—	.555	.603	APL_3	—	.809	.667
TPL_2		—	.661	TPL_3		—	.641
$EFPL_2$			—	$EFPL_3$			—

Where:
   S = Structure of participation;
   C = Content of participation;
   L_1 = Level 1;
   L_2 = Level 2;
   L_3 = Level 3;
   DM = Decision making;
   CE = Control and evaluation;
   EX = Execution;
   APL_1 = Administrative, social, and personnel problems at Level 1 (APL_2 and APL_3, at Levels 2 and 3, respectively);
   TPL_1 = Technical and production problems at Level 1 (TPL_2 and TPL_3, at Levels 2 and 3 respectively);
   $EFPL_1$ = Economic and financial problems at Level 1 ($EFPL_2$ and $EFPL_3$, at Levels 2 and 3, respectively).

ble for any firm to reach 150. To do so would require that all decision making between the state and worker representatives be conflictual, as well as other characteristics of dubious absolute import. Rather, the index is designed to determine which firms have more participation relative to the other firms in our sample. Given this intention and given the imprecision in measurement and some arbitrariness in weighting, we decided that it would be meaningless to distinguish between an index value of, say, 94.24 and 93.90.

Instead, we grouped our initial index values into eight categories, considering .5 standard deviations for each category. The firms fell into categories pretty much as we had impressionistically evaluated them during our survey (see

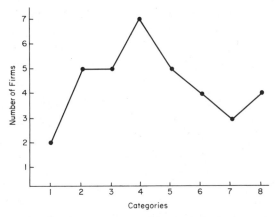

Figure 5.2.   Distribution of participation index by categories.

Figure 5.2). The category index was used for most of the statistical investigation discussed in the next two chapters.

THE STRUCTURAL COMPONENTS OF PARTICIPATION—BEHAVIORAL CHARACTERISTICS OF OUR INDEX

The most rudimentary breakdown of our index is between the formal structure of participation (S) and the content of participation (C). The correlation coefficient between (S) and (C) is .6589, indicating a strong positive relationship. It is likely that causality runs both ways. In the short run, structure is probably a prerequisite for substantial (beyond informal) content. In the longer run, substantial content is probably necessary to keep the structure working. That is, if workers have no real influence in decision making, there is no reason for them to attend meetings. Many workers expressed this idea to us in factories where the management tended to control meetings and looked upon participation solely as a means of legitimating their own power. To be sure, many authors attribute the workers' lack of interest and low attendance at European workers' councils (Garson 1975), Israeli's Histadrut joint consultation committees (Tabb and Goldfarb 1970), and many Yugoslavian workers' councils (Adizes 1971) to the inability of the workers to influence important decisions through these meetings.

As explained at the beginning of the chapter, we hypothesized that workers would participate in decision making first in Area 1 (social, administrative, and personnel problems), soon after in Area 2 (technical and production problems), and where the system was most developed in Area 3 (economic and financial

problems). Considering all the firms in our sample, this hypothesis can be formalized to the expectation that the mean value for participation in decision making in Area 1 (*SAPP*) will exceed that of Area 2 (*TPP*) which, in turn, will exceed the mean of Area 3 (*EEP*):

$$\overline{SAPP} > \overline{TPP} > \overline{EEP}$$

This turned out to be the case at Level 1 (L_1), i.e., at the highest level—the administrative council (see Table 5.4). However, at Level 2 (L_2, corresponding to the coordinating council) and Level 3 (L_3, corresponding to the general assembly, sectional assemblies, and the production committees) participation in technical and production matters exceeded participation in social, administrative, and personnel related issues. It makes perfect sense, of course, that shop floor committees concentrate more on production related matters and less on social and personnel questions (where policy regulations are generally standardized for the entire enterprise). These findings contradict prima facie prevailing notions to the effect that workers are only interested in bread and butter issues.

The 35 enterprises in our sample varied in length of time they spent in Chile's socialized sector from 8 to 28 months. If we consider the extent of worker participation at Levels 1, 2, and 3, we find the relationship between the length of time an enterprise was socialized (*TIME*) and the extent of participation at different levels in that enterprise to be that depicted in Table 5.5.

The first three equations suggest that participation at higher levels and lower levels is highly correlated, that participation at the top level tends to establish itself more quickly but grows less over time than participation at the lower level and that participation at L_3 tends to increase over time. It is also pertinent to point out here that the composite participation index (including all levels) and *TIME* were positive and correlated ($r = .32$). That is, enterprises which were socialized

TABLE 5.4

Levels and Areas of Participation

	Average	Standard deviation
L_1		
SAPP	5.90	1.68
TPP	4.57	1.61
EFP	3.76	1.66
L_2		
SAPP	3.81	3.34
TPP	4.46	3.42
EFP	2.66	2.56
L_3		
SAPP	6.35	2.02
TPP	7.44	2.31
EFP	4.75	1.65

TABLE 5.5

Levels of Participation and Time[a]

Equation number	Dependent variable	Constant	L_2	L_3	TIME	(TIME) $\times (L_3)$	R^2
(1)	L_1	12.9	.17 (.664)	.66 (3.49)			.492
(2)	L_1	28.3 (6.12)			.99 (1.18)		.040
(3)	L_3	16.4 (4.24)			2.25 (3.17)		.233
(4)	L_1	31.3 (3.20)		.177 (.465) .148 .166	−4.41 (−2.21) −.687 −.860	.132 (1.88) .597 1.16	.559

[a] Regression results are based on 35 observations in this and all succeeding tables. Numbers in parentheses refer to the t statistic; elasticity at the mean is below the t; and the beta coefficient is below the elasticity.

for longer periods of time tended to have higher overall participation levels.

Equation (4) attempts to gauge the interaction effect of TIME and L_3 on L_1. Namely, the coefficient of $(TIME) \times (L_3)$ represents $d\ [(dL_1)/(dL_3)]/d\ (TIME)$ with the functional form of $L_1 = F(L_3, TIME, L_3 \times TIME)$. We find this coefficient to be positive and significant and $t_{.10}$. That is, over time the impact of L_3 (lower level) on L_1 (higher level) becomes greater or, conversely, as L_3 increases the impact of TIME on L_1 becomes less negative (when you control for L_3).[6]

[6]There is strong multicollinearity in this equation which is lowering the t statistics. However,

	L_1	L_3	$L_3 \times TIME$	TIME
L_1		.696	.534	.201
L_3			.824	.483
$L_3 \times TIME$				.864
TIME				

the basic result is affirmed when L_1 is run on TIME and the sample is weighted by values above and below the mean of L_3. The chow test yields an $F = 12.25$ at 2 and 31 d.f. which leads to rejecting the null hypothesis of no structural shift at the $F_{.01}$ level of significance. In addition to the problem of multicollinearity, the equations in Table 5.5 probably suffer from a simultaneity bias. Perhaps due to the cross-sectional nature of our data, attempts to unravel this bias through instrumental variables and two stage least squares were not successful.

It is important to emphasize that our variable TIME refers to the length of time an enterprise was in the social area at the time of our survey. It does not explicitly reflect how specific enterprises changed through time. Temporal interpretations must always be qualified by this inherent data limitation.

This result is consistent with the hypothesis advanced by others (Pateman 1970; Karlsson 1973b; Jenkins 1973) that top level participation will only be sustained over time in the presence of active participation at lower levels. It may also serve in part to account for the disappointing codetermination experience in West Germany (Schauer 1973; Jenkins 1973).[7]

APPENDIX I BRIEF DESCRIPTION OF THE SURVEY

As mentioned in Chapter 1, our survey was designed to permit an analysis of the antecedents and results of worker participation. Previous attempts at such analyses have failed to go beyond drawing subjective and impressionistic conclusions. Because of our desire to present a systematic and statistical analysis, we chose to do a cross-sectional and representative survey of the enterprises in Chile's social area. Although much can be learned from case studies, as economists we did not feel adequately qualified to undertake them.

Our choice of the cross-sectional approach meant that, instead of being able to observe the process of worker participation directly in each enterprise, we would have to rely upon the impressions and subjective evaluations of the workers interviewed. For this reason, we structured our survey so that the questions relating to aspects of the participatory process were repeated at least twice and, in many cases, more frequently.

It should be pointed out that in seven instances other researchers have conducted case studies of enterprises included in our survey (Barrera, Aranda, and Diaz 1973; Cortés and Vivanco 1973; Riquelme and Gonzales 1973; Marotta and Urzúa 1973; de la Fuente 1973; *Experiencias de Masas* 1972). Our conclusions were, in general, consistent with those found in the more detailed case studies.

Our survey was composed of five separate but overlapping questionnaires.[8] One questionnaire deals with the production and financial performance of the firm. It was answered by direct reference to each firm's accounting records in consultation with the top production manager (*jefe de producción*). A second questionnaire was directed at the state appointed administrator.[9] This deals with the basic structural characteristics of the firm, as well as asking questions regarding participation also in

---

[7]Here, of course, other factors are at play. In West German public coal and steel enterprises worker representatives have sat on the supervisory boards since 1951. The supervisory boards, in turn, appoint the management boards. The general practice appears to be that the worker representatives on the supervisory board are not elected directly but selected by the union leadership. Once selected, the worker representatives receive higher salaries and certain perquisites. In 1976, a West German law seemingly extended codetermination to enterprises with over 2000 employees in all industrial sectors. However, actual nonmanagerial employee representation on supervisory boards is less than 50% according to the provisions of the new law (cf. Dreyer 1976).

[8]These questionnaires are 80 pages in length and hence are not included in the present text. A limited number of copies, in Spanish, are available from the authors.

[9]In most cases, the administrator was state appointed, but in several instances this person was removed by the workers. When this happened, at times the state would reappoint a new administrator and at times the workers, with state sanction, would select the new administrator. *Administrator*, as we use the term here, denotes two different words in Spanish: *administrador* and *interventor*. The latter applies to the administrator in those factories which still had temporary status in the APSM, i.e., those factories with an intervened or requisitioned status. The former applies to firms with permanent (during Allende) status in the APSM.

the third questionnaire. The latter was applied to two worker representatives in the administrative council (one production worker and one white-collar worker).[10] It deals with the formal structure of the participatory bodies, the content of the issues discussed in these bodies, the influence of the workers in decision making, and the communication system within the firm.

A fourth questionnaire was administered to the head of each coordinating committee (usually the president of the firm's largest union). It deals with the history and structure of the unions in the enterprise, the firm's passage to the APSM, the operation of the production committee, and the nature of participation in the coordinating committee.

The final questionnaire was directed at the presidents of two (in small firms), three (in medium-sized firms), or four (in large firms) production committees.[11] The questions deal principally with the structure and the content of participation in the production committee and the general meetings of the section.

It is necessary to recall that not all firms strictly followed the CUT–Government *normas básicas*. Thus in several cases we varied the formula for implementing our survey. One firm, for instance, had only one large production committee, but they had unusually frequent union meetings. In this instance, we applied questionnaires to two union leaders.

The questionnaires went through two preliminary forms that were discussed at meetings in CORFO, CUT, and CEPLA.[12] The third version was subjected to a test run, beginning on April 18, 1973, in three firms. The fourth and final version was applied during May and June and the first 2 weeks of July 1973. Because of national political and transportation problems, we were unable to complete our survey in 5 of the 40 factories initially selected.

The actual administration of the survey took between 1 and 2 days at each factory, depending primarily on its size and the availability of personnel. In addition to applying the questionnaires, we usually visited the inside of the factory and conducted informal conversations with the workers. These conversations were not considered in our measure of participation.

Another preparatory step was to define and collect data on our universe, which consisted of all firms in the APSM. In February and March, we visited the Ministry of Finance, the Ministry of Economics, the *sub-gerencias*[13] and sectoral committees of CORFO to assemble this information. By March 1973, there were 294 firms in APSM.[14] For the purpose of our survey, we restricted our universe to the industrial manufacturing subset. That is, we excluded mining, agricultural and livestock, services, commerce, and distribution. The industrial manufacturing subset had 223 firms in March 1973.

[10]We preferentially interviewed the professional or technical representative when this person was available because we believed that the point of view of the professional and technical people was more distinct to the production worker's point of view than was that of the administrative worker.

[11]It should be recalled that the production committee is the participating body at the level of the shop floor or section. The president of this committee, a worker in the section, was the closest to a rank-and-file worker that we interviewed. To have interviewed a representative sampling of rank-and-file workers in each factory would have required far more resources, on both our part and the factories', than were available.

[12]CORFO (*Corporación de Fomento de la Producción*), founded in 1939, is a state development agency encharged with gathering economic data and promoting industrial development. CUT (*Central Unica de Trabajadores*) is the national labor federation which first gained legal status under the Allende government. CEPLA (*Centro de Planeamiento*) is part of the Engineering School of the University of Chile where we were based.

[13]There were four *sub-gerencias* (heavy industry, light industry, basic consumer industry, and construction and cellulose) with some 15-odd sectoral committees dependent upon them.

[14]Many individual firms were conglomerated when they passed into the APSM. Thus, for example, the state enterprise ENAVI comprised five previously privately owned factories.

TABLE 5.6

Universe and Sample Breakdown of Distributional Characteristics

United Nations classification[a]	Percentage of firms in APSM	Percentage of firms in sample of 40	Percentage of firms in sample of 35
Division 31	24.7	22.5	22.9
Division 32	11.7	12.5	14.3
Division 33	9.9	7.5	8.6
Division 34	1.3	2.5	0.0
Division 35	8.6	7.5	5.7
Division 36	7.6	10.0	8.6
Division 37	10.8	12.5	14.3
Division 38	25.6	25.0	25.7
Division 39	0.0	0.0	0.0
Total number	223	40	35

	Percentage of firms in greater Santiago	Percentage of firms in Province Concepción	Percentage of firms in between Santiago and Concepción, including Valparaiso
Universe	62.8	18.3	18.9
Final sample of 35	65.7	14.3	20.0

	Percentage small firms	Percentage medium firms	Percentage large firms
Universe	41.5	36.0	22.6
Final sample of 35	34.4	42.8	22.8

[a] The U.N. classified divisions are the following: Division 31—food products, drinks, and tobacco; Division 32—textiles, garments, and leather products; Division 33—wood, cork, and furniture; Division 34—paper products, newspapers, and publishing; Division 35—chemical products derived from petroleum, coal, rubber, and plastics; Division 36—fabrication of nonmetallic minerals, except those derived from petroleum and coal; Division 37—basic metal industries; Division 38—fabrication of metal products, machinery, and equipment; Division 39—other manufacturing industries.

TABLE 5.7

Cross-Distribution Ratio of Percentage in Universe to Percentage in Final Sample

Division	Size			
	Small	Medium	Large	All
31	1.30	.91	1.05	1.08
32	1.00	.69	.79	.82
33	1.36	.97	1.10	1.15
34	1.36	.97	1.10	1.15
35	1.80	1.29	1.46	1.51
36	1.06	.78	.92	.88
37	.92	.64	.76	.76
38	1.20	.84	.99	1.00
39	1.00	1.00	1.00	1.00
All	1.21	.84	.99	

[a] Because of zero denominator in row 34, the ratios are assumed to be equal to those in row 33. In row 39, 0 divided by 0 is represented as equal to 1. If the distributional characteristics of the sample were identical to those of the universe with respect to size and industrial division, then each number would equal one. The number 1.30 in row 1, column 1 equals 10.3% (the percentage of small firms in the universe in division 31) divided by 7.9% (the percentage of small firms in the sample in division 31). The chi-square for the table, calculated assuming the expected frequency to be equal to 35 times the percentage of firms in universe, is equal to 2.077, and with 16 d.f. we cannot reject the null hypothesis that the sample and the universe belong to the same population at the .05 level of significance (chi-square equals 26.296 with 16 d.f.). That is, with a wide margin for error we cannot reject the null hypothesis that the sample is representative of the universe at the 5% significance level.

Our initial sample included 40 firms, 18.43% of the universe. To avoid possible distortions in selecting our sample, we divided the universe along three lines: (a) the nine-category United Nations industrial classification; (b) the size of the firms (small—0 to 250 employees; medium—250 to 750 employees; large—more than 750 employees); and (c) the geographical locations of the firms. In addition, only firms with a minimum of 8 months experience in the APSM were considered. Because of time and cost constraints, we further restricted our universe by considering only firms located in Chile's central valley region, i.e., those between the provinces of Valparaiso and Aconcagua to the north and Concepción to the south. Of the 223 firms, 164 (74%) were in this region. Our sample of 40 firms represented 24.4% of our restricted universe of 164.[15] The breakdown of our universe and sample by these three criteria are shown in Table 5.6.

Firms were first divided by industrial classification, then by size, then by location. We assigned representative weights to each category and then made random selections. When fewer than three choices fell in any category, we joined categories before making the selection. This helps to explain deviations from perfect proportionality between our universe and the sample. Two other such factors should be pointed out. First, the employment data we used to delineate our universe usually pertained to the last quarter of 1972, but the data reported in Table 5.7 are based on the employment information obtained at the time of the survey. Two firms passed from the small to the medium group during this time. Second, because of a schedule mix-up while in Concepción, we were forced to omit one of

[15] Of the 223 firms in the universe, approximately 185 had been in the APSM more than 8 months.

our selected firms. In any case, the distributional characteristics of the final sample of 35 firms bear a strong resemblance to those of the initial universe. At the 5% level of significance, we cannot reject the null hypothesis that the sample is representative of the universe (see Table 5.7).

Finally, a few additional comments on the organizational mechanics of the survey are in order. The period from September 1972 to January 1973 was dedicated to informal interviewing and attending meetings in factories. In January 1973, we began work on the design of the survey. We spent approximately 4 months discussing our experiences in the factories and our own and others' views of the process of participation and attending meetings with members of CUT and CORFO and our colleagues at CEPLA.

Our contact with the firms was greatly facilitated by our affiliation with CORFO and CUT. In most cases, it sufficed to call the factory administrator a week or two in advance, explain the purpose and nature of the survey and ask him to pick a date. In several instances, however, it was necessary to make a prior visit to the factory and bring credentials.

We went to each factory with one, two, or three assistants, depending on the size of the factory and the schedules of our assistants. We chose a team of eight assistants who were studying industrial engineering at the *Facultad de Ingeniería* of the University of Chile (our center, CEPLA, was part of this *Facultad*), were in their fifth or sixth year of the program and had some experience working in industry.[16]

APPENDIX II THE WEIGHTING PROCEDURE AND THE POINT SYSTEM OF THE INDEX OF WORKER PARTICIPATION

In this appendix, we present the point and weighting system employed in the construction of our index of participation in detail. We proceed by considering first the structure of participation and then the content of participation (Table 5.8).

Before detailing our codification of content of participation, we should cover a few procedural points. Our category *matters covered* or *matters taken up* is a multiplicative function of the *frequency* with which the matter is brought up and the *intensity* with which the matter is dealt by the worker representatives. Thus the area of social, administrative, and personnel problems has seven items or components, and for each component we make the following calculation (in the case of the administrative council):

$$\text{matter covered} = \text{frequency} \times \text{intensity}$$

where: high frequency = 2
          medium frequency = 1.5
          low or zero frequency = 1
          high intensity = 2
          medium intensity = 1.5
          low intensity = 1

Our guidelines were high frequency: at least every third meeting; medium frequency: at least every 10 meetings; low frequency: less than once every 10 meetings. In the case of the general assembly, the guidelines were high frequency: every 2 months; medium frequency: every 6 months; low frequency: less than every 6 months. Only in around 50% of the firms were there comprehensive records of all the meetings. In those cases, we tabulated frequencies and found them to correspond almost completely to the average of our respondents' answers.

[16]We had several sessions with them to acquaint them with the contents of the survey and the *normas básicas* and to clarify any confusions regarding our specific intention in asking each of the questions. This group worked with us throughout the three months of the survey.

TABLE 5.8

Index Construction: Structure of Participation

	Maximum raw score	W.C. (weighting coefficient)	Final score
I. Structure of participation			
A. Level 1—Administrative council	12	1.67	20
1. Weekly meetings = 6			
Biweekly meetings = 4			
Monthly meetings = 2			
PLUS			
2. All members attend = 6			
All but one attend = 4			
All but two attend = 2			
B. Level 2—Coordinating committee	12	.83	10
1. Weekly meetings = 6			
Biweekly meetings = 4			
Monthly meetings = 2			
PLUS			
2. All members attend = 6[a]			
More than 75% attend = 4[a]			
More than 50%, but			
less than 75% attend = 2[a]			
C. Level 3	29	.6896	20
1. Production committee (PC)	12		
a. Each section has PC = 6			
Half or more have PC = 4			
Less than half but more than			
zero have PC = 2			
PLUS			
b. Weekly meetings = 3			
Biweekly meetings = 2			
Monthly meetings = 1			
PLUS			
c. If one person attends			
for at least every 7			
workers in section = 3			
If one person attends			
for at least every 14			
workers in section = 2			
If one person attends			
for at least every 21			
workers in sections = 1			
2. Sectional assembly	8		
a. Weekly meetings = 3			
Biweekly meetings = 2			
Monthly meetings = 1			

continued

Table 5.8 *(continued)*

	Maximum raw score	W.C.	Final score
PLUS			
b. Attendance 75–100% = 5[b]			
Attendance 50–74% = 4[b]			
Attendance 30–49% = 3[b]			
Attendance 0–29% = 2[b]			
3. General assembly	9		
a. Monthly meetings = 5			
Bimonthly meetings = 4			
Quarterly meetings = 3			
Semiannual meetings = 2			
Annual meetings = 1			
PLUS			
b. Attendance 75–100% = 4[c]			
Attendance 50–74% = 3[c]			
Attendance 30–59% = 2[c]			
Attendance 0–29% = 1[c]			
Maximum total for structure of participation			50

[a] The *normas básicas* stipulate that all participation bodies with the exception of administrative councils should meet outside work hours. If the meetings were held during work hours, 2 points were deducted.

[b] If meeting held outside work hours, minus 0; if the meeting is between the shifts or during lunch and overlapping into work hours, minus 1; if the meeting is during work hours, minus 2.

[c] Minus 1 if meetings are during work hours and there are no problems with the scheduling of shifts.

TABLE 5.9

Instances of Participation: Characteristics of Measures

	Standard deviation	Weight in total index	Beta coefficient[a]
Decision making	7.08	.391	.712
Control and evaluation	10.40	.183	.168
Execution	12.35	.092	.145

[a]From equation, when P_F is run on these three variables. The relative contribution to the variance of the index of these three variables cannot be calculated, because the values of the variables available (used to calculate the standard deviation above) are gross values. The gross values were multiplied by the weighting coefficients for purposes of constructing the index. Unfortunately, the weighted values are not readily available.

TABLE 5.10

Characteristics of Structure and Content Measures

	Standard deviation	Weight in total index	Percentage variance[a] index due to
Structure of participation	7.49	.333	34.0
Content of participation	13.02	.666	66.0

[a] This calculation was made with the formula: $\text{Var } Y = \text{Var } X_1 + \text{Var } X_2 + 2 \text{ Cov } X_1 X_2$, when $Y = X_1 + X_2$. It is a coincidence that the weights and the contribution to the variance are virtually identical.

Our respondents were asked to give their appreciation of intensity based on the vocalness and degree of comprehension exhibited by the worker representatives. They were asked about the production worker representatives and the white-collar representatives separately. We marked the average of these two. Again, it is important to emphasize that we were relying upon the impressions of the respondents. Although we attended worker meetings both before and during the survey, our observations were not formally recorded. Nevertheless, we were impressed by the general correspondence of our perceptions, those in the minutes, and those reported by the workers.

It is perhaps appropriate, at this point, to make one further comment along these lines. In Chile, it was often suggested that the workers would have a tendency to paint a pretty picture of participation. We found, on the contrary, that the workers were highly critical of the shortcomings in the new management system. Criticism was often focused on the sectarianism within the firm, the paternalism of the Communist party leaders, the lack of cooperation from the Christian Democrats, the absence of clarification regarding workers' new rights and duties from CUT, the dearth of internal information from management, and the lack of responsiveness of the state bureaucracy.[17]

Our measure of workers' influence in the actual making of decisions was the most difficult to construct. Certainly, majority representation in and of itself does not guarantee that the workers will run the show. For example, although workers might talk at length and even possess a fairly high level of understanding, the opinions of administrators or state representatives might ultimately prevail. One way to unravel this issue was to ask who on the administrative council introduces each particular item. It was assumed that the person who brings up the matter has either particular interest in or knowledge about it. When the administrator introduces an item, it is likely that he informs the council on the problem, presents the alternative solutions, and then proposes a reasonable course of action. The worker representatives may immediately accept the proposal or bat the alternatives already put forth around and then accept the proposal. This power dynamic is unlikely to obtain when the worker representatives themselves introduce the item.

At each factory, we also asked the administrator and the two worker representatives whose opinion ultimately prevailed on each item and if there was usually agreement between the state and worker representatives or if there was conflict with the matter being resolved by a vote. With respect to the administrative council, our influence measure was composed of two further questions. First, we asked how many professional and technical people had left since the firm passed to the APSM and how many had been hired. We then asked who decided upon and approved the employment of the new people. Second, we ascertained the proportion of administrative council members who were workers from the firm to those from outside the firm.

According to the *normas básicas*, the administrative council was the only body in a firm endowed with the power to make decisions. So, the measure of worker influence is most appropriate at this

[17]Since we came to the factories under the auspices of CUT, the workers' honesty is apparently attributable to their desire to have CUT do something to improve the situation or to rebuke CUT for not having done enough in the past.

TABLE 5.11

Index Construction: Content of Participation

	Maximum raw score	W.C.	Final score
II. Content of participation			
A. Level 1			
1. Decision making			
a. Social, administrative, and personnel problems	78	.1324	10.327
(1) Matters covered (7 items) Frequency × intensity	28		
(2) Influence			
(a) Each time introduced by workers = 2	14		
(b) If there is general agreement and administrator's position prevails, each time = −1 If there's disagreement and administrator's position prevails, each time = −2	−14		
(c) If there is general agreement and the workers prevail, each time = 1 If there is disagreement and workers prevail, each time = 2	14		
(d) Who decided upon hiring of new professional and technical people: Administrative council or special worker commission = 8, other but approved by administrative council = 4	8		
(e) Worker composition of administrative council: If ½ are workers from the factory = 4;[a] If between ½ and ¾ are from factory = 6;[a] If ¾ or more are from factory = 12[a]	14		

continued

Table 5.11 *(continued)*

		Maximum raw score	W.C.	Final score
b.	Technical and production problems	94	.1098	10.321
	(1) Matters covered (10 items) Frequency × intensity	40		
	(2) Influence			
	(a) As above	20		
	(b) As above	−20		
	(c) As above	20		
	(d) As above	14		
c.	Economic and financial problems	86	.1201	10.328
	(1) Matters covered (9 items) Frequency × intensity	36		
	(2) Influence			
	(a) As above	18		
	(b) As above	−18		
	(c) As above	18		
	(d) As above	14		
1.	Total decision making			30.976
2.	⅓ control and evaluation	50	.1201	6.005
3.	⅓ execution	25	.1201	3.003
	Total Level 1 content	333	.1201	40
B.	**Level 2**			
1.	Decision making (4 items) Questionnaire 3, question 33 Frequency (high = 3) × intensity (high = 3)	36	.1801	6.484
2.	⅓ control and evaluation	50	.1801	9.005
3.	⅓ execution	25	.1801	4.503
	Total Level 2 content	111	.1801	20
C.	**Level 3**			
1.	Decision making			
	a. Matters covered (4 items each) Frequency (high = 2) × intensity (high = 2)			
	(1) General assembly	16		
	(2) Production committee	16		
	(3) Sectional assembly	16		

continued

Table 5.11 *(continued)*

				Maximum raw score	W.C.	Final score
b.	Influence					
	(1)	Questionnaire 4, question 34.1; on foreman or supervisor: If eliminated = 8 If elected by workers = 8 If appointed from above subject to workers' approval = 4		8		
	(2)	Questionnaire 2, question 9: On the influence of resolutions taken by the general assembly on the policy decisions of the administrative council[b]		8		
	(3)	Questionnaire 4, question 12; Every time a matter is introduced by the section supervisor (if he or she exists and attends the meetings) at the meetings of the production committee = -2		-8		
	(4)	Questionnaire 4, question 13; If there exist serious conflicts between the supervisor and the workers, and the conflict is resolved: By the supervisor = -8 By the workers = 8 If there are no serious conflicts, but problems are resolved: By the supervisor = -4 By the workers = 4		8		

continued

Table 5.11 *(continued)*

	Maximum raw score	W.C.	Final score
(5) Questionnaire 4, question 15; If the production committee has presented a suggestion or petition for the consideration of the administrative council = 4 If so, and the petition was accepted = 4	8		
(6) Questionnaire 2, question 10; If there have been conflicts between resolutions taken by the general assembly and those taken by the administrative council, and the position of the general assembly has prevailed = 5	5		
1. Total decision making	85	.25	21.25
2. ⅓ control and evaluation	50	.25	12.50
3. ⅓ execution	25	.25	6.25
Total Level 3 content	160	.25	40
Total content Levels 1, 2, and 3			100
Total structure, Levels 1, 2, and 3			50
Total participation			150

[a] Plus 2 if the administrator is also from the factory. This indicates that the workers had a say in the administrator's selection.

[b] If the influence is: decisive (the administrative council accepts more than 75% of the resolutions of the general assembly) = 8; adequate (the administrative council accepts between 40 and 75% of the resolutions of the general assembly) = 4; weak (the administrative council accepts less than 40% of the resolutions) = 2; null (the general assembly does not make resolutions, the general assembly only serves to disseminate information to the workers) = 0. The scores above are multiplied by: 1, if the general assembly meets four or more times annually; by ½, if it meets two or three times annually, and by $1/10$, if it meets once a year.

level. However, decision-making power on shop floor issues was often delegated to the production committee, and in most cases, suggestions from the production committee, when feasible, were accepted by the administrative council. Thus we had several questions regarding worker influence through the production committee (see Table 5.11).

There is little doubt that our most suspect measures were those of execution and control and evaluation. On the one hand, we asked fewer questions about them, and on the other, we had to spend more time explaining these concepts to the workers. For each item where control and evaluation was judged to be high in the second questionnaire, we allocated 6 points, for medium, 3 points, and for low or none, 0 points (this was rescaled for the first questionnaire). Item 6 of question 22, second questionnaire (wage and salary policy) was suppressed. This gave a total possible score of 150 (averaged over the three respondents) for control and evaluation, which was divided in three parts and allocated equally to Levels 1, 2, and 3.

With respect to execution, 25 points were allocated when the decisions in any one of the three areas were carried out in an organized fashion by the workers, e.g., when workers sat on the personnel or contracting committee or when there was a workers' commission to assure that the factory's products were not distributed on the black market. We allocated 12.5 points when workers participated in the execution in an unorganized fashion, e.g., when workers were informally consulted about the hiring of new personnel or the construction plans for a factory day-care center. This gave a total possible score of 75 (averaged over the three respondents) for execution, which was divided in three parts and allocated equally to Levels 1, 2, and 3.

The assertion that our measures of control and evaluation and execution are less reliable is supported prima facie by comparing their standard deviations with those of our measure of decision making (see Tables 5.9 and 5.10). However, it might be argued that control and evaluation and execution would naturally have more variability than decision making during the initiation period of democratic management. In any event, the size of none of these deviations is outlandishly large when compared to the standard deviation of structure or content of participation (the latter being composed of decision making, control and evaluation, and execution)—see Table 5.11.

APPENDIX III   ALPHABETICAL LIST OF ENTERPRISES SURVEYED

 1. Aceros Andes
 2. Cecinas Loewer
 3. Cintac
 4. Comandari
 5. Compac
 6. Compañía Cervecerías Unidas
 7. Consorcio Nieto
 8. El Volcán
 9. Enap
10. Enavi
11. Fabrilana
12. Fanac
13. Fanaloza
14. Ford
15. Fundición Libertad
16. Harling
17. Hilandería Andina
18. Immar
19. Indesa
20. I.R.T.
21. Mademsa
22. Maestranza Lo Espejo
23. Maestranza Maipú
24. Marco Chilena
25. Martonffy
26. Montero
27. Muebles Easton
28. Paños Bellavista Tome
29. Petroquímica Chilena
30. Rayonhil
31. Refractarios Lota Green
32. Sec Ingeniería
33. Sindelen
34. Socometal
35. Soleche

6

Analysis of the Factors
Affecting Participation

In this chapter, we attempt to identify the principal variables that affect the different levels of worker participation attained in the 35 socialized enterprises of our sample. Certain methodological limitations must be mentioned, however, before we proceed. First, the individual variables we consider are operating in the unique historical context of Chile during the Allende years. It is difficult, if not impossible, to imagine that these variables would behave identically in other countries or at other times. Thus any policy implications of our results must be qualified by these considerations. Second, the statistical techniques we employ (linear multiple regression and factor analysis) do not denote causality; rather they enable us, through theory, to infer relational patterns. Moreover, to the extent that our theory leads us to suspect causal relationships, it must be recognized that at best we are isolating the proximate, not the historical, antecedents of worker participation. Third, the independent variables employed represent a broad range of phenomena. Some are easily identifiable, others are attitudinal, social, political, or subjective in nature and consequently more difficult to measure. Many of the subjective or social variables overlap and interact with each other and, we can assume, influence worker participation not individually and directly but indirectly through their interaction—constituting a complex social phenomenon. It is, in part, for this reason that at the end of this chapter we follow the lead of Adelman and Morris (1971) and apply factor analysis to discern how our 29 independent variables behave together, and explore the relationships between the principal behavioral clusters and worker participation. We find that the results of our factor analysis reinforce the findings of our multiple regression analysis presented in the first part of this chapter.

In selecting our independent variables, we were guided by the large body of literature in the fields of management science, industrial psychology, labor rela-

TABLE 6.1

Variables Used in the Analysis

Independent variables	Intermediate variables	Dependent variable
I. Technostructure		
A. Technology		
1. Complexity		
2. Typology		
3. Intensity		
B. Organizational and bureaucratic structure		
1. Size		
2. Vertical differentiation		
3. Span of control		
4. Horizontal differentiation		
5. Administrative staff		
II. Labor force		P_F
A. Education		
1. Schooling		
2. Training		
3. Labor mobilization and consciousness		
B. Political organization		
1. Party composition		
2. Characteristics of unions		
	III. Disposition of the administration toward participation	
	IV. System of information	

tions, and sociology of organization.[1] Our previous experience visiting Chile's social area enterprises, the measurability or tractability of certain phenomena, and the inherent time and resource limitations of a cross-sectional study also informed our choice of variables.

In our ensuing discussion, we will treat the antecedents of participation according to the classification scheme shown in Table 6.1.

[1] In the discussion of our statistical results we treat categories of independent variables both separately and together with other independent variables. When treated separately we incur a specifi-

THE TECHNOSTRUCTURE

The relationship between technology and forms of organization has been commented on by several authors. Some hold that technology determines organization (e.g., Woodward 1965; Perrow 1967), while others maintain that (the needs of) organization determine technology (Marglin 1974). Others uninterested in which begat which maintain modern technology is so advanced and complex that the only efficient mode of organization centralizes decision making at the point of specialized knowledge (e.g., Weber 1947; Whisler and Leavitt 1958). As we shall see further on, sometimes this point is middle management and sometimes it is top management. Still others believe that there can be many different forms of social organization for any one technology (e.g., Blauner 1964; Jenkins 1973). A variation on these approaches maintains that organization is structured so as to maximize control regardless of the technology (Edwards 1972; Stone 1974; Gordon *et al.* 1974; Braverman 1974).

Most of the literature on the impact of technology and organization on the decentralization of decision making limits itself to a discussion of decentralization to the level of middle management. Moreover, there seems to be an underlying confusion in this literature between the delegation of decision making and the delegation of responsibilities (cf. Bates 1970). Perhaps the most useful discussion of technology's impact on the ability of the production worker to participate in decision making is *Alienation and Freedom* by Robert Blauner (1964). Despite the paucity of serious investigation on this matter, there appears to be a general conviction among social scientists (some social and industrial psychologists excepted) dating at least from Weber and F. W. Taylor that modern technology is too complex to be understood and managed by anyone below middle management.

We will proceed, then, by outlining some basic theoretical considerations for the study of the impact of technology on worker participation. In a static perspective, at least four intervening variables can be isolated to trace technology's influence on the potential for workers' participation.

cation bias. If our sample were large enough and there were no problems of multicollinearity, the preferred method would be to fully specify our model at the outset. However, given the limited size of our sample and the presence of multicollinearity, the t statistics in a fully specified equation would be low and unreliable. For instance, a significant variable may appear insignificant. Thus, in an effort to give full play to factors which have been treated as paramount in the literature, we regress participation on certain explanatory variables separately first. The results from these equations, therefore, must be considered as tentative. The variables which are found to be insignificant in less than fully specified equations did not become significant in equations where significant variables were added. For purposes of brevity and our desire not to overburden the presentation for the nontechnical reader, some of the latter equations are not included in the text. It was, in part, our concern with the question of specification bias that led us to employ factor analysis at the end of this chapter.

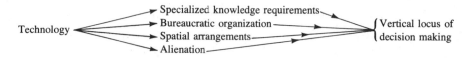

Each of these four variables has a complex relationship with both technology and participation. A priori, it would seem that more complex technologies have higher knowledge requirements and, all other things being equal, would tend to restrict worker participation potential. This would be the case, at least in the short run, while workers took training courses. However, even in the short run, it would be possible for workers to have a real input in the decision-making process through the employment of technical experts. These experts would explain available options to the workers' councils where the worker policy priority could be exercised. The majority of the administrative council meetings we attended in Chile availed themselves of such experts.[2] Even with such experts, it may be expected that there will be a short-run limitation of interest and understanding on the part of the workers and that this in turn will reduce the effective worker input.

It should be pointed out that there is nothing unique about this (expert–worker) consultation system. It is widely employed both in capitalist industry and in parliamentary government. A senator without researchers and consultants would have a difficult time getting reelected. Those who hold to a strict Weberian view of industrial management (that there is an hierarchy of knowledge, and hence efficiency mandates centralized decision making) also call into question a basic operating principle of parliamentary government (Pateman 1970, p. 97). In the Chapter 7, we discuss the efficiency or performance implications of worker participation under complex technologies.

Many organizational sociologists hold that technology determines organization, which in turn defines many of the characteristics of decision making. Charles Perrow (1967) divides technology into routine and nonroutine, the former mode greatly restricting participation. Joan Woodward (1965) divides technology into three types: unit and small batch, mass production, and process production. As one moves from unit to process, the system becomes more complex, there are fewer decisions, each decision commits the firm for a longer time, and decisions are more predictable. The fact that decisions are more predictable (i.e., are more defined by the environment and tend to be structurally

---

[2]It should be recalled from Chapter 4 that one of the five worker representatives on an administrative council was usually a technical expert. In many cases, one or more of the state representatives were also technical experts from either the same or other enterprises. In addition, other technical experts were often called upon to attend meetings of participatory bodies to explain technical aspects of various policy alternatives.

imperative), she argues, makes it less risky to decentralize decisions to middle management.

The element of reduced risk plays an important role throughout organization literature. Blau (1970) looks at two of Weber's chief characteristics of bureaucracy: formalization and standardization. He defines the former as the average number of words describing the different jobs in an organization and the latter as the proportion of employees who took the civil service exam. Weber, of course, argued that bureaucracy and centralization go hand in hand. Yet Blau finds the more formalization and standardization, the more decisions are delegated to middle management. Pugh *et al.* (1968) report a similar finding. The explanation here is that more formalization and standardization reduce the risk that the employee is incompetent or that he or she does not understand what is expected of the job; thus decentralization becomes less risky. However, they seem to be measuring delegation of tasks or responsibilities, not of decision making. It certainly does not seem that increased power is conferred to the employee whose job is more circumscribed by rules and regulations. The decision making is done by the person who draws up the rules or decides upon the hiring criteria. The notion that more bureaucracy leads to more decentralization, then, is not only counterintuitive, it is also unfounded.

To be sure, the meticulous study of Lawrence and Lorsch (*Organization and Environment,* 1967) suggests increasing decentralization to middle management in industries where market conditions and technology change most rapidly, i.e., under conditions of enhanced uncertainty and risk. Such organizations, when successful, are characterized by broad organizational charts. That is, they have many specialized departments at the level of middle management (referred to as the degree of specialization or horizontal differentiation). Alvarez (1972) in a 1969 study of 200 industrial firms in Chile also finds that more horizontal differentiation is associated with more reliance on middle management for decision making. It is significant that Lawrence and Lorsch connect the internal organizational structure of a firm with external conditions and not with the technology per se.

Vertical differentiation, the number of hierarchical levels between the top manager and the production worker, is also found to have a positive impact on decentralization (Blau 1970; Alvarez 1972). The logic here is that the further the top manager is removed from other levels of firm operation, the more he or she has to rely on those closer to that level of operation. Alvarez qualifies this relationship by saying that when both vertical and horizontal differentiation are high, decision making is encumbered and more centralized. Apart from this qualification, there appears to be nothing special about decentralization to middle management except, perhaps, that it is an ingredient of success. That is, no matter what kind of an organization you have—tall or short, formal or

informal—you always do better to consult your middle management professional and technical experts.

Three final organizational variables have an ambiguous relationship to decentralization in the literature. Size of the firm (number of employees), the percentage of administrative staff in total firm employment, and the span of control (number of workers per first line supervisor). Blau (1970) argues that the larger the administrative staff, the more the head manager is cushioned from middle management and the more decisions are centralized. Alvarez (1972) finds no relationship between decentralization and size of administrative staff. Pugh *et al.* (1969) find no relationship between size and concentration of authority, while both Alvarez and Blau find size to be positively associated with decentralization to middle management. These discrepancies in findings, it seems, could be accounted for by the differing measuring and controlling techniques employed.

Blau and Scott (1962) and Durbin (1965) find narrower spans of control to be linked with stricter control over subordinates, while Alvarez (1972) finds no relationship between the two. Alvarez explains his finding by arguing that narrower spans of control can increase contact between supervision and subordinates "increasing the latter's chances to exercise greater autonomy [p. 85]." The two effects, Alvarez suggests, balance each other off. Lipset, Trow, and Coleman in *Union Democracy* (1956, pp. 174–175) hold that wider spans of control are associated with deeper class consciousness. In small shops, the worker tends to be friendly with and to channel grievances directly through the foreman. In larger shops, the foreman is more isolated from the workers, who tend to channel grievances through the union. This is consistent with the Marxian notion regarding the increasing socialization of production under capitalism and the consequent growing class consciousness. In their essay, "Germany: Revolution and Counter-Revolution," (1942 [1851]) Marx and Engels argue that large factories increase the social distance between workers and management, reduce the loyalty of the work force to the enterprise, and heighten the potential for class consciousness. Class consciousness, it shall be argued later, is positively correlated with worker participation.

Technology also influences participation through the spatial arrangements in production and the consequent social relations it generates. It is presumed, all other things being equal, that technologies permitting more on-the-job contact between the workers would also be most propitious for worker participation. A variation of this principle is that contact plus severity of working conditions raises worker solidarity and the potential for worker participation. This relationship is suggested by Alvin Gouldner (1964) and various writings on the longwall coal getting methods in Great Britain (see, for one, Trist and Bamforth 1969).

Blauner (1964) and Woodward (1965), among others, argue that technology affects worker alienation. In addition to affecting spatial arrangments, technology influences the interest and diversity of tasks, job pressure, the pacing

mechanism (man or machine), and the distribution of manual skills. Blauner has developed a useful typology for exploring these relationships. He ranks four technologies according to their degree of mechanization or the order of their chronological appearance since the Industrial Revolution. The ordering is craft (e.g., printing trades or construction), machine tending (e.g., textiles), assembly line (e.g., automobiles and packaging) and continuous process (e.g., chemicals and oil refining).

Blauner cites several studies indicating that craft technology is associated with more personal initiative, less job pressure, greater manual skills, more interpersonal contact, smaller units of production, a greater understanding of the production process, and a narrower span of control. The two intermediate mass production categories essentially invert these characteristics and bring on more worker alienation. The most mechanized system of process production reverses the more alienating characteristics of mass production technology. Although the continuous process operator might have a monotonous job in watching panels and adjusting knobs, the operator has more free time, friendly relations with the supervisor who ceases to play a policing role, and, perhaps most significant, works in the cooperative atmosphere of a small work team. Thus, Blauner and Woodward concur: As production has become more automated the alienation of the industrial blue-collar laborer has followed the path of an inverted U.[3]

All this, of course, is not to deny the existence of alienation, but the underlying trend toward smaller production units and less pressure described by Blauner has potential implications for the development of working-class consciousness.[4] The implications for the potential of worker participation are more complicated. On the one hand, if class consciousness and cohesiveness determine worker participation, then it might be expected that machine-tending, assembly-line, and possibly craft workers will participate more than continuous process workers. On the other hand, if the ability for interworker contact and the exercise of initiative in job implementation are auspicious conditions for worker participation, then we might expect the opposite result. Putting these independent influences together, it is not clear how alienation or, in a larger sense, technology will affect participation. The only unambiguous expectation of this analysis is that craft technology will tend to lend itself more to worker participation than the other three types.[5]

---

[3]Braverman (1974) would take exception here. He argues that modern technology (continuous process, numerical control, word processing, etc.) has evolved continually to deskill both blue- and white-collar work.

[4]Of course, there are several other changes in the characteristics of the U.S. labor force that have equally serious implications. However, it is beyond the scope of the present study to discuss them.

[5]Further evidence along these lines is supplied by John H. Goldthorpe et al. in The Affluent Worker (1968). They found craft workers to be the only industrial group wherein a majority of the respondents upheld workers' control as a primary union objective (1:108–109). In addition, many observers (Herman 1974; Cahiers de Mai 1973) considered the initial motivation and immediate success of the Lip factory takeover in Besançon, France to be linked to the craft nature of watch production at Lip.

In attempting to gauge the impact of technostructure on participation, we constructed several distinct measures. We shall proceed by considering first, variables describing a firm's technology and second, variables describing a firm's organizational structure.

Technology

Three variables were used to describe a firm's technology: technological complexity (*TCOMP*), defined as the percentage of the firm's workers primarily dedicated to the maintenance of machinery and equipment; technological typology (*TTYP*), defined by the predominant type of technology in the firm; technological intensity (*TINT*), defined by the capital–labor ratio, where capital is the value of machinery and equipment on December 31, 1972.[6]

Our *TTYP* variable warrants further discussion. Here we used an expanded Blaunerian typology, where the mode *assembly technology* was added between machine tending and assembly line. The assembly mode was characteristic of certain sections of the metallurgy industry (e.g., boilers, plating, etc.) and other assembly processes (e.g., electrical instruments) without a conveyor belt. The variable *TTYP* was ordered according to the degree of mechanization: artisan = 1, machine tending = 2, assembly = 3, assembly line = 4, continuous process = 5. In doing this, we are imposing a discrete and equally spaced ordering in our variable describing technology types. As indicated above, different technological types not only influence participation potential through their respective degrees of mechanization, but also through the spatial arrangements and social relationships they engender. It is therefore likely that our imposed ordering throws away information about technology's impact on participation.[7]

When considered separately, the only significant technology variables are the two typology variables, *TTYP* and *TDUM*. Both are significant at $t_{.05}$. That is, our measure of mechanization is inversely correlated with participation. Artisan work and machine tending are the two least mechanized technologies and have equally the most positive impact upon participation. As we indicated, the spatial arrangements and social relations under these two systems are quite different. Machine tending combines minimal interworker contact and low skill with a broad span of control, large rooms, and harsh working conditions. In terms of

[6]To keep *TINT* a manageable size it was divided by 10,000 for purposes of the regression analysis. We call attention to footnote 1 of this chapter regarding our presentation of partial groupings of the independent variables.

[7]To adjust for this, the variable *TDUM* is constructed wherein technological types are allowed to weight themselves. P_F is run on the five different types as dummies. The coefficients of each of the five types are then used as the observations in *TDUM* (see Table 6.2).

worker cohesiveness or class consciousness, it is possible that these two sets of characteristics are offsetting in the general case.[8]

The effect of continuous process is different from the effects of artisan work and machine tending at the $t_{.20}$ level of significance, while assembly and assembly line are each different from artisan work and machine tending at the $t_{.10}$ level.[9] The continuous process variable, having a less negative impact than either assembly or assembly-line technologies, is the only deviation from a straight inverse linear relationship between participation and mechanization. Although this deviation could probably be explained by the spatial and social conditions of continuous process production, it should be noted that the effects of continuous process and assembly (at $t_{.88}$) and assembly line (at $t_{.70}$) are by no stretch of the imagination significantly different.

Our tentative conclusion, then, is that mechanization seems to have a negative immediate impact on the potential for participation. This impact is mediated through the spatial and social conditions engendered by the technology and finally manifests itself in two discrete stages (one, artisan–machine tending, and two, continuous process–assembly–assembly line).

If this result for Chile is generalizable, then it cautions against using the Woodward breakdown for studying the relationship of technology to participation. Woodward's category of mass production groups together assembly line and machine tending and thereby obfuscates a fundamental distinction.[10]

It can be objected that our typology method is imprecise since we are identifying the whole firm on the basis of its most prevalent technology. Blauner points out, for instance, that in a typical automobile factory only 20% of the employees work on the assembly line. However, when we look at the relationship between participation in a given section (P_S) and the technology in that section ($TDUM_S$), our basic relationship holds up:[11]

---

[8]By the general case, we mean that one does not know a priori whether alienation will produce apathy and inaction or anger and action. It depends on particular characteristics of the labor force.

[9]Several tests can be applied to the hypothesis $B_1 - B_2 = 0$. With dummy variables, however, one is obligated to omit one variable so the variance does not blow up. When this is done, the coefficients of the remaining variables actually represent the effect of the remaining variable minus the effect of the omitted variable.

[10]Assembly-line technology generally involves even less interworker contact and harsher conditions than machine tending. We might speculate that as working conditions became harsher up to a certain point the potential for worker consciousness and cohesiveness grows, but beyond this point the worker is so rapidly dehumanized that apathy is a more likely reaction. Again, this is suggested as a very general relationship and in no sense do we wish to argue technological determinism.

[11]Our index for P_S is identical to Level 3 (L_3) participation minus what happens in the general assembly. The sample size for the analysis of sections is 93.

$$P_S = 18.03 + .815\ (TDUM_S); R^2 = .032 \qquad\qquad (6.1)$$
$$(1.74)$$

Where $TDUM_S$:	Machine tending $= 1.75$
(rounded off to	Artisan $= .85$
the nearest	Continuous process $= -.03$
hundredth)	Assembly $= -1.71$
	Assembly line $= -3.07$

The relationship here is weaker than at the firm level, but this is true for all the relationships at the sectional level. It is probably accounted for by the increased importance of personality factors at the section level which tend to get neutralized over an entire enterprise. The greater dispersion of the coefficients of the $TDUM_S$ components reflects greater variability in their standard errors and not a greater difference in the effects of the distinct technologies.

The fact that machine tending has a higher coefficient than artisan production reemphasizes the problem with Woodward's mass production category, although the coefficients are not significantly different at $t_{.15}$. Nevertheless, the change in the ordering of artisan and machine tending might be explained by our classifying all maintenance sections as artisan. That is, individual sections of an assembly-line plant might be artisan. In this case, it is possible that assembly-line production is generating certain social relations that pervade the whole plant thus weakening the relationship between craft production in the section and participation in the section.[12] On the other hand, when a firm was classified as craft, it was not on the basis of a large maintenance section but rather on the basis of the main production system in the plant (e.g., furniture production).

Equation (5) in Table 6.2 indicates that our three technology variables together explain 27.8% of the variance of P_F. The typology variable remains significant at $t_{.10}$, but technological intensity and complexity become significant at this level. That is, if you control for the technological type and the capital–labor ratio ($TINT$), then technological complexity becomes significant and vice versa. Whereas, intensity (K/L) and mechanization are both inversely correlated to P_F, complexity ($TCOMP$) is positively related. This seems to be the case because $TCOMP$ is being measured as the relative size of the maintenance crew in each factory. As we have just seen, maintenance workers are engaged in craft-style jobs that are positively correlated with P_F and P_S.[13]

As discussed earlier, several social scientists have postulated that technology affects participation through its impact on organizational structure. We shall now

---

[12]This notion of plant social relations affecting the individual section is supported prima facie by the high correlation between P_S and P_F ($r = .48$).

[13]Again, these results should be considered as tentative, since we have not yet controlled for other significant explanatory variables.

TABLE 6.2

Technology and Participation[a]

Equation number	Dependent variable	Constant	TCOMP	TTYP	TINT	TDUM	R^2
(1)	P_F	4.3	.02 (.49)				.024
(2)	P_F	5.8		−.52 (−2.05) .298 .335			.113
(3)	P_F	4.7			−.007 (−1.03)		.031
(4)	P_F	4.4				7.84 (2.43)	.151
(5)	P_F	3.5	.159 (2.24) .335 .580		−.02 (−2.20) .115 .541	.656 (2.08) .01 .326	.278

Where *TDUM:*

Artisan = 1.00

Machine tending = 1.00

Continuous process = −.83

Assembly = −.96

Assembly line = −1.27

[a] The correlation matrix for this and subsequent tables in this chapter can be found in Appendix I to this chapter. Unless otherwise specified in this and subsequent tables in Chapters 6 and 7, numbers in parentheses refer to the *t* statistic; elasticity at the mean is beneath the *t;* and the beta coefficient is beneath the elasticity.

turn briefly to consider this relationship. In Tables 6.3 and 6.4, *VDIF* is vertical differentiation or the number of hierarchical levels in the firm defined in terms of accountability rather than income or perquisites; *SPANC* is the first line supervisory span of control or the average number of workers per first line supervision in the factory; *HDIF* is horizontal differentiation defined by the number of separate specialized departments at the level of middle management;[14] *SIZE* is the number of employees in the firm where every 100 employees equals 1 point; *PCTAD* is the percentage of employees classified as administrative workers, and *PCTSK* is the percentage of employees considered skilled (all white-collar plus skilled production workers).

[14]We assigned 2 points for departments with three or more people and 1 point for departments with one or two people.

TABLE 6.3

Technology and Organizational Structure

Equation number	Dependent variable	Constant	TCOMP	TTYP	TINT	R^2
(1)	VDIF	4.0	−.003 (−.053)	.405 (1.99) .207 .376	.0002 (.032)	.139
(2)	SPANC	24.7	.092 (.165)	−.105 (−.050)	−.03 (−.362)	.007
(3)	HDIF	21.7	−.741 (−2.23) 1.36 3.90	1.63 (1.29) .834 1.52	.08 (1.78) .411 3.13	.180
(4)	SIZE	5.2	.069 (.384)	.099 (.144)	−.004 (−.147)	.009
(5)	PCTAD	14.2	−.393 (−1.39)	.330 (.307)	.08 (1.96) .154 .592	.134
(6)	PCTSK	23.5	.340 (.548) .083 .116	2.01 (.857) 1.38 .121	.22 (2.55) .151 .559	.514

According to our results, we may say that in general, increased mechanization is associated with a taller executive hierarchy, while higher capital–labor ratios are associated with broader organizational charts (see Table 6.3). Average span of control and size do not appear to be related to technology, at least not in a linear fashion. As the capital–labor ratio increases, the relative size of the administrative staff and the proportion of skilled workers both rise. The high R^2 in Equation (6) of Table 6.3 indicates the presence of multicollinearity and suggests that mechanization and complexity ought also to be positively and significantly correlated with *PCTSK*. However, for our present purposes, it is sufficient to note that technology is related to organizational structure but their relationship is rather weak (with one exception) and scarcely indicates the determinism implied by Woodward.[15] The one exception stands out—more advanced technology is associated with a more skilled labor force.

[15]The Lawrence and Lorsch notion that organizational structure corresponds in large part to the external environment is given some prima facie credibility in light of these results. However, both because of the irregular market situation during the Allende period in Chile and inherent limitations in our study, we were unable to devise a suitable test of the Lawrence and Lorsch hypothesis.

TABLE 6.4

Organizational Structure and Participation

Equation number	Dependent variable	Constant	VDIF	SPANC	HDIF	SIZE	R^2
(1)	P_F	6.7	−.32 (−1.22)	.009 (.33)	−.05 (−1.24)	.037 (.425)	.098
			PCTAD	PCTSK	TINT		
(2)	P^F		−.052 (−1.07)		−.005 (−.690)		.064
(3)	P_F			−.032 (−1.42)	.002 (.256)		.088

Organizational and Bureaucratic Structure

If the relationship between technology and organizational structure is weak, the relationship between organizational structure and worker participation is even weaker (see Tables 6.3 and 6.4). In view of the efforts by organizational sociologists to demonstrate a relationship between characteristics of bureaucracy and decentralization of decision making this result may appear anomalous. It should be recalled, however, that (a) while these sociologists agree that organizational structure affects decentralization, they do not always agree on the specific mechanisms of their interaction; (b) they tend to confuse delegation of tasks with decentralization of power or decision making; and most significant, (c) they are concerned solely with decentralization to the level of middle management. It is not unusual that factors such as horizontal and vertical differentiation affect the locus of decision making within the management hierarchy, since these factors describe the organization of this hierarchy. It is another question whether the internal organization of management will have a direct and significant impact on the potential for workers to participate in decision making. Our results suggest it does not.[16]

THE LABOR FORCE

We shall discuss the impact of labor force characteristics on participation in terms of two central features—education and political organization. Other

---

[16]When technology and political variables are added to the equations in Table 6.4, the *t* statistics of the variables describing organizational and bureaucratic structure fall. The variable *TIME* loses statistical significance when added here.

characteristics such as age, sex, or family background will not be treated systematically, but a few fleeting remarks are in order.

Because of our cross-sectional approach, it was impossible to obtain information about individual workers. Some firms had data summarizing the age distribution of their labor force, others did not. Family background information (county of birth, social class, etc.) was even scarcer.

As far as we could determine from informal conversations, the effect of age in participation appeared to be ambiguous. Young workers without families had more free time after work hours, but some would participate in athletic programs or spend more time in their private social lives. Others would clearly take advantage of their free time to engage more heavily in factory and political life. Older workers had less free time and, perhaps, less energy to dedicate to the factory after work, but their personal lives were more settled and their athletic lives less active. The result was no clear distinction by age in the distribution of worker representatives or in attendance at councils or assemblies. However, it did seem to be the case that the more politically militant workers tended to be younger, and correspondingly the political leaders of the newer and more radical left-wing parties tended to be younger.

The relationship between women and participation was also unclear. When participation by sections (P_S) was run on the percentage of women workers in a given section, the relationship was insignificant. Women were proportionally underrepresented as worker representatives, especially at the level of the administrative council, in those enterprises where they constituted an important fraction of the labor force. Although day care centers (*sala cunas* for children under 2 and *jardines infantiles* for children between the ages of 2 and 6) could be found in most factories that employed more than a handful of female production workers and in many working-class communities, married women were still responsible for home and child care after work hours. This generally meant that they had less time to spend around the factory.

Finally, there appeared to be a tendency for workers more recently arrived to the cities to be both more radical and more politically active. Such workers were typically involved in illegal land takeovers. Violent repression was a constant threat they had to face or they would go homeless. Moreover, recent immigrants were thrust into new social roles and often into a social vacuum. This vacuum tended to be filled with political commitment.

Education

It is commonplace to stress the positive impact of education on the potential for worker participation. Yet, to our knowledge, the precise nature of the rela-

tionship between the quantity and quality of education and industrial democracy has not been studied.[17]

In addition to developing cognitive skills, schooling socializes an individual (Gintis 1971; Bowles and Gintis 1976). Working-class socialization tends to instill character traits suitable to a repressive and authoritarian work life. Higher levels of educational attainment correspond to increased expectation of rewards and identification with middle- and upper-class values. If these two assertions are correct, it is likely that any positive cognitive impact of formal schooling would be offset by its negative affective (or personality) and ideological impact. A study of 920 industrial workers in Chile in 1967 found that as a worker's education increases there is generally a marked rise in tolerance of politicians. Workers with high school educations were less likely to participate in unions, neighborhood associations or religious groups than workers with only grade school educations (Peppe 1971).

However, even the cognitive impact of education is unclear. It is unlikely that beyond basic literacy,[18] increased schooling (short of specialized training) would enhance the workers' understanding of labor relations or production methods. It was almost universally the case in Chile that foremen would tell us that workers understood the machinery better than either they themselves or their superiors. In the case of the United States, in the September 1970 issue of *Fortune*, Judson Gooding writes: "America's factory workers... can do more, and do it better, and contribute a flood of valuable ideas.... They know more about their jobs than anyone else—they spend forty hours a week doing nothing else—and hardly any of their suggestions for improving methods are impractical [p. 133]."

Reviewing over a dozen experiments in industrial democracy, David Jenkins (1973, p. 286) points out that they have been successful with workers of all levels of skill and in a wide variety of technical conditions. One of the most successful projects at Texas Instruments involved maintenance personnel with an average of below fifth grade education, while at a Proctor and Gamble experimental plant in Lima, Ohio, "one man who was a farmer... designed the plant's whole instrument control system [Jenkins 1973, pp. 233 and 286]."

Participation itself appears to be a very intense form of education (Pateman 1970, pp. 40–42; Freire 1973). Moreover, participation creates demand on the part of the workers for more general education and training courses (Jenkins

---

[17]An interesting project called "Educational Requirements for Economic Democracy" has recently been undertaken at the Center for Economic Studies, Stanford, California.

[18]The literacy rate in Chile during the Allende years was around 92%. In urban areas, literacy and educational levels were even higher. There, 98% could read and write, and 73% had completed primary education. In 1966, average schooling of agricultural workers was 2.6 years; whereas for industrial workers it was 5.7 years (Chile, Dirección de Estadística y Censos 1966).

1973, pp. 106 and 253). The interaction between participation and education is dynamic and therefore potentially one of the most threatening aspects of job enrichment programs to capitalists (see Chapter 2).[19]

Through our educational variables, we propose to test three different hypotheses regarding the relationship between the acquisition of knowledge, skills, or consciousness and participation. The first hypothesis regards the link between training levels of individuals and their participation. Some authors state that as peoples' training and schooling increase, they will be better able and more eager to participate. The studies done by Kolaya (1961) who found general apathy among Yugoslavian workers with low levels of schooling and Zupanov and Tannenbaum (1968) who observed higher aspirations and greater interest in participation among Yugoslavian workers with higher levels of educational attainment seem to support this view. However, it should be emphasized that participation is a long-established social norm in Yugoslavia, as well as a vehicle for individual advancement. As pointed out earlier, in nonparticipatory societies several authors have found that more schooling tends to make individuals adopt the goals of and passively accommodate themselves to the social and economic system. The second hypothesis, suggested by Crozier (1971) and others, argues that although training level is only one necessary condition to produce interest among workers about the problems of administration, the sufficient condition is the level an individual occupies in the enterprise's occupational hierarchy. The third hypothesis, which involves a broader interpretation of education, is typified by the approach of Paulo Freire. Freire (1973) stresses that more fundamental than an individual's formal schooling is the individual's "development of awareness" of his or her social situation.

In attempting to measure the influence of education on participation, we were again limited by our cross-sectional approach. Several firms did not have summary statistics on the educational attainment of their employees.[20] Since we were unable to survey the employees individually, we were forced to use proxy variables.

To test the first two hypotheses, we used the percentage of skilled workers in the enterprise's labor force (PCTSK) as a proxy for the level of education, and the percentage of professional, technical, and administrative personnel (PCTPTA) as a proxy for the position in the internal hierarchy of the enterprise as well as educational level.

---

[19]In this chapter, we are studying proxies for the preexisting level of formal education and their effects on participation. In the next chapter, we consider the effects of participation on the increase in worker training programs. Over time, therefore, one may postulate causality in both directions. However, we were unable to test the hypothesis of a dynamic interaction due to the short run and cross-sectional character of our data.

[20]Alvarez (1972) encountered the same problem in his 1969 survey of Chilean firms.

A few comments are in order to justify our proxy for the educational level. According to Chilean labor law (up to 1973), in order to be classified as a skilled worker, an individual must have either a high school education or its equivalent in trade school. The trade school requirement can also be met by 10 years of factory experience or a combination of schooling, certain jobs (e.g., lathe operator), and certified training courses. Administrative workers must have a high school education. Technical workers must have a technical training beyond high school, and professional workers must have a college education. That is, the different job categories imply minimum levels of educational attainment.

One serious defect in our *PCTSK* variable as a proxy for educational level should be mentioned before proceeding. In a handful of firms in our sample, large groups of production workers were promoted to the category of skilled workers according to a new, broader interpretation of the formal requirements specified in labor laws.[21] The workers reasoned that many more than those originally so considered were skilled. Since the workers were now in control of job classification, they promoted each other. These promotions constituted a change in status without a commensurate increase in education or money wages.

One other new variable was introduced as a measure of political ideology. It was important to control for this, since our model suggests that education has an ideological as well as cognitive influence. Our control is the percentage of workers per factory who voted for the liberal Christian Democratic party in the May 1972 CUT (National Labor Organization) elections (*PCTCD*).[22]

The results shown in Table 6.5 are difficult to interpret. The only education proxy (*PCTSK*) which is significant at $t_{.10}$ when considered alone loses its significance when ideology is controlled. The negative significant coefficient in the first equation might be interpreted to be reflecting the ideological and affective effects of education. To be sure, the technostructure of a firm also socializes. The higher status of a skilled job undoubtedly affects worker attitudes. *PCTSK* could be reflecting the status influence more than the educational.

Since technology is significantly correlated with both skill mix and participation, it was controlled for in equations (4), (5), and (7). In Equations (4) and (5), *PCTSK* lost significance at $t_{.10}$. Equations (6) and (7) add *AVGR* (average remuneration in the enterprise) as a control variable, which is highly correlated with both *PCTSK* ($r = .736$) and *TINT* or K/L ($r = .598$). Interpretation here is very tricky. One could argue that once you control for the proportion of skilled workers and the capital–labor ratio in each factory, average remuneration would

---

[21]It should be mentioned that the labor law provision allowing production workers to be classified as skilled by virtue of 10 years of job experience also introduces a distortion in our proxy.

[22]The Christian Democrats were the only major party to the right of the UP who ran candidates in this election. The election included all government and educational workers as well as all white- and

be highly associated with educational level. Thus education is positively and significantly (at $t_{.10}$) correlated with participation. On the other hand, one might argue on the basis of studies for the United States, that individual income does not seem to be highly correlated with formal education (Becker 1964; Bowles 1972), so that it is unlikely that *AVGR* proxies for education regardless of the control variables. Another interpretation might be that *PCTSK* proxies for education and when you control for this and ideology together, the positive coefficient on *AVGR* supports the Maslow thesis (1973), i.e., as individuals satisfy their basic material needs, other needs (e.g., self-fulfillment) become evident. All of these propositions, it strikes us, are dubious. Probably the safest conclusion to draw from the evidence presented is that *PCTSK* and *PCTPA* are simply inadequate proxies for the level of educational attainment.

However, as presented in more detail in the next chapter, the introduction of factory training courses (a possible measure of worker training levels free from the distortion of socialization) is highly correlated with participation ($r = .49$). Viewed dynamically, training increases skills and knowledge, which increases the ability to participate and participation increases worker involvement and

blue-collar factory workers. The results of this election (the first of its kind in Chile) were as follows:

CUT Vote	Votes	Percentage
Partido Comunista	173,064	31.8
Partido Socialista	148,117	27.1
MAPU	25,970	4.7
Partido Radical	21,810	4.0
Izquierda Cristiana	3,336	0.6
Partido Social Demócrata	1,601	0.3
Acción Popular Independiente	1,599	0.3
Total UP	375,597	68.8
FTR (MIR)	10,192	1.8
USOPO	5,420	1.0
P.C.R.	3,216	0.6
M.S.L.	676	0.1
Total other groups	19,504	3.5
Democracia Cristiana	147,598	26.6
PIR	3,572	0.6
Total of Anti-UP coalition (CODE)	151,170	27.6
Total valid votes	546,271	100%
Active labor force	ca. 3,000,000	18.2% voted

If blue-collar vote alone is considered, then the UP plus parties to its left obtained upwards of 85% of the vote.

TABLE 6.5

Education and Participation with Control Variables

Equation number	Dependent variable	Constant	PCTSK	PCTPTA	AVGR	PCTCD	TCOMP	TTYP	TINT	R^2
(1)	P_F	5.5	-.03 (-1.77) -.251 -.320							.086
(2)	P_F	5.5		-.0005 (-1.36)						.053
(3)	P_F	6.7	-.013 (-.764)			-.073 (-2.08)				.195
(4)	P_F	5.6	-.032 (-1.42)						1.002 (.256)	.088
(5)	P_F	5.5	-.032 (-1.59)				.198 (2.85)	-.487 (-1.84)	-.01 (-1.31)	.333
(6)	P_F	6.1	-.042 (-2.02) -.350 -.448		.0002 (2.14) .615 .579	-.101 (-2.83) -.543 -.509				.299
(7)	P_F	5.7	-.052 (-2.37) -.434 -.554		.0002 (2.34) .615 .579	-.072 (-2.11) -.386 -.363	.165 (2.50) .338 .602	-.481 (-1.91) -.275 -.310	-.01 (-1.06) -.057 -.271	.473 (corrected) .360

stimulation, which increases the demand for education. This result is consistent with our earlier claim that participation and education are mutually reinforcing.[23]

The third hypothesis takes into consideration the affective and ideological as well as the cognitive aspects of education. Herein education is construed broadly to refer to the process by which the individual develops a social awareness of his or her condition and a critical capacity to evaluate and advance this condition. This process has obvious implications for the development of a system of worker participation. Such a transformation of consciousness, Freire asserts (1973), normally occurs outside of and despite formal education.[24]

Thus, Freire affirms that knowledge results only from the discovery and rediscovery of reality, from one's hopeful and unceasing search and struggle together with others. The alternative of self-realization, regardless of the initial condition of "ignorance" or material misery, emerges from one's ability to view the surrounding world critically in constant dialogue with others. To the extent that the personal and social conditions are propitious for this encounter, the individual is able to transcend the paternalistic student–teacher relationship, and a simple worker can transfer the capacity to experience life critically to a fellow worker or neighbor much more effectively than a teacher or another superior with a different life experience.

In this manner, people who have been completely deprived are radically transformed and are no longer content to respond as passive objects to the changes occuring around them. Those who have achieved this awakening of consciousness are ready to begin the struggle to change the structure of a society that had previously served to oppress them.

Critical capacity makes it possible for individuals to be in a state of mobilization and protest directed toward social change. Mobilization and protest, in turn, form part of a larger educational and political process that enhances and diffuses critical awareness.

[23]A production worker from a Santiago furniture factory we visited had the following to say about education: "The majority of us haven't gone beyond primary school . . . but we have knowledge from our experience and we have gotten in touch with professors who will come to teach us in the factory. That is, instead of going to the university, we want to make this factory into a university, where everyone of us will be a professor and we will teach each other."

[24]In this connection, Freire points out that "the teacher speaks of reality as if it were stationary, static, compartmentalized, and perfectly predictable . . . and the students are considered as 'containers' or receptacles to be filled by the teacher [1973, pp. 57–58]." This system of learning Freire calls the "banking concept of education," where the teacher is the depositor and the students mere depositories of the truth handed down by the teacher. The students patiently receive, memorize, and repeat, which helps in transforming them into adaptable and manageable beings. The more the students work at guarding the "deposits" entrusted to them, the less is the development of their critical consciousness. The latter can only come about through active intervention in their environment and through the effort to change it. That is, the more they accept the passive role they are assigned, the more they will tend to simply adapt to their world and the more they will tend to accept the fragmented view of reality that is entrusted to them.

Through the variable labor mobilization (*LMOB*) we attempt to gauge the degree of worker mobilization, critical consciousness, and militance in each enterprise, as opposed to the average level of formal education in each plant. The two principal components of *LMOB* are (*a*) whether the enterprise was socialized by top-down decree or by worker initiative (*LMOB*$_1$); and (*b*) the number of strike days during the 5 years prior to socialization (*LMOB*$_2$).[25]

We found labor mobilization to be very highly correlated with participation: The correlation coefficient between P_F and *LMOB*$_1$ is $r = .50$ and between P_F and *LMOB*$_2$ is $r = .34$ (see Table 6.6).

Since *LMOB*$_1$ (form of socialization) and *LMOB*$_2$ (prior strike activity) both measure labor mobilization before the firm's passage to the APSM, it is interesting to see if their effect on P_F is sustained. Consequently, the number of months a firm had been in the social area (*TIME*) was controlled for. From Equations (2) and (3) of Table 6.6, we see that when *TIME* is included, the significance levels

[25]The precise construction of this variable involves some arbitrariness in point assignment, yet it clearly captures the trend of labor mobilization. Our regressions would have yielded stronger results had we allowed the components to weight themselves through dummies. The details of its construction follow:

I. *LMOB*$_1$: Passage of firm to APSM

  A. Without labor conflict
    1. but with some rank and file involvement = 6
    2. but with involvement of labor leadership only = 2
    3. with no labor involvement = 0

  B. With a labor conflict
    1. through a strike = 12
    2. through a takeover or a takeover and strike = 24
    3. (every 5 days of conflict = 5) times
      1, when participation in conflict by 75–100% of workers,
      3/4, when participation in conflict by 50–75% of workers,
      1/2, when participation in conflict by 30–49% of workers,
      0, when participation in conflict by 0–20% of workers.

II. *LMOB*$_2$: Strikes in 5 years preceding passage.
  A. Every legal strike = 1; every illegal strike = 2
  B. Sum of the number of days of the two longest strikes; every 10 days = 1, up to 12

III. *LMOB*$_3$: minus 2 for every month the firm delays (after first 2 months in APSM) in setting up the participation organisms.

IV. *LMOB*$_4$: if the workers had some participation in the change of the (government appointed) factory administrator, 10

V. *LMOB*$_5$: if the workers had asked for some form of participation in their contract negotiations prior to their incorporation into the APSM.

  A. To audit company books or to share profits, 2

  B. To have representatives on the management board, 4

The aggregate variable $LMOB = LMOB_1 + LMOB_2 + LMOB_3 + LMOB_4 + LMOB_5$.

TABLE 6.6

Labor Mobilization and Participation

Equation number	Dependent variable	Constant	*TIME*	$LMOB_1$	$LMOB_2$	R^2
(1)	P_F	2.5	.391 (1.90)			.099
(2)	P_F	3.1		.088 (2.58)	.045 (.806)	.266
(3)	P_F	.47	.48 (2.76)	.087 (2.80)	.069 (1.36)	.411
			PCTCP	*PCTCD*		
(4)	*LMOB*	50.5	−.395 (−1.69)	−.865 (−3.38)		.325

of both $LMOB_1$ and $LMOB_2$ increase, suggesting the presence of a sustaining effect.[26]

Finally, Equation (4) suggests that the percentage voting for the Communist (*PCTCP*) and Christian Democratic (*PCTCD*) parties have a negative effect on worker mobilization. This reflects paternalistic patterns in both parties and is consistent with our analysis of these parties in the next section. However, the Chilean Communist party has always been an effective, militant strike leader ($LMOB_2$). This probably accounts for the negative correlation being stronger between *PCTCD* and *LMOB* than between *PCTCP* and *LMOB*.

In our analysis, labor mobilization has been considered as a manifestation of workers' critical consciousness, which in turn reflects the broad and dynamic view of education suggested by Freire. Labor mobilization accounts for over 26% of the variance in our dependent variable, P_F, and thus is the single most powerful explanatory variable introduced so far. Although treated as an educational variable, labor mobilization has clear political overtones. In the next section, we turn to consider additional political variables.

Political Organization

Many writers have stressed the intrinsically political nature of worker participation. Both radical and liberal theorists have emphasized that worker participation is principally characterized by a shift of *power* to the workers. The more power shifted, the greater the potential for participation. Since power is not

---

[26]It is germane here to recall that the entire Chilean experience with worker participation in social area firms lasted only 32 months. Thus our analysis of time effects applies more appropriately to the medium run than the long run.

generally given away for nothing, it is usually gained by the workers as a result of the level of struggle and political organization of the working class. A sociologist who studied the question of power in industrial firms in Chile just prior to Allende's election came to much the same conclusion (Alvarez 1972): "Participation in the final analysis originates in a political decision to redistribute power, and its occurrence will depend on changes in the power relations of the external society [p. 3]."

In this section, we consider two factors which describe the political organization of the working class. They are specific to the enterprise, but it should be kept in mind that there was a favorable external political environment that affected all the enterprises in our sample. It is also important to remember that the period in question was one of great political flux and institutional instability. Politics conditioned not only participation but also practically everything else in Chile during the Allende period.

The first political factor is the composition of political party support in each firm. Again, we refer to the May 1972 CUT elections. We were given access to CUT's records of that election and were thereby able to calculate the relative strength of the major parties in each factory. We isolated four variables to describe the results of the CUT elections: *PCTCP,* the percentage of votes in each factory that went to Luis Figueroa, the Communist party (CP) candidate for national CUT president; *PCTCD,* the percentage of votes going to the Christian Democratic (CD) candidate, Ernesto Vogel; *PARHOM,* party homogeneity, the percentage of votes going to the largest party in each factory; and, *PARORD,* party ordering, where the parties are ordered a priori on the basis of their expected influence on participation.[27]

We expected the increased presence of either Communist or Christian Democrat workers to be associated with lower participation because of (a) the ideological and organizational influence of these parties on their followers; and (b) the actions based on party programs taken by the elected officials of these parties at the factory level.

The Communist party in Chile was a very tight, bureaucratic, top-down organization. Its program was revolution by steps. The Communists believed that by nationalizing the large monopolies and reforming other aspects of the dependent Chilean economy, the UP would be able to increase production and win the country over to socialism. The Party's main slogan was *A Ganar la Batalla de la Producción* ('To Win the Battle for Production'). Ideological struggle was minimized. The masses were to be mobilized to increase production and to attend the mammoth marches of the UP, but for little else. Mobilized masses were a threat to the Communist party's goal of controlling and molding the process.

---

[27]When the Socialist party received the most votes in a factory, we allocated 4 points; when MAPU did, 3 points; when the Communists did, 2 points; when the Christian Democrats did, 1 point. The justification for this ordering is provided in the text.

The Communist party in Chile was closely linked to Moscow. Ever since the spring of 1918,[28] when Lenin embraced Taylorism ("The Immediate Tasks of the Soviet Government," April 1918), the Party in Moscow has subverted worker control. It happened again in Czechoslovakia, 1945–1948 (Kovanda 1974), Hungary 1956–1958 (Horvat 1975), Poland 1956–1958 (Babeau 1968), and Czechoslovakia in 1968 (Pelikan 1973; Bernstein 1973). The Communist strategy is generally to replace the independent workers' council with a trade union and then attempt to gain Party control over the union. When this fails, there is intervention. The Chilean Communist party saw the more advanced factory committees in Chile taking on autonomous functions, e.g., forming *cordones industriales* or *comandos comunales*.[29] The Communist strategy for gaining control of these organizations was familiar: They argued that the unions should control the factory committees.

The Christian Democrats had maintained a proparticipation position since the early days of the Frei government. Yet, as we saw in Chapter 3, the Frei government did more to frustrate worker participation than to advance it. The party contained many ideological factions, but it was strongly dominated by the more conservative, procapitalist Frei wing. When Allende was elected, the Christian Democrats had one overriding concern—to remove Allende and bring the presidency back to their party. Their strategy involved resisting and, in some cases, sabotaging aspects of the UP program, including the nationalization of industry and worker participation.

According to our results (see Table 6.7), the Communist and Christian Democratic parties both have a significant and strong negative impact on the level of participation. When *PCTCP* and *PCTCD* are merged (through a weighted linear combination) into *PCPCD,* we explain 40.6% of the variance of P_F which is considerably more than the explanation provided by our three technology variables taken together (27.8%).

The converse of this result is that the Socialist party, MAPU, and other progressive parties on the left had a positive impact on participation. This is seen in the *PARORD* variable.

PARHOM was added as attempted index of (the inverse of) sectarianism in the firm. Sectarianism between the Christian Democrats and the UP parties, as well as within the parties of the left, was one of the most destructive forces to the entire political–economic process during the Allende period. Rivalry and divisionism were a lot stronger at the level of party leadership than among the rank

---

[28]We do not mean to imply that this date constitutes a break with the past. Rather, it is a clarification and crystallization of earlier tendencies in the Bolshevik party.

[29]Such organizations were intended to establish a basis for parallel political power modeled after the *Soviets* in Russia, 1904 and 1917. See Zimbalist and Stallings (1973) for a more detailed description of these organizations.

TABLE 6.7

Political Parties and Participation

Equation number	Dependent variable	Constant	PCTCP	PCTCD	PCPCD[a]	PARHOM	PARORD	R^2
(1)	P_F	6.9	-.093 (-3.42) -.549 -.513					.262
(2)	P_F	6.5		-.084 (-2.70) -.451 -.424				.180
(3)	P_F	8.61	-.086 (-3.50)	-.076 (-2.80)				.407
(4)	P_F	8.6			-.082 (-4.75) -.924 -.639			.406
(5)	P_F	2.2				.059 (1.27) .509 .217		.047
(6)	P_F	1.8					.976 (4.17) .591 .586	.345
(7)	P_F	.13				.046 (1.21) .397 .169	.953 (4.08) .576 .572	.373

[a] $PCPCD = PCTCP + PCTCD$. This operation is justified by the practically identical coefficients on $PCTCP$ and $PCTCD$ in Equation (3).

and file. The very existence of such sectarianism was another failure of political leadership in Chile. By driving artificial wedges between workers, by creating unnecessary competition, and by fostering ideological confusion it hindered the growth and solidarity of workers at all levels. At times, what started with the political leadership would then filter into the rank and file and damage the development of participation in the factories.

Equally prejudicial for participation was sectarianism in the bureaucracy. The appointments of state representatives to administrative councils were delayed in some factories for several months because of feuds for the positions between UP parties.[30] Also, Christian Democratic as well as right-wing bureaucrats, most of whom were retained at middle- and lower-level positions in government offices, would delay petitions for loans, raw materials, or import permits from "social area" firms.[31] Such complications could cause economic problems for the firms affected or, in certain instances, disillusion the workers.[32] While we were unable to measure sectarianism outside the firm, our measure of the inverse of sectarianism inside the firm, $PARHOM$, is positively related to P_F. However, it is insignificant at the $t_{.10}$ level. The low level of significance can probably be attributed to the inadequacy of our measure (percentage of votes of largest party) and not to the actual relationship.[33]

The second political factor we consider is the role of the union. With virtual unanimity, political theorists and social scientists have found that unions play a conservative role with respect to workers' control.[34] The reasoning goes that unions either: (a) are reluctant to witness the creation of parallel bodies to represent worker interests; (b) have a historical role which is, in essence, defen-

[30]For instance, here are the remarks of a production worker in a Santiago appliance factory: "There was a split in the Popular Unity in our factory ... on one side the Communist Party, with the conciliatory position toward the Christian Democrats. . . . I won't say what they agreed upon, but it is true that together they delayed, arbitrarily, the election of the Administrative Council."

[31]An excellent treatment of bureaucracy, sectarianism, and revolutionary leadership in the Chilean countryside can be found in Marchetti and Maffei (1972). Also, see *Mayoría* February 16, 1972, p. 5. Another interesting study is Castillo and Larrain (1971).

[32]This would depend, naturally, on the previous state of organization of the workers. Where they were already well organized, bureaucratic problems would sometimes make them more militant. Ultimately, bureaucratic inaction could lead to workers of one or many factories taking over government offices.

[33]The support in the largest party represents the potential, not the actual, state of sectarianism. If one party has 100% support, the potential is practically nil. But with 40, 50, or 60% support, there is a potential, and the actual extent of sectarianism will depend on local leadership and relations between the parties.

[34]Some of these authors are: Aronowitz (1974); Babeau (1968, p. 222); Barrera, Aranda, and Diaz (1973); Brecher (1972); Cohn-Bendit and Cohn-Bendit (1968, p. 345); Gorz (1970); Gramsci (1973); Shearer (1974); Trotsky (1972); and Zwerdling (1973).

sive in looking after the workers' economic interests; or (c) have been in-stitutionalized and, to one degree or another, are sold out to management.

Industrial trade unions in Chile have a long history.[35] Since the writing of the labor code in 1924, there have typically been at least two unions in every company. According to the law, three types of unions were authorized in Chile: industrial, professional, and employees unions.[36] Collective bargaining was done at the local level since federations were illegal.[37] During the Allende period, there was a tendency for the distinct unions within a firm to merge into one "class-unified" union.

As mentioned in Chapter 4, the unions, according to *Las Normas Básicas de Participación,* were encharged with initiating the participation process, i.e., explaining the *normas básicas* to the workers, clarifying the new system of management, spelling out workers' rights, and calling the initial elections. When the union did not undertake this task, usually no one else did (for a while at least), and the participation process would be delayed. In the meantime, internal frictions and conflicts would develop that debilitated worker unity. Similarly, if the union called the elections without making an adequate educational effort, the start of the process would be slowed. Also in accordance with the *normas básicas,* union leaders were to preside over the coordinating councils, which had the vital function of channeling information and suggestions from top to bottom and vice versa. In some instances, unresponsive or reluctant unions could be bypassed with local party cadres playing the union's part, but most often the attitude of the union toward participation had an important influence on how the process developed.

We used four variables to look at the influence of the unions. One, the union attitude (*UNATT*) toward participation was measured by asking each of our

[35]Cf. Peppe (1971); Barria (1967 and 1970); Barrera (1971a); Morris (1973); L. Castillo (1971); Campero and Jaramillo (1971); Noe (1971); Castillo, Saez, and Rogers (1970); Ribeiro and DeBarbierre (1973); and Castillo, Echeverria, and Larrain (1973).

[36]*Industrial unions* could be organized in any industrial establishment with more than 25 workers over 18 years of age, provided that 55% of them agreed to form the union. Once the union was legally organized, affiliation was obligatory. *Professional unions* could be organized by at least 25 workers having the same profession or trade or doing the same work, without the requirement of belonging to the same establishment. The recruiting area was not restricted to one company, but was rather of a regional nature. *Employee unions* were the same as professional unions, except that they were adapted to the employees of one or more firms depending on whether or not the number was sufficient. Here the word "employee" corresponds to *empleado* which refers to skilled production and white-collar workers.

[37]In our opinion this was an important feature that kept Chilean unions from becoming overly bureaucratic and helped to maintain a certain degree of democracy and rank-and-file participation in the union. This is consistent with the idea on the process of union federation put forth in Lipset, Trow, and Coleman (1956).

respondents if the union has actively pushed participation, actively resisted it, or acted ambivalently.[38] The second union variable is the political ideology of the president of the largest (or only) union in the plant (*UNID*). Here, we asked the respondent "which of the following five ideas best justify the participation of the workers in the firm's management": (1) It increases production; (2) it deepens the political consciousness of the workers; (3) it lowers the level of conflict in the firm; (4) it is a concrete way of transferring power to the working class; (5) because of the concept of work itself, i.e., the right to administer a factory belongs to those who work in it. The respondent was asked to select two from this list. If the respondent chose (4) and (2) or (4) and (5), this was considered a "very progressive" position; including either (2) or (4) was considered a "moderately progressive" position; choosing neither (2) nor (4) was considered a "conservative" position. The variable *UNID* was ranked according to the progressiveness of the response (very progressive = 3, moderately progressive = 2, conservative = 1). Since it would have been indiscreet to query directly as to the workers political party leaning, *UNID* was intended to reveal party sympathies, e.g., the Communist party's position emphasized that participation was a means to raise productivity (basic idea number one). It seems, however, that *UNID* has given us more information than simple party affiliation, because within each party there is a substantial variation in political attitudes among the rank and file (and, in some cases, among leadership as well). It was our hypothesis that the political ideology of the elected union official would determine to a large extent the role of the union in the process.

The third union variable is the number of unions per firm (*UNNO*). The fourth variable is the average age of the unions in the plant (*UNAGE*, every 5 years = 1 pt.). This fourth variable is motivated by several writings by James Petras (1972a, 1972b) where he suggests that younger unions and other organizations tend to be less institutionalized, more democratic, and more radical. In particular, he maintains that this factor explains much of the variations in participation in different Chilean firms and communities during the Allende years.

Union attitude was confirmed to be a very important variable (see Table 6.8). The positive, significant, and strong correlation between *UNID* and P_F reveals that the more progressive the ideology of the union leader, the more developed the worker participation. It also suggests the importance of political leadership.[39] SLID, the ideology of the leader of the production committee at the sectional level, is also significantly and positively correlated with participation in the section (P_S).

---

[38]If the union pushed participation at first and still pushes it = 2; if pushed it at beginning and now does not or vice versa = 1; if it has been inactive = 0. The different respondents' scores were summed and averaged over the different unions in the plant. The potential scores varied from -10 to $+10$.

[39]The correlation coefficient between *UNATT* and *UNID* is .530.

TABLE 6.8

Union Attitude, Ideology, and Participation

Equation number	Dependent variable	Constant	UNATT	UNID	UNNO	UNAGE	UNATID[a]	R^2
(1)	P_F	2.8	.408 (4.44) .382 .611					.374
(2)	P_F	1.2		1.67 (4.13) .744 .584				.341
(3)	P_F	4.6			−.043 (−.256)			.002
(4)	P_F	4.3				.068 (.258)		.004
(5)	P_F	1.2					.269 (5.38) .731 .682	.468
			SLID	P_F				
(6)	P_S	12.4	3.22 (3.44)					.115
(7)	P_S	8.3	2.06 (2.31)	1.41 (4.44)				.274

[a] Our variable, *UNATID*, combines union attitude and union ideology. *UNATID*, by itself, explains 46.8% of the variance of P_F. Neither *UNNO* nor *UNAGE* is significant. *UNATID* equals $4 \times (UNID) + 1 \times (UNATT)$. This linear combination is justified by the ratio of the variables' coefficients in the following equation:

$$P_F = 1.25 + 1.03 \ (UNID) + .280 \ (UNATT); R^2 = .468$$
$$\qquad\qquad\quad (2.37) \qquad\quad (2.77)$$

The *very progressive* category more or less corresponds to the position of the groups which criticized from within or outside the UP for not having a strategy to win state power. The results on union attitude and ideology, along with the results on party composition, suggest that those groups which sponsored a clearer, more aggressive strategy for the taking of state power were the same groups that developed more effective systems of workers' power at the level of the enterprise.

It is now appropriate to summarize the results obtained for our independent variables. Despite the plethora of literature on the importance of the firm's bureaucratic organization in conditioning the vertical loci of decision making, our organizational variables are not significantly correlated with our index of worker participation. On the other hand, each of our two political variables (*PCPCD* and *UNATID*) individually explain over 40% of the variance in P_F. It might be objected that both *PCPCD* and *UNATID* are measuring the same intangible and generalized political impact. For instance, a good case could be made that *UNID* and *PCPCD* seriously overlap.[40] However, when *PCPCD* and *UNATID*, along with the politically related variable, *LMOB*, are regressed together with P_F, each of these three variables is significant at $t_{.05}$ (Table 6.9, Equation [2]).

When the three most significant nonpolitical variables (the technology variables) are added to these three political variables, none of the technology variables retain significance at the $t_{.10}$ level. The technology variables as a group are also insignificant.[41] This suggests that technology has no independent impact on participation.[42] Rather, its 27.8% (Table 6.9, Equation [1]) is being absorbed by the political factors.[43]

The three political variables in Equation (2) of Table 6.9 explain 64.9% of the variance in P_F. Their measurement, it should be emphasized, is completely independent from the measurement of P_F. The only possible conclusion to draw

[40]This is borne out in the correlation matrix of Table 6.8 found in Appendix I to this chapter.

[41]The F (4, 28) test on all the coefficients of the technology variables in Equation (3) of Table 6.9 being equal to zero is not significant at $t_{.10}$, i.e., the null hypothesis that the three technology coefficients equal zero cannot be rejected at this level.

[42]It is important to remind the reader that we refer here not to the results of participation (to be discussed in the next chapter), but to the extent of its presence. For instance, it is still possible that increased participation be associated with lower productivity for complex technologies. Our general result, that political factors rather than technology or size determine the development of participation, is supported by similar findings for the case of industrial undertakings on Israeli kibbutzim (Fine 1973, p. 288). Of course, the variation of technology is rather limited in kibbutz industry.

[43]In the long run, it is possible that technology influences participation indirectly through its effect on political variables. Although crudely exemplified, this is consistent with the Marxist notion on the interaction between technology and class consciousness discussed earlier. In any case, these results caution against looking only at the simple correlation between technology and participation. Those who do so are underspecifying the actual relationship.

TABLE 6.9

Technology, Political Variables, and Participation

Equation number	Dependent variable	Constant	TCOMP	TDUM	TINT	LMOB	UNATID	PCPCD	R^2
(1)	P_F	3.5	.159 (2.24)	.656 (2.08)	-.02 (-2.20)				.278
(2)	P_F	4.5				.033 (2.20) .141 .292	.225 (3.12) .408 .380	-.041 (-2.50) -.462 -.319	.649
(3)	P_F	3.8	.071 (1.39)	.292 (1.26)	-.007 (-1.01)	.031 (1.95)	.209 (2.91)	-.033 (-1.92)	.689

from this result is that participation in Chile, at least in its first stages of development, was an intensely political process. Workers' power at the enterprise level was a function of political organization, ideology, and struggle of the local work force. It was made possible by and reflected the temporary, changing balance of class power in the whole society.[44]

THE INTERMEDIATE VARIABLES

The two intermediate variables we defined are the disposition of the administration toward participation (DISPAD) and the extent (quantity and depth) of internal information flows (INFO).

We expected that participation would result from a dialectical interaction between the organization and mobilization of the rank and file (force from below) and the organization of the administration (force from above, DISPAD). Even when power is nominally transferred to workers, there is no guarantee they will exercise it. Specifically, it has been the historical experience, with a few exceptions, that those interpreting the workers' priorities and needs have grown apart from the workers they are supposed to represent. There is a tendency for the leaders to bureaucratize themselves and become a new class of privileged administrators. In some cases, they are bureaucrats to begin with. The more this happens, the more power is alienated from the rank and file and the less interest the rank and file have in attending assemblies and councils with little or no influence. This relationship has been illustrated neatly for the case of two textile factories in Yugoslavia by Ichak Adizes (1971); see also Wachtel (1973, pp. 90–94).

In China, the *hsia-fang* system was institutionalized in 1957 (Lee 1966), obligating administrators to spend a certain amount of their work weeks doing manual labor. Since 1957, this system has been expanded. The Chinese have also experienced one cultural revolution and periodically initiate campaigns to fight the tendency toward bureaucracy and privilege (Bettelheim 1974; Meissner 1972; Hoffman 1975; Robinson 1973; Andors 1977b). Elsewhere, bureaucratic privilege and isolation have been minimized by narrowing wage differentials. Bureaucracy does not disappear by itself; it is minimized in direct relation to the pressure from those on the bottom.

For our purposes, bureaucracy's minimization is contained in *DISPAD*. The more favorable is the disposition of the administration to participation, the more

[44]Andors surveys 85 enterprises through articles in the Chinese press in attempting to identify the factors affecting the speed of the establishment of the participatory revolutionary committee management system during China's Cultural Revolution. He concludes: "[It] depended more on political, organizational and historical factors than on economic, geographic or technical ones [1977b, pp. 186–187]."

TABLE 6.10

Disposition of the Administration and Participation

Equation number	Dependent variable	Constant	DISPAD	LMOB	INFO	R^2
(1)	P_F	1.98	.312 (6.66) .588 .756			.574
(2)	P_F	2.00	.242 (3.88) .433 .587	.028 (1.65) .119 .248		.607
(3)	P_F	.07	.149 (3.11) .266 .361		.065 (5.01) .714 .583	.761
(4)	P_F	.13	.089 (1.62) .159 .216	.025 (1.99) .107 .221	.065 (5.15) .703 .574	.788

			PCTCP	PCTCD	LMOB	UNATID	R^2
(5)	DISPAD	2.4	−.018 (−.345)	.0001 (.002)	.129 (3.20)	.588 (3.11)	.603

effort there will be to decentralize decision making, the more information will be provided to the workers, the more understandable the information will be (e.g., graphs instead of traditional balance sheets), the more there will be an effort to clarify the operation and function of the different participation bodies, the more often meetings will be called, and the closer will be the contact of administrators and workers. All of these items, in turn, are directly related to demands of and pressure from the workers.

DISPAD, as we measure it,[45] is very highly correlated with P_F ($r = .758$). When LMOB, as an index of pressure from the base, is controlled for, various

[45]DISPAD has four components: (1) the ideological justification of participation (used to measure UNID) is asked of the chief administrator and the two interviewed worker representatives on the administrative council (scored 3, 2, 1); (2) if the chief administrator was named by the workers of the enterprise equals +5 and, if the chief administrator was formerly a worker (nonmanagerial) in the same enterprise equals +5; (3) the union leader who headed the coordinating committee was asked to evaluate the stimulus for participation provided by the administrative council, scored 1 for no stimulus to 5 for strong stimulus; (4) our impressions of the chief administrator based on our interview, scored 1 to 5. In this last point, we attempted to isolate objective characteristics. For

TABLE 6.11

Information and Exogenous Political Variables, Plus *DISPAD*

Dependent variable	Constant	*DISPAD*	*UNATID*	*LMOB*	*PARHOM*	*PARORD*	R^2
INFO	19.2	1.75	1.51	−.038			.519
		(2.74)	(1.85)	(−.21)			
		.433	.190				
INFO	11.2	1.82	1.39	−.21)	.789	1.13	.606
		(2.98)	(1.80)	(−1.12)	(2.52)	(.528)	(corrected)
							.538

measures of the significance of *DISPAD* fall (see Table 6.10).[46] When *INFO* is controlled for as well, as in Equation (4), *DISPAD* becomes insignificant at the $t_{.10}$ level. This may be attributable in part to multicollinearity, but it nevertheless seems that most of the impact of *DISPAD* on P_F is explained by *LMOB* and *INFO*. That is, *DISPAD* does not appear to add any explanatory power beyond what is provided by labor mobilization and the system of information. Equation (5) indicates the intermediate character of the *DISPAD* variable.

Our second intermediate variable, information (*INFO*), is extremely highly correlated with P_F ($r = .831$). This result could be interpreted to mean that *INFO* and P_F are practically the same variable. It must be emphasized, however, that P_F and *INFO* have been constructed on the basis of completely independent components, i.e., no element of *INFO* appears in P_F and vice versa.[47] An alternative interpretation is that "there is no participation without information." This slogan was used by the department of participation of CUT, and it was stressed at meetings with the government appointed administrators. It is, in fact, a convincing slogan. Participation that is not based on adequate information will be self-destructive. Furthermore, knowledge dissemination will stimulate workers to utilize the knowledge (information causes participation) and the endeavor to

instance, how did the administrator refer to the workers (disparagingly, condescendingly, paternalistically, or equally, positively, comradely)? Was an effort made by the administration to put technical information passed on to the workers in accessible, understandable form?

[46]These measures include the *t* statistics, the elasticity at the mean, and the beta coefficient.

[47]*INFO* attempts to measure the frequency of information, the intensity of information, and the extension (how many people it reaches) of information. Questions regarding these three aspects of information were asked of the general administration and each of the participatory bodies. In the latter case, we were also interested in whether they distributed an agenda and relevant information before meetings and how the representatives informed their constituents following meetings. In all, our questionnaires included 16 different questions pertaining to the system of information. We followed the usual procedure of taking averages where there were several respondents. *INFO* varied from a low of 20 to a high of 93, with an average of 49.3 and s.d. of 18.4.

TABLE 6.12

Participation and Strongest Explanatory Variables

Dependent variable	Constant	LMOB	UNATID	PCPCD	DISPAD	INFO	R^2
P_F	4.6	.033 (2.20)	.225 (3.12)	−.041 (−2.50)			.649
P_F	3.6	.007 (.427)	.142 (1.99)	−.040 (−2.66)	.156 (2.84)		.723
P_F	2.4	.010 (.795)	.053 (.974)	−.039 (−3.60) −.439 −.304	.058 (1.19)	.059 (5.28) .648 .530	.859 (corrected) .835

utilize knowledge will eventually generate demand for its greater dissemination (participation causes information).[48] Similar to *DISPAD,* information is assumed to be not exogenous and seems to be determined by other variables (see Table 6.11).

Table 6.12 combines our three exogenous political variables with our two intermediate variables. Because of multicollinearity, the *t* statistics are deflated, but the R^2 (.859) is quite impressive.[49] These five variables explain over 83% (corrected R^2) of the variance in P_F.

In summary, we have attempted in this section to isolate those factors which contribute to explaining the variance of P_F. Before considering the apparent causal model, we present corroborating evidence derived from a factor analysis treatment of our data.

FACTOR ANALYSIS AND EMERGING CAUSAL MODEL

The primary purpose of factor analysis is to reduce the original number of explanatory variables to a smaller number of independent factors in terms of which the entire set of variables can be understood. The factors are groupings of the original variables into clusters, wherein the component variables are highly intercorrelated with each other. Each cluster or *factor* captures a pattern of

[48]Since, in the longer run, it is expected that P_F will play back and affect *INFO,* it is possible that there is a simultaneity bias in the equations with *INFO* present. However, since the time period in question is short and our sample is cross-sectional, it is not likely that this play back effect is strongly reflected in our data. Attempts to gauge this effect statistically were not successful.

[49]When the three technology variables are added to this equation, the *F* test on their coefficients shows them to be insignificant at the 10% level. The same is true for various combinations of our variables representing organizational and bureaucratic structure when they are included here.

interaction among the various independent variables. In a broad sense, each factor represents a particular phenomenon through a linear combination of the independent variables. Resulting factors are orthogonal or independent from each other and hence minimize the problem of multicollinearity in interpreting the significance level of each factor in multiple regressions of the dependent variable (P_F) on the independent variables (factors).[50] The central problem with factor analysis lies in interpreting what underlying phenomenon each factor (linear combination of independent variables) represents.

From the set of observations, treating all variables equally, factor analysis proceeds by forming a new artificial variable (first factor) that has the greatest possible variance. The first factor, therefore, simply summarizes, as far as is possible with one variable, the variance of the whole set of original variables. The analysis may proceed by calculating a second factor, with the restriction that it be independent of the first factor and with the greatest variance after allowing for the variance explained (of the whole set of original variables) by the first factor.

Further factors, independent of all the previous ones, can be estimated in similar fashion.[51] The procedure is stopped when a further factor accounts for less than a predetermined proportion of the total variance of all the variables.[52]

According to our results, there seems to be a clear phenomenal pattern in only our first 3 factors. The remaining 7 factors are difficult to interpret and, in any case, are not significantly correlated with P_F (at the 10% level).[53] We shall confine therefore our discussion to the first three factors which collectively

[50]The mathematical principles for forming each factor out of the independent variables have been outlined by Adelman and Morris:

(1) Those variables that are most clearly intercorrelated are combined within a single factor.

(2) The variables allocated to a given factor are those that are most nearly independent of the variables allocated to the other factors.

(3) The factors are derived in a manner that maximizes the percentage of the total variance of the original variables attributable to each successive factor (given the inclusion of the preceding factors).

(4) The factors are derived so as to minimize the correlation between them [1971, p. 93].

[51]In our case, the model could be visualized in the following set of equations:
$$F_i = f (\text{Var } 001, \text{Var } 002, \dots , \text{Var } 029), i = 1, 2, \dots , 29.$$
$$P_F = f (F_1, F_2, \dots , F_{29}), \text{ where } F_i \text{ stands for the various factors.}$$

[52]This is done through the eigenvalues estimated in the analysis. The standard procedure recommends considering only those factors with an eigenvalue greater than 1. In our case, of the 29 factors derived from our 29 original independent variables, the first 10 factors met this criterion. The eigenvalues of these 10 factors are given in Table 6.22 in Appendix II to this chapter.

[53]In Appendix II to this chapter, the varimax rotated factor matrix (Table 6.20) and the factor score matrix (Table 6.21) of the first 5 factors have been included. In our computation, we used a varimax orthogonal rotation. The varimax criterion, in contrast to the quartimax orthogonal rotation which centers on simplifying the rows of a factor matrix, centers on simplifying the columns of a factor matrix. Such a simplification is equivalent to maximizing the variance of the squared loadings in each column and is the most widely used.

account for 43.5% of the variance of the set of all the standardized independent variables.[54]

The first factor appears to be representative of the "human factors," such as labor mobilization and consciousness, and the other political variables discussed elsewhere, or those variables affected by political pressures. In order of importance, the five most important variables making up the first factor (in terms of their values in the varimax rotated factor matrix and their factor score coefficients) are the attitude of the new administrators toward participation, the extent of labor mobilization and consciousness, the attitude of union leadership toward participation, the system of internal informational flows, and the basic idea (ideology) of the union leadership. Each of these variables figure in the first factor with a positive coefficient. The correlation coefficient between the first factor and our relative index of participation is positive and highly significant ($r = .814$).

The second factor appears to represent variables which chiefly describe the enterprise's technology. The three most important variables are, in order of importance, technological complexity or the percentage of workers in the factory doing maintenance work (positive coefficient); the percentage of skilled production workers, administrative workers and technical and professional employees in the enterprise's labor force (positive coefficient); and the capital–labor ratio (positive coefficient). The correlation coefficient between our relative index of participation and the second factor is negative but insignificant at the 10% level ($r = -.044$). That is, more complex technologies do not seem to have limited the development of worker participation.

The third factor appears to represent the internal bureaucratic organization of the enterprise. The four most important component variables in this factor are, in order of importance, the horizontal differentiation of the enterprise or the number of middle management departments (its coefficient is positive); the percentage of the enterprise's labor force engaged in nonproduction work (positive coefficient); the extent to which blue- and white-collar workers' evaluations of the level of participation differed (positive coefficient); and the percentage of the firm's white-collar employees classified as professional, technical, or managerial staff (positive coefficient). The higher the value of this third factor, then, the more bureaucratic the enterprise's internal organization. The third factor has a negative and insignificant (at the 10% level) relationship to our index of worker participation ($r = -.154$).

Table 6.13 summarizes the results of our factor analysis. The preponderant importance of the labor mobilization–political factor and the apparent insignificance of the technology and bureaucracy factors in explaining the variance of P_F seem to confirm the results of our multiple regression analysis presented earlier in this chapter.

[54]It must be remembered that the total variance of the 29 variables under analysis not only corresponds to the particular phenomenon we are concerned with (participation), but goes beyond it.

TABLE 6.13
Factor Analysis of Worker Participation[a]

Equation number	Dependent variable	Constant	Factor 1 (political variables)	Factor 2 (technology variables)	Factor 3 (bureaucracy variables)	R^2
(1)	P_F	4.5	1.69 (67.4) .814		−.320 (2.43) −.154	.687
(2)	P_F	4.5	1.69 (66.0) .814	−.091 (.190) −.044	−.321 (2.37) −.154	.688

[a] Numbers in the parentheses refer to the F statistics; beneath the F statistics are the beta coefficients.

Accordingly, we may sketch the emerging model relating the significant independent variables to participation in the following way:

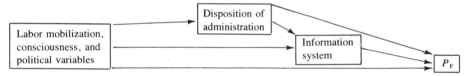

The arrow indicates the main causal direction but does not imply that participation does not eventually play back and affect the other variables. In fact, it is reasonable to assume that these factors are, through time, constantly interacting and changing each other. As such, they constitute a whole, dynamic social system. In the next chapter, we consider the influence of this new social system on enterprise performance.

APPENDIX I   CORRELATION MATRIXES OF TABLES 6.2, 6.3, 6.5, 6.7, 6.8, AND 6.10

TABLE 6.14
Correlation Matrix of Table 6.2

	P_F	TCOMP	TTYP	TINT	SIZE	VDIF	SPANC	HDIF
P_F		.0854	−.3364	−.1764	.0016	−.2203	.0722	−.1971
TCOMP			.4048	.8052	.0910	.1441	−.0448	−.1118
TTYP				.4587	.0551	.3726	−.0414	.2193
TINT					.0610	.1690	−.0770	.1181
SIZE						.2136	.3205	.2365
VDIF							−.1391	.0283
SPANC								.2116
HDIF								

TABLE 6.15

Correlation Matrix of Table 6.3

	P_F	VDIF	SPANC	HDIF	TCOMP	TTYP	TINT	PCTAD	PCTSK	SIZE
P_F		-.2203	.0722	-.1971	.0854	-.3364	-.1764	-.2245	-.2937	.0016
VDIF			-.1391	.0283	.1441	.3726	.1690	.1693	.4900	.2136
SPANC				.2116	-.0448	-.0414	-.0770	-.0268	-.2131	.3205
HDIF					-.1118	.2193	.1181	.7125	.0680	.2365
TCOMP						.4048	.8052	.0906	.6126	.0910
TTYP							.4587	.1608	.4230	.0551
TINT								.2812	.7048	.0610
PCTAD									.3720	.0533
PCTSK										-.0938
SIZE										

TABLE 6.16

Correlation Matrix of Table 6.5

	PCTSK	PCTPTA	AVGR	FCOR	PCTCD	TCOMP	TTYP	TINT
PCTSK		.4588	.7355	.2005	.4346	.6126	.4230	.7048
PCTPTA			.1079	.2985	.1839	.1567	.1366	.3809
AVGR				.1533	.5466	.5018	.4528	.5975
FCOR					−.3260	.3628	−.0617	.2761
PCTCD						.2250	.3842	.4171
TCOMP							.4048	.8052
TTYP								.4587
TINT								

TABLE 6.17

Correlation Matrix of Table 6.7

	PCTCP	PCTCD	PARHOM	PARORD
PCTCP		.008	.160	−.506
PCTCD			−.115	−.536
PARHOM				.082
PARORD				

TABLE 6.18

Correlation Matrix of Table 6.8

	UNATT	UNID	UNNO	UNAGE
UNATT		.530	.082	−.022
UNID			−.037	−.059
UNNO				−.034
UNAGE				

TABLE 6.19

Correlation Matrix of Table 6.10

	P_F	DISPAD	UNATID	LMOB	INFO	PCPCD
P_F		0.7574	0.6556	0.6497	0.8300	−0.6370
DISPAD			0.6495	0.6811	0.6729	−0.4553
UNATID				0.4735	0.5917	−0.4073
LMOB					0.4814	−0.5379
INFO						−0.3477
PCPCD						

APPENDIX II   FACTOR ANALYSIS DATA

TABLE 6.20

Varimax Rotated Factor Matrix

Independent variables	Factor 1	Factor 2	Factor 3	Factor 4	Factor 5
PCTSK	−.203	.822	.142	−.164	.366
PCTPTA	.032	−.547	.467	−.232	−.284
AVGR	−.084	.656	−.050	.026	.491
PTCAD	−.166	.170	.878	−.090	.130
SIZE	.026	−.017	.160	.813	.066
NO. SHIFTS	.110	.128	−.150	.725	.121
TCOMP	.110	.876	−.050	.138	−.032
TTYP	−.214	.340	.189	.208	.263
TINT	−.062	.822	.190	−.020	.036
LIM.FAC.	−.491	−.035	.178	.451	.332
UNATT	.783	.012	−.104	−.162	.067
UNID	.558	−.195	−.212	.049	−.259
UNNO	.003	−.143	.220	.241	.050
UNAGE	.021	−.067	−.060	.581	−.194
PCTCD	−.376	−.035	−.204	.059	−.075
PCTCP	−.496	.313	.197	.306	.356
PARHOM	.453	.142	.073	.048	−.024
LMOB	.790	−.253	−.121	.217	.003
TIME	.173	.089	.125	−.028	−.078
VDIFF	−.127	.237	.078	.110	.805
SPANC	.148	−.064	.199	.363	−.419
HDIFF	−.164	−.068	.879	.150	−.063
INFO	.768	.130	−.117	.037	−.066
FINGD	−.192	−.672	−.011	.270	.083
AUTOPL	−.534	.415	−.002	.044	−.507
AUTOGOV	.346	−.657	.102	−.191	.031
COMPMGR	.164	.156	.067	−.130	.025
DISPAD	.833	−.016	−.045	.150	−.163
DIFFBW	−.330	.144	.498	.045	.222

TABLE 6.21

Factor Score Matrix

Independent variables (standardized)	Factor 1	Factor 2	Factor 3	Factor 4	Factor 5
PCTSK	.020	.170	.050	−.100	.108
PCTPTA	.024	−.091	.204	−.175	−.084
AVGR	.011	.102	−.060	−.013	.200
PCTAD	.062	.039	.385	−.069	.029
SIZE	.024	−.009	.036	.342	.009
NO. SHIFTS	.059	.036	−.057	.301	.049
TCOMP	.051	.229	−.016	.070	−.118
TTYP	−.020	.044	.044	.106	.034
TINT	.017	.199	.061	−.004	−.086
LIM.FAC.	−.083	−.057	.034	.134	.150
UNATT	.221	.039	.044	−.080	.116
UNID	.067	−.019	−.080	.044	−.083
UNNO	.079	.008	.108	.072	.100
UNAGE	−.008	−.004	−.018	.273	−.146
PCTCD	−.091	.001	−.125	.059	−.052
PCTCP	−.116	.003	−.005	.100	.110
PARHOM	.141	.057	.086	.025	−.019
LMOB	.197	−.039	.028	.097	.067
TIME	.020	.031	−.006	.036	−.021
VDIFF	.040	−.032	.006	−.000	.418
SPANC	.002	.013	.126	.137	−.275
HDIFF	.023	−.016	.385	.032	−.082
INFO	.172	.063	−.007	.020	.013
FINGD	−.123	−.213	−.098	.118	.106
AUTOPL	−.151	.154	−.019	.006	−.353
AUTOGOV	.062	−.179	.086	−.070	.077
COMPMGR	−.017	.007	−.006	−.070	−.008
DISPAD	.213	.050	.057	.080	−.031
DIFFBW	−.024	−.005	.163	.051	.047

TABLE 6.22

Factors with Eigenvalues Greater Than 1

Factor	Eigenvalue	Percentage of variance[a]	Cumulative Percentage
1	6.11	21.1	21.1
2	3.98	13.7	34.8
3	2.53	8.7	43.5
4	2.46	8.5	52.0
5	1.85	6.4	58.4
6	1.59	5.5	63.9
7	1.44	5.0	68.8
8	1.39	4.8	73.6
9	1.23	4.2	77.8
10	1.02	3.5	81.3

[a] Percentage of variance of the whole set of original variables explained by factor.

7

The Influence of Worker Participation on Enterprise Performance

INTRODUCTION

In this chapter, we analyze the relationships between worker participation and the economic and social performance of the 35 enterprises in our sample.

Arguments against worker participation often include the contention that modern technology and organizational structure are too complex to permit an economically effective system of democratic management. Such arguments, however, rest on ideological grounds and not on systematic analysis. While no studies have demonstrated that worker participation has negative consequences on the economic performance of modern enterprise, suppositions to this effect are commonly encountered. This situation is hardly surprising, given the newness of the idea, the relative paucity of serious investigation on the subject, and inadequate dissemination of the information available. Thus, although there is a wide consensus on industrial democracy's potentially positive psychological, social, and political effects, it is necessary to demonstrate its compatibility with the goal of efficient production in the context of the modern economy. Such a demonstration is important if the concept of industrial democracy is to gain broader acceptance.

The scope of our investigation is doubtlessly reduced when one considers the extensive possibilities for evaluating the question of worker participation at the macro and micro levels, in the political, economic, and social spheres. Nonetheless, although our analysis is confined to the level of the individual enterprise, it can be readily appreciated that the variables studied can be projected on a global level under the usual assumptions in this type of study. It is relevant here to recall the orientation toward greater participation at the sectoral and national levels exhibited by participatory enterprises which was discussed in Chapter 4.

Furthermore, it is necessary to underscore that the systems of worker participation being developed in the enterprise were introduced in the context of broader social and political change. The societal context did not fail to influence strongly both the process of change in the enterprises and the performance results of the enterprises.

In this respect, it is interesting to mention André Babeau's (1968) study on the introduction of worker councils in Poland between 1956 and 1958. Babeau records that the index of industrial production in Poland rose from 100 in 1955 to 109.6 in 1957 after stagnating for the five previous years. Although one-quarter of all industrial establishments were run by worker councils, Babeau hesitates to attribute the industrial growth to the councils. He notes that the whole social and political atmosphere changed during this period, as did the tax structure. Under such circumstances, he maintains, it is impossible to isolate the councils themselves as the cause of growth. However, 45 experimental firms during this period were given almost total decision-making autonomy. Babeau observes that these firms, which had a more active internal democracy, were also characterized by a more highly skilled labor force. In these 45 firms, production rose between 6% and 33% during 1956 and 1957 with just one exception (1968, p. 233).

Babeau's point on controlling for other factors is important to keep in mind during our discussion of the effects on performance of worker participation in Chile. When feasible, we control for certain factors, but it is not possible to control for an entire social process. The absence of institutional stability and the degree of political flux were very notable in Chile between 1970 and 1973. Generalization from the specific results we describe must always be qualified with this consideration. Nevertheless, most of our results are common to other experiences with industrial democracy.

We shall proceed by examining two broad areas of performance—social and economic. Within each area, the following changes will be considered:

Independent variable	Dependent variables
	1. Social changes
	a. Social services
	b. Training and education
	c. Changes in product line
	d. Changes in distribution system
	e. Changes in work organization
	f. Changes in wage structure
P_F	2. Changes in economic performance
	a. Discipline
	b. Absenteeism
	c. Strikes
	d. Thefts and defective products
	e. Innovations
	f. Investment
	g. Productivity

Furthermore, in the analysis some assumptions of causality suggested by the International Institute for Labor Studies will be used.[1] That is, the effect of participation on performance can in some cases be directly identified, and in others it is indirectly manifested through intermediate variables. Specifically, our initial assumptions regarding causality might be simply depicted as follows:

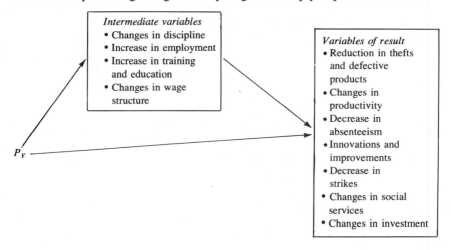

This division of the final variables into two groups arises chiefly from the aim of seeking the strongest possible explanation for the variation in the variables of result, particularly in the economic variables. The classification and choice of the variables are ours, although we were naturally confined to variables both readily quantifiable and available to us in all 35 enterprises.

As can be appreciated, the variables classified as intermediate might also be considered results or objectives in themselves. They have been designated in this way for the sole purpose of achieving greater clarity in the causality of the analysis. Finally, it should be recognized over time that the chain of causality in most cases runs in both directions as the variables are constantly interacting and affecting each other.[2] This point will become clearer as we proceed with our discussion.

SOCIAL CHANGES

The simple passage of an enterprise to the social area implied substantial social policy and organizational changes. Whether or not workers actively took part in

[1]See, for example, "Plan of Investigation," International Institute for Labor Studies Bulletin, No. 2 (February 1967), pp. 111–117.

[2]Again, due to the cross-sectional approach we employ, these dynamic effects are difficult to capture in our statistical analysis.

decision making, the disappearance of the top owners and managers in itself drastically altered the balance of power in an enterprise in favor of the workers. The executive hierarchy, the technicians, the professionals, the supervisors were now working for the workers, not for the capitalists. The time study persons and the foremen ceased to play their disciplinary roles. If they resisted the new social order in the enterprise, they were subject to worker criticism or even reassignment. This was also true of the government appointed administrator.

With the exception of the largest foreign companies, where the professional and technical staff were typically remunerated in dollars, expropriation of an enterprise was not generally accompanied by an extensive flight of highly skilled employees. In 17 of the 35 enterprises in our study, 10% or fewer of the professional and technical personnel left after expropriation; in 13, between 11% and 25% departed; and in only 4 cases did more than 51% leave.

As the participation system developed in an enterprise, so did the new system of discipline and social control. Social control exerted by the majority when developed, we shall see presently, was more effective than social control imposed by a small minority.

Although attitudinal changes were beyond the scope of our survey, it was clear from informal conversation and ever-present gratuitous comments that the workers were more comfortable and that they far preferred the new system. *Ahora uno se siente mas libre* ('one feels more free now') or *Ahora los obreros se pueden realizar* ('now the workers can realize themselves') were virtually unanimous sentiments. There was a strong sense of liberation, of new-found dignity and pride. Even the worker who was not making decisions felt that he or she mattered now. The clear change in power relations and attitudes is reflected in the following retrospective comment by a foundry production worker (this particular foundry ranked nineteenth out of 35 in our index of participation):

> We tried to break down the barriers which had been erected to divide us. We dissolved the three trade unions and formed a single one. Any executive or foreman could be submitted to the Discipline Committee. A collective bonus system was set up. In general, there was a qualitative change in human relationships. The executives and technicians attended the worker assemblies with everyone else—and their vote wasn't worth more than that of a worker. We were all "workers" with different functions—but the difference in function didn't define social privilege. It was the birth of a new sort of society—the reflections of our hopes and aspirations. Great perspectives opened—and for this we were ready to sacrifice ourselves—and so we did, simply because we were convinced that this would mean a better world for ourselves and our children.

The workers were running their shops without the old managers. They were helping each other out, and they were producing not for the profits of a few but for all Chileans. Put theoretically, alienation from the process of production, from fellow workers, and from the product were gradually being eliminated.

Of course, people do not change overnight. Workers were still materialistically motivated. Abuses developed and sometimes got out of hand. But

where the political leadership was strong and unified and the participation system became effective, a transformation in consciousness and behavior was evident.

Social Services

Increased provision and construction of social services were prevalent throughout all the enterprises in Chile's social area. Our variable which reflected this increase in social services (*SOCSER*) is positively and significantly correlated with P_F ($r = .436$).[3] That is, the more the workers were organized for decision making in general, the more they were organized to decide upon and construct social services (almost all social service construction was undertaken by the workers themselves during their free time). Increased social services, representing a fruit of participation, probably also played back to give the workers more confidence and make them more enthusiastic about participation.

Typical investments in the sphere of social services included: improvements in working conditions (e.g., ventilators, heating, elimination of gasses, noise level reduction); acquisition of work clothes, gloves, goggles, and so on for the workers; improvements in hygienic and sanitary conditions (baths, kitchens, etc.); construction of a new or expansion of an old cafeteria;[4] formation of consumer cooperatives; rest homes or summer houses; building of sports grounds; construction of day care centers in factories with a sizable number of female workers; installation of medical, dental, or first aid clinics and the purchase of ambulances (which were often for the benefit not only of the workers but also of members of their families and the surrounding community as well); initiation of various cultural activities (construction of libraries or classrooms, publication of worker-run newsletters, formation of folksong groups and theater troupes)[5] and the provision of liberal arts, administration, and technical courses to the workers.

---

[3]The variable *SOCSER* was constructed on the basis of an extensive list of social services. When a service was provided before the firm passed to the social area and maintained at the same level after passage, or if the service was not provided before or after passage, it was scored 0; if the service was provided before passage and extended after passage, it was scored 1; and if the service did not exist previously and was created after the changeover, it was scored 2. The maximum score attainable was 30. In practice, *SOCSER* varied between 2 and 27, with an average value of 13.11 (see the appendix to this chapter).

[4]In the past, where cafeterias existed the blue-collar workers were either denied access or ate separately from the white-collar workers. In social area enterprises, workers would either share the existing cafeterias and eat in shifts or facilities would be expanded. In all but a few cases, blue- and white-collar workers ate together. It was an important point and often an item of pride to the workers that they had a *casino único*, a class-unified cafeteria. Everybody got the same menu. Depending on the work schedule, in many cases, meals and snacks were provided free during the work day.

[5]The folksong and theater groups would often perform at popular fairs, rallies, and other factories. One of the authors attended a theater night where three factories got together and their theater troupes presented political skits. Two of the skits were about how the workers organized to take over their factories. After each skit, the actors and the workers in the audience discussed the political message, the acting, and the organization of the skit. Future performances would reflect the criticisms and comments received by the actors.

Naturally, on many occasions the realization of social service investments was used by the expropriated capitalists as evidence in arguing that the enterprise had degenerated into a charitable society, where "technical" criteria to study the investment of money were no longer applied. However, when the size of the investments in social services is considered, it turns out to be very small. In the 35 enterprises of our sample, these investments constituted less than 1% of net worth on the average. Much of the investment was realized with voluntary labor and scrap or surplus materials. Anyone acquainted with living and working conditions in underdeveloped countries would concur that the bulk of these investments was more than justified.

Along with participation, the extent of social service investments was a function of a firm's size. Larger firms generally had access to more resources and were in a better position to realize economies of scale in the production and consumption of social services. This relationship can be appreciated in Equation (7.1):

$$SOCSER = 5.5 + 1.21 \ (P_F) + .36 \ (SIZE); R^2 = .273 \qquad (7.1)$$
$$(2.89) \qquad (1.90)$$

Training and Education

The introduction of training courses was widespread. Everyone was aware that increasing the level of qualification of the work force was an important ingredient in the success of worker management. Training programs were set up by arrangement between individual factories or industrial sectors and various training institutes, e.g., *Instituto Laboral, INACAP, Universidad Técnica del Estado, Universidad de Chile*. New institutes for worker training and education were created, and the Department of Instruction and Culture of CUT achieved a level of activity never before seen. CUT called a national conference on education for workers which took place the last week of November 1972. The conference attracted 169 worker delegates who discussed their training needs and drew up a temporary plan for coordinating the relevant educational resources. Although training programs expanded during 1973, the implementation of a central plan was postponed by mounting political difficulties.

It is likely, in this case more than in others, that our variable representing increases in education and training is only a pale reflection of the enormous expansion produced in the cultural field, in training and general education. Nevertheless, we expressly wished to restrict the field to courses or political instruction concerning (a) greater education or qualification pertinent to the firm's production and administration and (b) learning about the content and functioning of the new system of worker participation.[6]

[6]Besides the subjects considered in the survey, there were courses in music, theater, political education, community literacy, first aid, history, economics, and other subjects.

TABLE 7.1

Percentage of Workers Taking Courses in 1970, by Level of Skill

Courses	Skilled	Semiskilled	Unskilled	Total
Inside or outside the firm	5.6	1.6	1.6	8.8
Other courses	1.4	0.4	0.2	2.0
On their own account	8.1	4.6	5.0	17.7
Did not take	18.9	18.6	30.1	67.6
No response	1.2	0.9	1.8	3.9

Source: Chile, CORFO, *Obreros Industriales Chilenos, Publicación* No. 12-A/70, Santiago, 1970, *Cuadro* No. 22, p. 80.

The variable denoting increase in education and training (*INCR. EDUC.*) directly represents the quotient between the total number of hours of training or instruction received by workers and the total number of persons employed in the firm.[7] The correlation coefficient between *INCR. EDUC.* and P_F is .490 and between *INCR. EDUC.* and the system of information (*INFO*) it is .575. Participation and information promote demands for more education on the part of the workers. At the same time, education and training facilitate participation. The dynamic relationship between participation and education has been highlighted by several authors (cf., in particular, Freire 1973; Pateman 1970).

The previous results mark a sharp contrast to the situation of worker education which prevailed in the great majority of Chilean industrial firms in 1970. As may be observed from Table 7.1, only 10.8% of industrial workers had access to any kind of course financed by the firm or state, and the large majority of workers who took courses had to finance them with personal funds. In addition, one clearly notes that the semiskilled and unskilled workers were relatively less favored than the skilled workers in terms of their participation in instructional programs—reinforcing skill differentials in the Chilean labor force.

Although at times they seem to be arguing the opposite, capitalist managers are opposed to sponsoring substantive training for their workers. It is cheaper to hire skilled workers from other firms or workers who have received personally or state-financed training. As Paul Strassman notes, it is often dangerous to over-train semiskilled and unskilled workers: "When work is simple and repetitive, managers fear that vocational training gets workers into thinking habits and makes them think they know enough to argue [1968, p. 89]."

[7]As shown in Table 7.12, the values of *INCR. EDUC.* varied between 0 and 45.5 course hours per worker, with an average of 11.5. The labeling of this variable as *increase* in education is justified by the virtual absence of previous enterprise-sponsored worker education programs (See table 7.1).

On the other hand, there is an extensive body of literature which demonstrates the stimulating effect of worker participation on worker education (Dickson 1975; Andors 1977b; Jenkins 1973; Kolaya 1960 and 1961; Pateman 1970; Teillac 1965). When Adam Smith says of the factory worker that he or she "generally becomes as stupid and ignorant as it is possible for a human creature to become" or F. W. Taylor writes that the "pig iron handler shall be so stupid and phlegmatic that he more resembles an ox than any other type [1947, p. 61]," they are not describing an inevitable condition of the industrial laborer; rather, they are describing a condition which is most suitable in a nonparticipatory, hierarchical workplace.

Changes in Product Line

Where the product line was amenable, there was generally a shift in production away from luxury toward common consumer items. Since the prices of most basic consumer items were controlled throughout the Allende period, the move away from luxury production often meant lower revenues for the enterprise.

One example of such a case occurred in a porcelain products faactory where the workers stopped putting designs on their dishware and shifted labor and other resources to the production of sinks, tubs, washbowls, floor and wall tiles, and the like, which were in great demand because of an ambitious government housing program. A similar example can be found in the case of a food processing and canning factory in Santiago where, within a month after passing to the social area, the workers denounced one of their former products for having practically no nutritional value. The product was redesigned with the help of a technical team to contain 85% more protein, and the price was lowered by 35%. In all, 12 of the 35 factories in our sample changed their line of products. Equation (7.2) represents line of product changes (LOPC) in relation to the level of participation in the enterprise, controlling for whether the firm produces finished or intermediate goods (FINGD).[8]

$$LOPC = .16 + .080 \ (P_F) + .288 \ (FINGD); R^2 = .199 \qquad (7.2)$$
$$(2.09) \qquad (1.91)$$

In many cases a change in product line in social area firms did not represent a shift toward production of mass consumption items. Such was the case in 2 of the

---

[8]*LOPC* equals 1 where a line of product change occurred and 0 where it did not. *FINGD* equals 1 where the factory produces a finished good and 0 where it does not. Textile production is considered a finished good, because cloth and yarn were often sold directly to the consumer. Since we are using a dichotomous dummy as our dependent variable in Equation (7.2), the coefficients on the right-hand side are not normally distributed and conventional significance interpretation of the *t* statistics cannot be made.

12 firms in our sample where product line changes occurred. For instance, several firms in the metallurgy sector got together and decided that given the layouts and endowments of their respective plants it would make sense to specialize—some in plating, others in structures. This denoted a rationalization of the production process that was improbable so long as the firms were controlled by competing capitalists. The change toward mass consumption items reflected a priority to meet basic needs before superfluous ones and, in this sense, was also a rationalization. This too was unlikely to occur so long as firms' behavior was motivated by profit.

Rationalization in Chile took place mostly on this ad hoc basis. The central planning apparatus was built in the 1930s and had since grown out of proportion to its function. It was essentially involved in making studies and gathering information. Even during the Allende period, plans were not drawn up in great detail, and the guidelines established were generally not followed. An opposition Congress vetoed most of Allende's budget proposals, and most production was still in private hands. Given these insuperable constraints, CORFO made progressive efforts to plan production and to involve the workers in this planning. Under pressure from the workers who began organizing themselves by sector with the *Encuentro Textil* in July 1972, CORFO was planning to introduce 50% worker representation on its sectoral planning commissions in 1974.

Even without effective planning, there was invaluable cooperation among many enterprises in the social area. Enterprises exchanged machinery, raw materials, and labor. One textile factory served as a machine and repair shop for the other textile factories in Santiago. When the textile factory at Chiguayante near Concepción was blown up by right-wing saboteurs, other factories sent workers and money to help undertake reconstruction. Factories shared day-care centers and held joint courses on factory administration. In some cases, as we shall see, economic surplus was voluntarily transferred from one enterprise to another.

Changes in the Distribution System

One of the most serious problems during the Allende period was the extensive black market. Even by August 1973, the government controlled only about 28% of wholesale food distribution. Most distributors were private and organized against the government. There is no space to go into this problem in depth here,[9] so suffice it to note that many social area firms discovered their products were not getting to their intended destination. They responded in one of three ways: (a) by appointing a workers' guard to follow their products to their destination; (b) by ceasing to trade with private distributors and sell only to government distributors; and (c) by selling directly to the public—either at popular fairs or to community

[9]For a fuller discussion of hoarding and the black market, see Zimbalist and Stallings (1973).

and worker organizations.[10] When the factory followed either of the latter two strategies, it was considered a change in the distribution system (*DISTC*).[11]

It is interesting that *DISTC* and *LOPC* are highly and positively correlated ($r = .566$). There are a number of possible interpretations of this result; but on the basis of our interviews, the following seems the most plausible: the more the factory changes its distribution, the more it is exposed to consumer needs and the more likely it is to change its line of products.

Changes in Work Organization

The question of work reorganization is very broad and complicated. We shall touch only its surface in the following paragraphs.

Of the 93 sections surveyed, 70 had an ongoing system of either job rotation or job enlargement. In 30 of those cases, the system existed before socialization. Many sections had tried it and given it up because they found it caused production problems. Many others said they were thinking about doing it, and some said it never crossed their minds. In a handful of instances, the workers explained that the old boss tried to make them do several jobs. They regarded this as a form of speed-up and wanted nothing to do with it now that they defined their own work organization. Rotation and enlargement are not panaceas for alienation or worker militance and indeed are only attractive for certain jobs and under certain conditions.

In Table 7.2 we consider four different measures of the change in work organization and their relation to participation at the section (P_S) and firm (P_F) levels.[12]

JROT was found to be significantly correlated neither with the preordered technology type variable, nor with P_S, nor with P_F (not shown). *JENL,* on the other hand, varied positively with the level of participation in the section. The coefficient on P_S is significant at the $t_{.01}$ level in Equations (3) and (5).

Workers reported that job conditions had improved a lot in 46 sections, some in 23 sections, and not at all in 24 sections. The nature of improvement varied

[10]This, of course, occurred only where the enterprise produced a finished good.

[11]*DISTC* equals 1 when the distribution system changes and 0 when it does not.

[12]*JROT* stands for job rotation; *JENL* for job enlargement; *COND* for work conditions; *ELSUP* for the elimination of supervisors and *TTYP_S* is the technology type in each section. The multiplication of $TTYP_S$ and P_S was an attempt to test the interaction effect of these two variables with respect to *JROT* and *JENL*. Unfortunately, multicollinearity seems to have impeded this effort.

Each of these variables is measured at the section level. *JROT* and *JENL* equal 2 when job rotation was introduced after socialization, 1 when it exists now (time of survey) and existed before, and 0 when it does not exist now. *COND* equals 2 when working conditions improved a lot since socialization, 1 when they improved some, and 0 when they did not improve. *ELSUP* equals 2 when the first-line supervisor is eliminated, 1 when there is still a supervisor but he or she no longer plays a policing role, and 0 when the supervisor plays the same policing role as before.

TABLE 7.2

Work Organization, Technology, and Participation

Equation number	Dependent variable	Constant	$TTYP_S$	P_S	$(TTYP_S) \times (P_S)$	P_F	R^2
(1)	JROT	.281	.093 (1.44)	.010 (.841)			.027
(2)	JROT	.272	.097 (.581)	.022 (.473)	−.0003 (−.030)		.027
(3)	JENL	.190	−.067 (−.895)	.041 (3.03)			.107
(4)	JENL	.159	−.052 (−.270)	.042 (1.68)	−.0008 (−.080)		.107
(5)	JENL	.039		.043 (2.80)		−.005 (−.093)	.099
(6)	COND	.665		.043 (3.23)		−.05 (−1.10)	.107
(7)	ELSUP	.545		.022 (.856)		.287 (3.30)	.172

Correlation matrix

	P_S	$TTYP_S$	$(TTYP_S) \times (P_S)$
P_S	1.00	−.117	.452
$TTYP_S$		1.00	.764
$(TTYP_S) \times (P_S)$			1.00

widely: new safety equipment (e.g., goggles, gloves), more cleanliness, new temperature controls, reduced noise level, improved exhaust systems, or improved maintenance of machinery. In 73 of the 93 sections, the traditional disciplinary role of the foreman was eliminated.[13] Most studies agree that close supervision is a cause not only of decreased worker satisfaction but of increased turnover and absenteeism and decreased productivity (Argyle, Gardner, and Cioffi 1973, p. 172; Gouldner 1964, pp. 159–164; Vroom 1973, p. 93; Melman 1958; Blumberg 1973, p. 117). Conversely, the elimination of close supervision increases satisfaction, decreases turnover and absenteeism, and increases productivity, as well as lowering supervisory costs.

Equation (6) of Table 7.2 shows that improved working conditions were positively correlated with participation in the section at the $t_{.01}$ level. Equation (7) shows that the changes in supervision are more related to participation at the

[13]Included in the 73 are a half-dozen or so sections where there never was a disciplining agent.

enterprise level than in the section. This result makes sense since changes in supervisory control imply a fundamental alteration in power relationships. It is unlikely that an individual section would succeed in changing power relationships if they had not changed in the entire firm.[14]

Changes in Wage Structure

The final social change variable we shall consider is changes in the wage structure. According to traditional wisdom, wage differentials are necessary to bring about an efficient allocation of labor and motivate workers to exert maximum effort. When a laborer is hired, the employer does not purchase actual labor; rather, the employer purchases potential labor. The employer attempts to organize work and work incentives in such a way as to motivate the laborer to produce as close to his or her potential as possible. Threats of layoffs or disciplinary action as well as close supervision are expected to keep the laborer working hard. Without wage differentials, however, they are not expected to do the full job.

Wage differentials and monetary incentives are generally considered essential in motivating maximum worker effort. Theoretically, wage differentials offer the industrious worker the possibility of promotion and higher income. Premium plans, piece-rate systems, and overtime arrangements directly connect a workers' pay to his or her efforts. Thus an individual worker reveals his or her own preferences regarding the trade-off between leisure and income. However, many studies have called into question the effectiveness of close supervision and piece-rate or bonus systems in motivating worker effort.

Conceptually, worker effort can be seen to have three dimensions: duration, intensity, and quality. In any work environment, the laborer has ultimate control over at least the intensity and quality of her or his work. Material incentives and organizational controls are external to the worker. However elaborate, external incentives are generally recognized to have failed in stimulating top productive performance (cf., HEW 1972; Leibenstein 1966b; Vroom 1969). However intensive, organizational controls do not wrest from the worker the ability to control the intensity and quality of effort. Participatory work environments, however, enhance the probability of the worker internalizing the goals of the enterprise. Once the process of goal internalization begins, sources of effort untapped by external incentives are progressively opened, and potential effort comes closer to being realized.[15]

Naturally, goal internalization is a long process, and participatory enterprises

---

[14]William F. Whyte illustrates this point with the case of the Hovey and Beard Co. (1955, Chapter 10). Power relations began to change in one section, and although productivity was increasing in that section, the experiment was ended because it threatened the hierarchical division of labor in the rest of the firm.

[15]For an elaboration and graphic illustration of this point, see Vanek and Espinosa (1972).

usually maintain some wage differentiation. A substantial body of evidence nevertheless suggests that inequality in remuneration and reliance upon personal incentives are significantly reduced in participatory work environments.

MacEwan (1974); Zimbalist (1975a, 1975b); and Karl (1975) note the importance of narrow wage differentials and collective incentives in the case of Cuban industrial enterprises. They find that collective incentives encourage the collective behavior essential for the exercise of worker power. Riskin (1974) and Andors (1977b) observe a trend toward increasing wage equality in Chinese firms which has accompanied the democratization of industrial management since the Cultural Revolution. In both Cuban and Chinese firms, the ratio of the highest wage to the lowest seems to vary between 2 to 1 and 3 to 1, with a maximum of 8 grades. Babeau (1968; p. 228) notes a trend of narrowing wage differentials in Poland after October 1956 when workers' councils and workers' management were introduced for a period of approximately two years. Fine (1973) and Jenkins (1973, p. 77) both suggest that the growing employment of outside wage labor with unequal benefits from the members of Kibbutzim factories in Israel is threatening to undermine the democratic principles of Kibbutz management. Wachtel (1973, p. 146) argues that increasing democracy within Yugoslav firms after 1959 led to a narrowing of interskill wage differentials.[16]

In the United States, the Scanlon Plan has generally eliminated individual bonuses and replaced them with collective bonuses in firms where it has been implemented. The worker-owned Puget Sound Plywood Corporation pays each worker from janitor to supervisor exactly the same wage (Zwerdling 1973). The same was true for a worker-managed grain-processing and natural foods purveying company (Llama, Toucan and Crow) in Brattleboro, Vermont. In England, the introduction of the self-recruiting work gangs at the car plant in Coventry described by Melman (1958) and the work teams of the composite longwall coal-getting system (Pateman 1970, pp. 61–62) brought substantial wage equalization. In Meriden, England, at the Triumph Motorbike Workers' Cooperative all workers receive the same pay, £50 per week (Carnoy and Levin 1976). At the large producer cooperative in Mondragon, Spain, the director's wage is only three times that of the lowest paid worker, and the latter's increases by 20% after the first year of membership (Oakeshott 1975).

This partial list makes clear that worker-created wage structures are more equal than wage structures imposed upon workers by capitalists. Equalized wages, far from interfering with motivation, are a basis for worker solidarity. Many wage levels, wide disparities, and private incentives, on the other hand, divide the work force and foster internal rivalries.[17]

[16]Wachtel's data go through 1967.

[17]For further elaboration of this point, see Espinosa (1975, pp. 243–252). After examining the effect of piece-rates in the Soviet Union, Kirsch (1972, p. 58) comes to much the same conclusion. Also see, Deutscher (1950, pp. 107–114); Marx (1967, 1:554–555); Trotsky (1972, pp. 80–83).

The experience in Chile lends support to these observations. There was a dramatic change in the wage structure of the 35 enterprises we surveyed. Before their passage to the social area, the ratio of highest to lowest wage in the firm varied between 3.5 to 1 and 225 to 1, with an average of 22.6 to 1;[18] the number of distinct wage grades rose as high as 60 or 70 in some cases, and 16 firms were using individual piece-rates. At the time of the survey, the ratio of the highest to lowest wage varied between 1.8 to 1 and 15 to 1, with an average of 7.6 to 1; the number of grades in no case rose above 10, and the piece-rate system had been reduced or eliminated in 14 of the 16 firms.

It is significant that the change to a more equal wage structure is positively associated with participation for all of our measures of wage structure. Our variable representing change in the piece-rate system $(CH.P.R.S)$[19] is positively correlated with P_F $(r = .342)$, with union ideology $(UNID, r = .388)$ and with $TIME$ $(r = .366)$. The latter two coefficients suggest first, that political ideology is important in influencing wage structure and second, that the longer an enterprise was in the social area, the more likely it was to have reduced or eliminated the use of piece-rates.

A second wage variable denotes changes in wage disparity $(CH.W.DISP.)$ or the percentage reduction in the ratio of the highest wage to the lowest in each enterprise from before passage to the social area to afterward. Although the correlation coefficient between $CH.W.DISP.$ and P_F is positive $(r = .346)$, there might be some question here as to whether $CH.W.DISP.$ merely reflects lopping off the top two or three salaries with no substantial change below that level. Although we were unable to obtain interquartile ratios, several factors indicate that there were changes throughout the wage structure. First, the *average* wage disparity ratio prior to socialization was 22.6 to 1, while the *highest* postsocialization ratio was 15 to 1. Second, $CH.W.DISP.$ is positively correlated with the reduction in the number of wage grades $(RE.NO.W.G.)$,[20] the correlation coefficient being .438. Third, the observed wage policy in almost all firms (and of the government) called for progressive wage readjustments to the rate of inflation. During the first 2 years, this meant giving lower paid workers readjustments greater than the rate of inflation and higher paid employees readjustments equal to the rate of inflation. During the third year, it meant giving all workers up to 5 *sueldo vitales* (a sort of minimum wage) a full percentage readjustment and all

[18]The firm with a ratio of 3.5 to 1 was a clear anomaly: This firm was in the state sector prior to 1970 but had no system of worker participation.

[19]$CH.P.R.S.$ equals 1 when there was a reduction in or elimination of the use of piece-rates, 0 when there was no change, and -1 when there was an increase in the use of piece rates. Simple correlation coefficients are significant at the 5% level for values above .35 given our sample size.

[20]$RE.NO.W.G.$ equals 1 when the number of wage grades was reduced and 0 when there was no change.

wage earners above that level the same absolute amount as the worker with 5 *sueldo vitales*.[21]

Finally, collective bonuses were used in 21 of the 35 sample firms after their passage to the social area. Our variable representing the presence or absence of collective bonuses (*COLL.BON.*)[22] is also positively correlated with P_F ($r = .365$).

Our evidence, then, is entirely consistent with the proposition stated previously: Capitalists structure wages in such a way as to create arbitrary and invidious distinctions in their work force; workers structure wages to eliminate those distinctions and to stimulate collective effort and cooperation.[23] By affecting the social relationships within an enterprise, the wage structure also has a powerful influence on productivity. We discuss the relationship between wage structure and productivity later in this chapter.

CHANGES IN ECONOMIC PERFORMANCE

Those who assert that worker participation in or control over modern industry is unfeasible ultimately point to their expectations of bad economic performance. The recorded experience of worker participation, however, passes a favorable verdict on its economic performance.[24] In this section, we consider various aspects of economic performance and their relation to participation.

Changes in Discipline

On the average, according to our measure, worker discipline improved in our 35 sample firms. Where worker participation was most developed, improvements in discipline were more notable. In some firms, where the new system of worker participation was slow to emerge, worker discipline deteriorated. The correlation coefficient between our measurement of changes in worker discipline (*CH.DISCI.*) and P_F is .493.[25]

---

[21]Although it would have been interesting to study the relationship between changes in the average real wage and the level of participation in each firm, we were unable to consistently obtain reliable data on the former. Rapid inflation, staggered contract periods, variations in fringe benefits, and other factors impeded our effort here.

[22]*COLL.BON.* equals 1 where collective bonuses were present and 0 where they were absent.

[23]In the Soviet Union, workers do not participate in structuring wages. Kirsch (1972, pp. 42–45) points out that since unemployment does not exist in the Soviet Union to discipline the work force, piece rates serve to fulfill part of the disciplinary function.

[24]See our discussion of productivity.

[25]*CH.DISCI.* was determined by direct consultation with trade union leaders. The consultation consisted of a detailed classification of each of the groups and levels within the firm; in this way it

Worker discipline in a traditional, nonparticipatory work environment is largely the responsibility of foremen or first-line supervisors. Recalling Equation (7) from Table 7.2, we see that higher levels of worker participation are not only associated with better discipline but are also strongly associated with the elimination of supervisors. This result makes sense, since the development of a profound process of participation ought to signify a substantial modification in the distribution of power within an enterprise. The elimination of supervisors and the improvement in internal discipline are outcomes intimately linked to this process of power redistribution.

Our findings categorically contradict arguments opposing participation on the grounds that a strong and rigid authority is the only solution to worker insubordination. According to this view, any relaxation of controls imposed from above is quickly translated into a weakening of discipline, norm fulfillment, and respect for superiors. This view receives generalized acceptance among managers not only in Chile but also in the great majority of developed and underdeveloped countries.[26]

For capitalist managers, increased supervision may serve another function by obviating more training for their work forces. Here two factors are at work: first, it is common practice in Latin American industry to place untrained workers at a job and expect them to learn by trial and error, sometimes at the risk of serious injury. The successful worker stays on the job, the unsuccessful is removed by the foreman and easily replaced by a member of the large surplus labor force. Second, according to a well-known principle of Taylorism, mental labor, understanding of the production process, and task coordination are to be displaced from the shop floor. The planning of production is done in the office; the coordination of production is transmitted to the shop floor by the supervisors. In this vein, Strassman observes: "More supervision can make up for a worker's

---

was possible to identify the conduct of each group at each level in six separate categories. For each group of employees who had improved greatly in discipline, a value of 2 was assigned; some improvement received 1; no change equaled 0; some deterioration equaled -1; and a large deterioration equaled -2. Scores vary between -12 and $+12$, with an average of $+1.45$ (see Table 7.12). Although one might object, in the specific case of this variable, that the values have been determined by the subjective opinion of union leaders, it should not be forgotten that first, a marked tendency toward giving answers asserting improvements in discipline would have resulted in an insignificant relationship between $CH.DISCI.$ and P_F which we did not find; second, the union leaders had varying political leanings which, in some cases opposed both participation and the government; and third, since our survey was cross-sectional, it was not possible for the union leaders in different firms to come to prior agreement regarding their answers.

[26]Paul Strassman, for example, quotes the opinions of Puerto Rican entrepreneurs with regard to the criteria employed in hiring supervisors. One of them, selected as representative, pointed out that: "finally a policy was adopted of hiring only former U.S. Army personnel—not because they had previous contact with advanced technology, but because they understood military discipline (1968, p. 85)."

inexpertness in materials and processes, his nonchalance about coordinating one task with another, and his disdain for long hours of gray captivity [1968, p. 93].''

Thus, in the capitalist firm, the increase in supervisory personnel arises not only from a desire to reinforce vertical authority but also from a desire to avoid, wherever possible, the costly and potentially troublesome increased training and education of the work force.

Changes in Absenteeism

One of the most important specters for the capitalist manager is worker absenteeism, as it is reflected in the majority of Latin American countries where labor legislation is replete with guidelines regarding timetables, absences due to illness or accident, rest periods during working hours, special leaves, internal discipline, and the like. In the specific case of Chile before 1970, three absences from work without previous notice constituted sufficient cause for dismissal.

Bringing an end to this persecutory and enervating system is, perhaps, one of the most obvious gains from worker participation. Such gains will not emerge because those previously controlled develop new schemes for watching over one another more closely, but on the contrary, because of the rise of a climate of mutual confidence and positive solidarity. A new consciousness must develop: perceiving the meaning of the new system of working together; feeling that each is doing her or his part; that negligence, laziness, or absence from work is prejudicial to one's work mates and oneself; and that this is a system where persecution and threats have no place.[27]

This level of consciousness and understanding is not always easy to achieve. For example, observers of the Cuban economy during the 1960s saw a country struggling with moral incentives and absenteeism. The connection between work effort and purchasing power had become very tenuous, and the traditional methods of discipline (firing, fines, close supervision, unemployment, etc.) were practically nonexistent. The transformation of work came too quickly and strongly for the prevailing state of ideological and organizational preparation. A period of worker undiscipline and high rates of absenteeism ensued. It appears the problem in Cuba has been brought under control,[28] but it is a problem that

[27]The personal experience of one of the authors in one of the first producer cooperatives formed in Chile prior to 1970 is relevant to this point. In this cooperative, a ''Committee to Supervise Absenteeism'' was formed. The committee members would visit the homes of workers who had missed several days of work, the basic assumption being that absence was due not to mere laziness or irresponsibility, but to some important problem which their workmate needed help to solve.

[28]Cuba's success in controlling this problem appears to be attributable to increased worker participation and the limited introduction of material incentives (usually in conjunction with collective decision patterns and moral incentives). The worker absenteeism committee described in footnote 27 exists in all Cuban workplaces and functions in much the same manner (cf. Zimbalist 1975b).

future experiments in democratic socialism or worker management are likely to confront.

The problem was confronted in Chile's social area in a moderated form. One apparent reason for its lesser severity in Chile was the full preservation of material incentives (albeit they were collective material incentives). A more important reason, however, was the rapid development of worker participation. Participation permitted a new social control system to emerge, which, when developed, was considerably more effective than the old because it was worker generated and worker controlled.

When an enterprise was first socialized, the level of worker abuse was understandably very high in many cases. The old managers were gone: Workers could say what they wanted to say now, they could have meetings, they could stay out of work when they were sick, all without the fear of being fired. Not only that, they could stay out of work when they were not sick or *sacar la vuelta* ('goof off') without getting fired. Absenteeism usually shot up, but the picnic atmosphere soon died away. Workers had a point to prove—they could manage their enterprises as well as or better than the capitalists. How well they proved this point depended on the development of the new social control system, that is, of participation. As participation grew, absenteeism fell, first to, and then below, its previous level.[29] (See Figure 7.1.)

The decrease in absenteeism (*DCR. ABSENT*)[30] is given in Equation (7.3):

$$DCR.ABSENT = 1.49 + .330 \, (P_F); \, R^2 = .302 \qquad (7.3)$$
$$(3.46) \; (3.78)$$
$$.490$$
$$.550$$

[29]In most factories, the workers formed their own discipline committees. A worker in a Santiago factory that prepares chicken feed explained:

At first, the very existence of the discipline committee produced certain frictions, because the workers did not understand that discipline could be controlled by a group of work mates even though this group was elected by the workers themselves. We conceived of discipline only as a blind obedience to the orders of our hierarchical superior. Today, there are no problems. Attendance at biweekly meetings is 100%, without there being any pressure exerted on the workers. The days when workers were absent on Mondays are far away and nobody remembers the words 'lackey' (*chupamedia*) or 'fink' (*soplón*).

[30]*DCR.ABSENT* is the inverse of the percentage change in the rate of absenteeism. It is grouped into the five levels shown on the vertical axis of Figure 7.1 where an increase in the rate of absenteeism of over 25% equals 1, an increase between 10% and 25% equals 2, a change between + 10% and − 10% equals 3, a decrease in the rate of absenteeism between 10% and 25% equals 4, and a decrease greater than 25% equals 5. Actually, because of the scale, the slope represented in the figure is steeper than the estimated least squares slope.

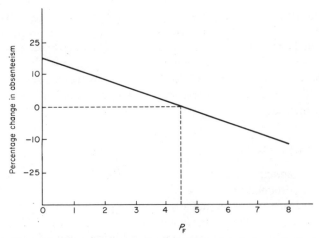

Figure 7.1. Change in absenteeism and the level of participation. In the vertical axis, 0% indicates level of absenteeism prior to socialization.

In terms of participation, the average firm experienced no change in its rate of absenteeism (average of *DCR. ABSENT* = 2.97).[31] Equation (7.3) demonstrates the significant (at $t_{.001}$) and strong effect of participation in lowering absenteeism.

$$DCR.ABSENT = 2.09 + .16 \ (P_F) + .012 \ (CH.DISCI.); \ R^2 = .489 \ (7.4)$$
$$(1.99) \qquad (3.65)$$

Equation (7.4) depicts the relationship between changes in absenteeism and discipline when controlling for the level of participation. It suggests that absenteeism is only one part of the wider problem, namely, the attitude of the worker in his or her place of employment. This attitude is reflected not only in sporadic absence from work, but also in slipping away or goofing off during work hours, reluctant work, negligence, insubordination, apathy, sabotage, etc.

$$DCR.ABSENT = 1.62 + .18 \ (P_F) + 4.65 \ (INCR.EDUC.); \ R^2 = .401$$
$$(2.05) \qquad (2.58) \qquad\qquad\qquad (7.5)$$

Equation (7.5) shows a significant and positive relationship between increases in worker training courses and decreases in absenteeism, when controlling for the level of participation. Worker training courses, it appears, promote deeper comprehension of the participatory system and the work process and lead to increased worker responsibility, dedication, and commitment to the enterprise.

[31]If anything, our grouping process causes an underestimation of the average of *DCR.ABSENT*. This occurs because firms that experienced decreases greater than 25% in the rate of absenteeism had greater displacements from 25% than firms that experienced increases in excess of 25%.

Finally, it is interesting to note that decreases in absenteeism were significantly correlated with the variables denoting union attitudes toward participation ($r = .425$) and the basic idea of participation held by worker representatives ($r = .648$). That is, where it was thought that the right to manage enterprises belonged to those who worked in them and consequently that the success of the new system was a challenge to the workers, this had a marked influence on reductions in absenteeism.

Changes in Strike Activity

As might be anticipated from the previous discussion, the number of strikes and strike days dropped drastically with a firm's changeover to the social area. This change can be traced principally to the application of the new system of participation. The correlation coefficient between P_F and *STRIKE* ($r = -.380$) expressly shows the inverse relation between higher levels of participation and the number of strike days in each enterprise.[32] It should be borne in mind that between 1970 and 1973 there was no modification in labor legislation that would have restricted the right to strike. On the contrary, new guarantees were incorporated into the statutes, and the government followed a strict policy of not intervening with public force to quell labor conflicts.[33] Furthermore, with greater job security and full employment, and the elimination of supervisory control and employer initiated espionage of labor organizations, there is little doubt that opportunities to strike were greater than before.

Despite the increased attractiveness of strikes, the average number of strike days per year, per enterprise in the 35 sample enterprises dropped from seven for the 5 years prior to socialization to one for the period of the social area.[34] This

[32]*STRIKE* is based on the number of strike days since the passing of the firm to the social area, a score of 1 being allotted for every 3 strike days.

[33]The refusal of the Allende government to repress worker strikes physically is in distinct contrast to all of Chilean union history, past and recent. A clear testimony to the leniency of the Allende government was its failure to use public force in the major 1973 strike at the *El Teniente* copper mine, which was instigated by the opposition. United States government complicity in this strike has been suggested by several authors (NACLA 1973b; Zimbalist and Stallings 1973; Petras and Morley 1975; and U.S. Congress, Senate Foreign Relations Committee 1975).

[34]Prior to Allende's election there was a trend in the country toward increasing strike activity (Barrera, 1971b; Zapata, 1976):

Period	Average number of strikes per year	Workers involved
1960–1964	377.6	108,589
1965–1967	979.4	202,120
1968–1970	1406.6	436,991

TABLE 7.3

Production Quality and Participation

Equation number	Dependent variable	Constant	P_F	$LMOB_2$	CH.W. DISP.	R^2
(1)	DEF.PROD.	−1.2	.418 (3.76)			.299
(2)	DEF.PROD.	−1.3	.345 (3.04)	.072 (1.93)		.373
(3)	DEF.PROD.	−2.3	.269 (2.89)		.685 (4.61)	.579

drop of 85.7% in frequency of strike days reveals an increased identification of the workers with the goals of their enterprises. In this sense, STRIKE is another variable reflecting a changing attitude toward work which can also be appreciated in the inverse correlation between STRIKE and DCR. ABSENT. ($r = −.307$), STRIKE and decreases in defective products and thefts ($r = −.418$), and STRIKE and increases in innovations and improvements ($r = −.405$).

Changes in Thefts and Defective Products

It was frequently alleged by Allende's opposition that where worker participation brought increased production it did so at the expense of consistent product quality. Because product quality itself is a subjective notion and cannot be directly measured, we used a closely related variable for which we were able to obtain information, changes in thefts and defective products (DEF.PROD.).[35] Insofar as DEF.PROD. proxies for product quality, our results directly contradict this allegation.

As may be observed in Table 7.12, an increase in thefts and defective products arose in only 4 of our 35 sample firms. On the average, there was an overall decrease in thefts and defective products of 2.06%.[36] Table 7.3, Equation

[35]The changes in thefts and defective products were added together because in a few instances the data were available only in aggregated form. The aggregation probably creates only minimal distortion since defective products and thefts tended to move together.

The variable DEF.PROD. measures the inverse of the percentage change of thefts and defective products added together. The value for DEF.PROD. was calculated as follows: a decrease in thefts and defective products of over 6% equals +3; a decrease between 3% and 6% equals +2; a decrease between 0% and 3% equals +1; an increase between 0% and 3% equals −1; an increase between 3% and 6% equals −2, and an increase of over 6% equals −3.

[36]The average value for DEF.PROD. was .686, which by interpolation yields an average decrease in thefts and defective products of 2.06%.

(1) shows that this decrease was greater, the greater the participation. The coefficient of P_F in Equation (1) indicates by interpolation that an increase of one category in P_F lowers thefts and defective products by 1.2% (this coefficient is significant at $t_{.001}$). Equation (2) indicates that strike activity in the 5 years prior to socialization has an independent positive, significant (at $t_{.10}$) impact on *DEF.PROD.* Such activity represents cohesive organization which apparently can be utilized equally to fight for higher wages or to regulate production quality successfully.

In Equation (3), the narrowing of wage disparities stands out as having a very significant (independent of P_F) influence on reducing thefts and defective products. It again appears that *CH.W.DISP.* results from and fosters worker cohesiveness and cooperation.[37]

Innovations

The term *innovation* is sufficiently broad to allow for some ambiguity in its interpretation. To the sociologist, for example, it might signify "any idea perceived as new by the individual [Rogers 1962, p. 13]," but the economist prefers to think of it as the first attempts to introduce a new commodity or process on a commercial scale. For the economist, therefore, the process of innovation "may subsume applied research, invention, and development while excluding imitation or diffusion [Machlup, 1962, p. 179]."

However, the stages of research, invention, and development, which can often take considerable time, are not what is typically observed as innovation in underdeveloped countries with capitalist economies. In these countries, the process of industrialization is generally based on the substitution of imports or foreign investment to exploit cheap labor and natural resources. It essentially consists of technological imitation, without applied research, invention, or innovation. That

---

[37]Furthermore, in relation to the political parties, Equation (7.6) shows that when P_F is controlled for, the more Christian Democrats in a firm, the more thefts and defective products tend to increase.

$$DEF.PROD. = 2.3 + .278 \ (P_F) - .040 \ (PCTCD); \ R^2 = .356 \qquad (7.6)$$
$$\qquad\qquad (2.78) \qquad (-1.68)$$

$$DEF.PROD. = -4.3 + .364 \ (P_F) - .019 \ (PCTCP); \ R^2 = .314 \qquad (7.7)$$
$$\qquad\qquad (2.79) \qquad (-.818)$$

This finding corresponds to less enthusiasm for the process and, in some cases, sabotage on the part of the Christian Democrats. Such behavior was not typical of rank-and-file workers who voted for Christian Democratic candidates. Rather, where more workers voted Christian Democrat, there was more Christian Democratic representation in leadership positions. From leadership positions on union committees and workers' councils, certain Christian Democrats were able to frustrate the development of the participation process and at times coordinate action against it. The same was not true of the Communists, as shown in Equation 7.7, where the relevant coefficient is not significant.

is, nothing resembling the scientific, investigatory world which the big multinational firms can finance or the specialized laboratories or investigation centers in the United States or Europe exists in the underdeveloped capitalist countries.[38] The mere presence in an underdeveloped country of eminent scientists in national laboratories, especially at universities, obviously does not assure connections with industry. Third World factories may borrow scientists from abroad, while local scientists may shun applied research, emigrate to more developed countries, or (more rarely) export their own discoveries for application elsewhere.

Thus it should be clear that in speaking of innovations and improvements in underdeveloped countries, one is not referring to major innovations derived from applying new principles of nature or from major scientific discoveries. Rather the reference is to the search to increase production through changes in production methods, in fitting the imported technology to the local medium, or, in the final instance, to inventions which are real but based on mechanical discoveries rather than scientific breakthroughs.

It is typical in most capitalist firms that workers are not consulted about ways to increase productivity.[39] This is overwhelmingly the case in underdeveloped countries (see Lauterbach 1964) and generally the case in developed countries. For instance, the HEW task force, in *Work in America,* states:[40]

> Perhaps the most consistent complaint reported to our task force has been the failure of bosses to listen to workers who wish to propose better ways of doing their jobs. Workers feel that their bosses demonstrate little respect for their intelligence. Supervisors are said to feel that the workers are incapable of thinking creatively about their jobs [U.S., HEW 1972, p. 37].

Closing off the workers' line of communication is an effective tool for reinforcing the workers' sense of isolation, impotence, and even inadequacy. Workers who consider themselves powerless may not help raise productivity, but they are less likely to cause trouble.

---

[38]A caveat is necessary here: Large corporations account for well under one-half of major inventions in the United States, and the federal government finances almost two-thirds of scientific research (cf. Adams 1974; and "The Silent Crisis in R and D" 1976).

[39]Whatever one may say about the absence of democracy in the Soviet Union, there is a very effective system of worker consultation there. David Granick (1966, p. 201) points out that in 1956 in the Soviet Union 1.3 million workers (5% of the active industrial population) presented one or more suggestions—of which, 1.4 million suggestions were carried out. It seems that this system has been substantially expanded since 1956 (cf. Zammit 1973, pp. 206–207; Khitrov 1975).

Andors finds a strong correlation between the emphasis on the participatory three-in-one teams (workers, cadres, and technical personnel) during the Great Leap Forward and Cultural Revolution in China and the number and importance of innovations (1977b, p. 217).

[40]The major exception in the United States is the systematic solicitation of worker suggestions in firms using the Scanlon Plan (cf. Whyte 1955, Chapter 14). A more passive suggestion system is operative in several hundred large U.S. firms, but it generally fails to stimulate active worker involvement (cf. James (1976).

It is natural that as workers' initiative and imagination are called upon for the first time there will be an abundance of useful suggestions. Such a process was evident in Chile. Several Chilean newspapers and journals began to publish the innovations or improvements introduced by the workers in social area enterprises. Doubtless this inventive activity was bolstered by the growing difficulties firms faced in finding spare parts and special inputs caused by the U.S. parts and credit blockade of Chile during the Allende years (cf. NACLA 1973a; Boorstein, 1977, Petras and Morley 1975). A 30-year-old Santiago textile worker, for example, had this to say:

> Before, one had to be a foreigner to be important in this factory. Before we received orders about moving machines or replacing parts, nobody ever consulted us. . . . We now have an understanding with the comrade supervisors who give us an opportunity to expose our ideas, to discuss them and to implement them. . . . After working five years here without understanding how the machinery worked or how it was made, I decided to run the risk of taking apart a motor. I was a bit scared at first but I had enough confidence to succeed in putting it together and learning how it works.

The same worker invented a delay relay for a cloth spinning machine which cost 100 *escudos* (around $2 at that time) and was estimated to save the country $2000 annually in reduced imports.[41] This textile factory also reported several other worker inventions: a new heating apparatus saving $5000 over 5 years; dyeing equipment saving $1000 over 3 years; a system for recovering gas escaped from a condensor reducing petroleum consumption by 60,000 *escudos* monthly; increasing the generating capacity of the boiler; replacement a magnetic clutch with an electrical system for a wreathing machine saving $24,000 over 3 years; a mechanical press for dyeing saving $6000; a mechanical transporting device for giant spools saving $20,000; the design of an air-conditioning system, projected saving of $500,000. In addition, this same factory enlarged its machine shop and began producing and modifying tools and equipment for other textile factories. The machine shop of another social area textile firm in Santiago was producing 80% of the spare parts they formerly imported (*Panorama Económico,* September 1972, pp. 26–27).

Innovations and improvements (*INNOV*), as expected, varied positively with P_F ($r = .37$).[42] Of the 93 sections sampled, 36.3% of them experienced at least one significant innovation.

[41]This savings estimate and those that follow come from the factory itself and it is likely that some of the figures are exaggerated.

[42]Innovations were identified at the section level within each firm. If the section leader responded affirmatively to the question "Has your section experienced any significant changes in its production system?" we would discuss the change to ascertain whether or not it led to an increase in productivity. If there was at least one significant change in the section, a score of 1 was assigned. The scores for each section were added up to obtain a score for the entire enterprise. *INNOV* had a minimum of 0 and potential maximum of 4. The average score was 1.45.

TABLE 7.4

Innovations and Participation

Equation number	Dependent variable	Constant	P_F	TTYP	TINT	PCTSK	CH.P.RS	R^2
(1)	*INNOV*	−.93	.338 (2.84)	.335 (1.81)				.217
(2)	*INNOV*	−.16	.308 (2.74)		.009 (2.11)			.243
(3)	*INNOV*	−.83	.314 (2.72)			.0004 (1.81)		.217
(4)	*INNOV*	.57	.181 (1.54)				1.24 (2.11)	.242

In Table 7.4 Equations (1) and (2) show a positive and significant correlation between innovation and technological mechanization (at $t_{.10}$) and technological intensity (at $t_{.05}$). Any notion about workers not being able to understand more complex technologies is called into question by these results. On the contrary, it appears that the more mechanized the technology, the more there is to innovate with and the more workers innovate.[43] Equation (3) shows a positive and significant (at $t_{.10}$) correlation between innovation and the skill level of the work force.

Equation (4) of Table 7.4 suggests that the elimination or reduction of individual piece rates (*CH.P.R.S.*), an intermediate variable, fosters worker innovation. Here two factors appear to be at work. First, to motivate workers to innovate at all, it is usually insufficient simply to ask for suggestions. The worker must identify with the goal of increased production. This identification comes either from a social commitment or from a moral or material incentive—which is where the second factor comes in. Second, when the incentive is individualized (e.g., piece-rates), the distribution of the reward often creates conflict. For instance, two or more people may have discussed the change although it was first suggested by and attributed to a single worker. The ensuing tension produces a reluctance on the part of the workers to present suggestions.[44] Collective incentives, then, encourage worker cooperation, which is important in stimulating innovative behavior.

[43]This result is consistent with Leibenstein's notion that the isoquant is more discontinuous (fewer technological alternatives available) for low capital–labor ratios than for high. See Leibenstein (1966a).

[44]For a fuller and excellent discussion of this problem, see Whyte (1955, Chapter 14). A related point is that where suggestions raise productivity, worker lay-offs become a threat. Thus, worker control over employment practices removes another impediment to worker innovations.

Changes in Investment

It is important to situate our discussion of investment in social area firms in the context of the nature and role of investment in underdeveloped countries generally and in Chile specifically. It is not easy to find the link between the economic theory of production and capital and the investment behavior observed in underdeveloped countries. Common distortions in the labor and capital markets becloud the determination of factor opportunity costs and place economic theory almost entirely outside the world where actual decision making occurs.

Capital is reified in traditional economic theory to exclude consideration of the actual social and economic relations it engenders. It follows from this reification that capital has been mystified and glorified to be the engine for economic growth in underdeveloped countries.[45] This approach has been, at least implicitly, accepted by governments in the undeveloped capitalist world where one encounters development policies replete with tax incentives for foreign investment and reinvestment of profits and low interest public and foreign loans with no relation to existing capital scarcities or labor surpluses. This situation is compounded by what Strassman aptly calls "asymmetry of promotion [1968; p. 31]," that is, the huge systems of promotion, propaganda, and sales the big multinational corporations maintain in the nations importing technology and capital goods. These systems include training courses, manuals to explain the use of machinery and equipment, service and permanent replacements, etc. In contrast, who promotes the hiring of an additional worker in a similar fashion? As H. J. Habakkuk points out:

> More often, labor-saving ideas are embodied in a saleable piece of capital equipment. Replacing capital with labor, however, may take more than a purchase: the manager might have to be converted to the subtleties of efficient organization, a far more taxing teaching assignment [1967, pp. 164–165].

This bias toward capital intensive technologies is crucial to understanding the industrial structure and economic problems of underdeveloped countries. It creates a monopolistic potential, a lower level of employment, and a more unequal distribution of income; and it often imbalances international payments. Until recently, if the tide of automation has not resulted in chronic high unemployment in the developed economies, it is largely because when workers are replaced by machines in consumer goods industries, new jobs are created in the capital goods sector. However, underdeveloped countries typically import the major share of their technology and capital goods (in Chile over 85% of capital goods are imported). Thus, heavier capitalization in consumer goods production is not offset by new employment opportunities in the production of capital goods.

[45] A thoughtful critique of this notion is presented in Griffin (1969).

The result, given heavily concentrated land ownership patterns, is bulging cities, swollen service sectors, and massive unemployment.

It is not surprising, therefore, that Chilean workers perceived new investments to jeopardize their employment situation. In Table 7.5, it can be seen that 62.1% of Chilean industrial workers surveyed in 1969 felt that the introduction of new machinery meant more unemployment and 63.1% that despite reductions in personnel and increases in productivity their income would not be improved or could even be reduced.

Despite all the incentives and subsidies to investment, private investment activity remains insufficient. It has been necessary for the state to undertake investment itself, generally transferring funds and benefits to the private sector. In Chile, between 1961 and 1969 the proportion of gross private investment in gross domestic product fell from 10.6% to 7.6%. Moreover, the actual investment contribution of the private sector was considerably less than these figures indicate, since they include public funds passed over to the private sector (see Table 7.6). In 1969, the public sector contributed 75% of gross investment in fixed capital. Sergio Molina (1972), one of Frei's ministers of finance, accurately portrays the important role of the state in investment activity during the late 1960s:

> The conduct of private investment in that period was very different from that of the Public Sector in that its rate of increase fell and it was necessary to transfer savings from other sectors (government and foreign) to complete its financing. This transfer of public savings to the private sector and the fact that some State organizations were guaranteeing certain firms so that they could obtain financing from outside was the cause of criticisms of the Government; it was argued that they were encouraging a neocapitalist system, strengthening the centers of economic power and financing a new kind of capitalism more destructive than the preceding one [p. 82; our translation].

TABLE 7.5

Workers' Opinions Concerning the Effects of the Introduction of New Modern Machines

Unemployment	Percentage	Salaries	Percentage
Increases it	62.1	Increase	36.5
Keeps it the same	20.8	Remain the same	50.7
Decrease it	16.2	Decrease	12.4
No response	0.9	No response	0.4
Total	100.0		100.0

Source: Chile, CORFO, *Obreros Industriales Chilenos,* Publicación No. 12-A/70 (Santiago, 1970), cuadros 44 and 45.

TABLE 7.6

Chile: Sources of Investment in the Private Sector (millions of 1965 *escudos*)

Year (1)	Gross domestic product (2)	Total gross private investment (3)=(5)+(6)	Coefficient of private investment (4)=(3)/(2)	Indirect public investment[a] (5)	Effective investment private sector (6)	Percentage of changeover from public sector to private sector (7)=(5)/(3)
1961	14,638	1,552.7	10.6	194.5	1,358.2	12.5
1962	15,477	1,293.8	8.4	259.0	1,034.8	20.0
1963	16,091	1,589.2	9.9	203.2	1,386.0	12.8
1964	16,864	1,438.5	8.5	178.4	1,260.1	12.4
1965	17,956	1,418.4	7.9	301.3	1,117.1	21.2
1966	19,769	1,305.7	6.6	288.8	1,016.9	22.1
1967	20,002	1,449.1	7.2	543.4	905.7	37.5
1968	20,693	1,577.4	7.6	710.4	867.0	45.0
1969	21,785	1,666.9	7.6	838.6	828.3	50.3

Source: Chile, ODEPLAN, *La Inversión Pública en el período 1961–1970* (Santiago, June 1971), cuadros T and III.

[a] The indirect public investment is those public funds which pass over and remain under the authority of the private sector with the object of being invested under the form of long range credits or transfers of capital.

After 1970, with the changeover of each firm to the social area, investments faced increasing difficulties stemming from the process of change itself. At the same time, these difficulties were translated into important obstacles to the measurement of this variable. For example, the absence of legislation regarding the definitive ownership of these firms was one of the crucial problems. In addition, the growing number of judgments (*decretos precautorios*) in the courts that went against the workers regarding their rights over the realized investments in the firms transferred to the social area induced the firms' administrative councils to clothe investment procedures in complications or disguises so as to avoid the former proprietors also claiming part ownership over the new installations.[46]

Despite these difficulties, the size of investments in social area firms was impressive. In the 35 firms surveyed, the average annual rate of gross investment in machinery and equipment (as a proportion of fixed assets) was 15.47%.[47] This

[46]Because of this situation, obtaining investment figures required special applications to the authorities in each firm to clarify the forms and amounts of the realized investments. In the end, there was no certainty as to whether there still remained an important volume of investment which had not been considered.

[47]The variable *INVEST* is the annual rate of investment in machinery and equipment as a proportion of fixed assets. Both investment and fixed assets are measured in *escudos* of December 1972. From 1960 to 1969, the average annual rate of gross domestic capital formation in Chile was 19.85% (calculated from Chile, ODEPLAN 1970, pp. 32–36). This figure includes investment in building

figure does not include social service investment, which was reckoned separately.

A few words about institutional arrangements are in order to elucidate the circumstances of this investment. The rate of investment was not significantly correlated with the rate of profit ($r = .115$).[48] The reasons for this were varied: As pointed out in Chapter 3, around one-half of the firms in the social area were either intervened or requisitioned. That is, the state had "temporarily" assumed the management responsibilities of these enterprises, but the ownership was still private. In these cases, any profits shown by the enterprises would go to the owners. Thus, it behooved these firms to hide their profits. This was usually done by investing an amount equal to their anticipated profits and adjusting their books. In our sample, 17 of the 35 firms were either requisitioned or intervened:

Legal status	Number of firms[a]
Intervened	9
Requisitioned	8
Bought by state	15
State owned before 1970	3
Total	35

[a] Several firms were both intervened and requisitioned, including 2 of our 35 firms, and one was put in each category.

Some of the firms which did the most investing in our sample, therefore, showed no profits.

It is also important to point out that profits often reflected political priorities more than the state of the market or the efficiency of management. This was because the state deliberately controlled the prices of basic consumption items. It was the partial failing of the government economic policy that it did not also adequately control the prices of the inputs used to produce these goods. Thus, firms producing certain basic goods tended to show losses, but because the state wanted to increase production in these areas, these firms also tended to receive

and grounds as well as machinery and equipment and excludes (i.e., does not subtract) foreign liabilities. If we assume, as does Kuznets (1966, p. 421), that the capital–national income ratio in underdeveloped countries is 4 to 1, then gross investment averaged under 5% of capital stock in Chile during the 1960s. Assuming that the public and private investment rates are equal, we can safely assert that the rate of 15.4% is well above average.

[48]"Profits" were taken from the enterprises' accounting books. Although they are readily calculable, their theoretical significance in a worker-managed enterprise is questionable. In a capitalist firm, profits represent the residual after subtracting total costs (including the wage bill) from total revenues. In a worker-managed firm, "profits" can exist in an accounting sense, but the meaning of the residual changes. Here, the relevant magnitude is income per worker. Moreover, if the enterprise is socially owned, "profit" in the sense of return to ownership has no meaning. For an extended discussion of this point see Vanek and Espinosa (1971, p. 22).

large loans and import permits for investment. In some cases, there was a direct transfer of funds from one enterprise in the black to another in the red.

Investment also tended to be correlated with the amount of sabotage the enterprise had suffered. The more sabotage, the more reconstruction. Sabotage often took the form of owners anticipating expropriation and withdrawing or destroying as much equipment and inventories as possible. Sabotage also took the form of right-wing groups and paramilitary organizations blowing up machinery. In the case of *Textil Chiguayante,* near Concepción, practically the whole factory was blown up. Other factories sent money, equipment, and workers to help reconstruct it.

For all these reasons, it is not surprising that investment and profits (although positively) were not significantly correlated. Investment was dictated in essence not by the market per se, but by social priorities and political exigency.

Finally, it is necessary to explain the relatively high rate of investment, 15.47% per year. Given the difficult economic conditions and, in particular, the shortage of foreign exchange during Allende's last 18 months how were these firms, most of which used foreign machinery, able to invest? There are two answers: first, much of the investment took place in the first 2 years; and second, there was virtually no new investment in the private sector during the Allende period. Practically the entire assignment of foreign exchange for capital goods imports went to the social sector.

With these institutional limitations in mind, we can cautiously proceed to look at the relationships between participation and investment. Contrary to the hypotheses of those who assert that worker-managed enterprises will distribute more earnings in the form of wages and consequently underinvest, participation was found to be positively and significantly correlated with *INVEST* ($r = .470$).[49] This and other relations presented in Table 7.7 would undoubtedly be stronger if the macroenvironment had been more stable.

Equation (1) indicates that the looser the supervision, the higher the rate of investment, controlling for P_F. The looser supervision gives the workers more responsibility and more possibility of knowing the machinery away from their posts. These two factors could be stimulating the increased investment. Equation (2) says that at the $t_{.001}$ level of significance a change away from piece rates (when P_F is controlled for) increases investment by 26.8%.[50] This strong impact

---

[49]It might be objected that this result is not contrary to the behavioral assumptions of the underinvestment school since in Chile there was no effective trade-off between present consumption and investment. It is probably the case that the trade-off was not as clear as it would have been under normal conditions, but it nevertheless existed. Three points should be made in this regard. (*a*) loans had to be paid back, although the threat of foreclosure was not very strong; (*b*) workers in requisitioned or intervened enterprises chose to invest in productive assets rather than social services; and (*c*) investment funds often came out of retained earnings, despite the fact that the decision to invest was more related to social and political priorities than the financial situation of the enterprise.

[50]The beta coefficient in this relation is .542.

TABLE 7.7

Investment, Participation, and Other Variables

Equation number	Dependent variable	Constant	P_F	SPANC	CH.P.R.S.	PCTCD	R^2
(1)	INVEST	−26.5	3.87 (2.55)	10.9 (1.94)			.303
(2)	INVEST	1.24	2.83 (2.11)		26.8 (3.99)		.480
(3)	INVEST	32.6				−.711 (−2.23)	.131

might partly be a result of psychological factors, but it is more probably a reflection of the fact that without individual piece rates any benefits from plant expansion accrue to all workers. Finally, it is to be noted in Equation (3) that the increased presence of Christian Democrats lowers investment. This result is somewhat ironic because the Christian Democrats accused the UP of not investing in socialized industry.

In conclusion, as a brief evaluation of the results obtained for this variable, it can be stated that its change in quantity and orientation as a consequence of the new process of participation was considerable. Regarding the change in quantity, it could be argued that this was largely the result of an even greater contribution from the state, in comparison with the preceding period. This is obviously true if it is considered that the private sector during the Allende period almost completely stopped its already reduced investments and the government naturally concentrated its investments in the social area. However, it cannot be ignored that through the registered rate of investments, resources were now actually used in new installations and machinery. In addition, realized investments did not produce stagnation in employment, nor were they directed toward increased differentiation of products for the small group of high income earners. Instead a search was made to simplify consumption and give durability to what was being produced, avoiding the accelerated obsolescence imposed on products in capitalist economies to maintain a high level of consumption demand.

Changes in Productivity

Several studies have attempted to explain the differences in the level of productivity between developed and underdeveloped countries. The results, on the whole, fail to identify conclusively the most relevant factors in determining these differences. Explanations have been traditionally sought in variables representing the intensity of technology, the scale of operation, the size of the market, the management techniques employed, or the training of the labor force. Apart from

the limited notion of investment in human capital, rarely has an explanation been sought in the human factor.

Although the arguments used to support this hypothesis seem solid and coherent in theory, in practice they have turned out to be far from significant. So, for example, Edmar L. Bacha (1966), studying the hypothesis of A. Hirschman (1958, pp. 146–147), who asserts that the differences in productivity between developed and underdeveloped countries are fewer in industries with higher intensity of technology than in those with greater intensity of labor, found that:

> The intensity of technology does not explain (in the statistical sense) more than 10% of the variations in the differences of productivity from labor, although the coefficient of regression has the correct sign. In Mexico, the 100% increase in the intensity of technology is accompanied by a 22% increase in the relative productivity from labor [p. 667, our translation].

In the face of the differences in productivity between the developed and underdeveloped parts of the world with capitalist economies and the uncertain explanation for it, it is appropriate to inquire into the results observed when firms come to be managed by workers.

Although concrete cases and comparable studies are scarce, they are sufficient to support and substantiate three different aspects of the problem: (a) the existing differences in the level of productivity, as well as other indicators of performance, between the developed and underdeveloped worlds seem to be less when self-management is extensively introduced in backward countries; (b) there is a clear consensus in all existing literature that productivity is enhanced in firms where worker participation is introduced; and (c) the extent of the positive effects will depend on the importance and intensity of worker involvement in the decision-making process.

In relation to the first point, a comparative study of the type carried out by Edmar Bacha (1966) for Mexico and the United States or Carlos Diaz-Alejandro (1965) for Argentina and the United States would only be possible in an economy like that of Yugoslavia where the system of participation has been in practice for many years and extends to the majority of productive sectors. Naturally, a thorough investigation of the Yugoslavian case would take this study away from the Chilean experience, but it is interesting to recall certain benefits achieved in Yugoslavia under their system of worker self-management.

Bearing in mind the underdeveloped condition of Yugoslavia before World War II and the damage suffered during the war itself, the growth and consolidation of the economy have been considerable. In the period 1953–1972, the average annual rate of growth of social product was around 7% in real terms (Jović 1975, p. 6). Over the same period, industrial output rose at an average annual rate of 10.7%, fixed assets at 9.2%, employment at 5.3%, labor productivity at 5.1%, and industrial exports at 13.6% (Jović 1975, p. 8). Even though it is difficult to establish a direct link between indicators of productivity and

growth in the whole economy and the yield of each particular firm, it cannot be ignored that the growth rate of the Yugoslav economy in the past two decades has been among the highest in the world.[51]

In relation to the second point, ever since the Elton Mayo experiments at the Hawthorne Works of the Western Electric Company in the 1920s, social scientists have studied the effects of job enrichment and participation on worker attitudes and productivity. In his study surveying 17 experiments in worker participation, Paul Blumberg (1969) concludes:

> There is hardly a study in the entire literature which fails to demonstrate that satisfaction in work is enhanced or that other generally acknowledged beneficial consequences accrue from a genuine increase in workers' decision-making power. Such consistency of findings, I submit, is rare in social research [p. 123].

Carole Pateman (1970) has criticized Blumberg saying that the experiments he reviewed entailed short-lived changes and only minor participation. Further, Blumberg develops no useful taxonomy of participation. We come, then, to the third point: namely, the extent of the effects derived from different degrees of worker involvement in the decision-making process. Is it the case, from the least consequential form of worker participation to the most advanced form of worker control or self-management, that satisfaction is enhanced and productivity increased? Virtually all the evidence we have seen suggests the answer to this question is affirmative—provided that the change toward a participatory situation in question is a real change, small or large.[52] The mechanisms by which the change brings results or the longevity of the results will, of course, depend on the nature of the change.

In this regard, available evidence suggests that the more substantive the change in work organization, the more substantial are the results. For example,

[51]Arguing for causality between self-management and this high rate of growth in Yugoslavia is, of course, problematic, although some authors have attempted to control for other sources of growth such as the high investment ratio and make this argument (cf. Horvat 1976). As we point out in earlier chapters, the market-oriented Yugoslavian economy has suffered from many economic problems. Developments in the country's economic and social structure, particularly since the economic reforms of 1965, appear to be moving the economy away from meaningful self-management and democratic socialism.

[52]By *real,* we mean that in some concrete sense the workers have more control over their work or actual influence in certain aspects of the decision-making process. Thus, minority representation on management boards is generally tokenistic and an example of spurious change. It is not surprising from this perspective that the European experience has not yielded either appreciable economic or social results. A possible interpretation of a real change is provided by Walker and de Bellecombe:

> In conclusion, the positive direct influence of participation in management on productivity seems to have been proved with some precision only when the said participation has taken the form of a reorganization of labor within the framework of autonomous and responsible groups [1967, pp. 104–105; our translation]

after reviewing 34 cases where worker participation was introduced to some degree, the HEW (1972) task force in *Work in America* concluded:

> It is imperative, then, that employers be made aware of the fact that more thorough efforts to redesign work—not simply 'job enrichment' or 'job rotation'—have resulted in increases in productivity from 5 to 40%. In no instance of which we have evidence has a major effort to increase employee participation resulted in a long-term decline in productivity . . . *it appears that the size of increase in productivity is, in general, a function of the thoroughness of the effort* [p. 112; emphasis added].

Several studies by the Tavistock Institute in textile factories in India (Rice 1963), in coal mines in Great Britain (Trist *et al*. 1963), in industrial factories in Norway (French, Israel, and Aas 1960), lead to the same conclusion.

Many other studies support the previous assertions and findings in the same manner. For present purposes, it suffices to divide the literature into two categories: experiments involving increased worker participation at the shop floor level and experiments in worker management or comanagement.

The following authors have written about cases where the introduction of some participation at the shop floor level has yielded positive results: A. Gouldner (1964, p. 141) on a gypsum mine in Ohio; L. Karlsson (1973a and 1973b) on several experiments in Swedish industry; D. Jenkins (1973) on 14 industrial experiments in the United States and many others elsewhere; J. Gooding (1972) on two additional industrial experiments with work teams in the United States; P. Blumberg (1969) on 17 experiments; Trist and Bamforth (1969) on the composite longwall system of coal getting in Great Britain; S. Melman (1958) on the "gang system" of production at the Standard Motor Company in Great Britain; W. F. Whyte (1955 Chapter 10) on an assembly line experiment in the Hovey and Beard Toy Company; P. Dickson (1975), Emery and Thorsrud (1976), and U.S. HEW (1972) on experiments in the United States, Sweden, Norway, Holland, and elsewhere; Argyris (1973); R. Likert (1967, pp. 13–29); Vroom (1969); McGregor (1960); Katz and Kahn (1966, p. 463); C. Riskin (1974); and D. Zwerdling (1974) are some others who have also argued on the basis of their work that participation or democratic management stimulates improved performance.

The second category—where the workers organize and essentially run the whole show—includes producer cooperatives and self-managed and comanaged enterprises. A growing body of literature suggests that this more total form of participation either improves efficiency or is consistent with efficient performance: R. Oakeshott (1975) on the producer cooperative complex, Mondragon, in Spain; S. Dolgoff (1974) on the worker-managed factories in Catalonia, 1936; D. Jones (1974) on some 25 British producer cooperatives; Carnoy and Levin (1976) on the Triumph Motorbike Cooperative in Meriden, England; C. Bellas (1972) on 21 worker-owned plywood companies in the Pacific Northwest;

Zwerdling (1974) and Albelda (1976) on the Vermont Asbestos Group in northern Vermont; A. Babeau (1968) on the 1956–1958 Polish experience with workers' councils; S. Melman (1970); M. Rosner (1970); and K. Fine (1973) on the industrial establishments of the Israeli kibbutzim; O. Narkiewicz (1970) and G. Gurvitch (1966) on the approximately six- to eight-month period of worker control in the Soviet Union following the October Revolution; Harnecker (1975) and Zimbalist (1975a and 1975b) on the Cuban comanagement experience since 1970; and Wheelwright and MacFarlane (1970), C. Bettelheim (1974), S. Andors (1977a and 1977b); J. Robinson (1973), and C. Hoffman (1975) on the Chinese comanagement experience since the Cultural Revolution.

In summary, a wide-ranging group of studies are virtually unanimous in concluding that real participation has a positive impact on productivity. Our results for Chile corroborate these earlier studies.

Our productivity variable (*PROD*) attempts to measure the average annual change in product per worker since the passage of the enterprise to the social area. *PROD* was constructed in the following way:

$$\overline{\quad\underset{(T_0-18)}{|}\qquad\underset{(T_0-6)}{|}\qquad\underset{T_0}{|}\qquad\underset{(T_s-12)}{|}\qquad\underset{T_s}{|}\quad}$$

If T_0 was the date of the passage of the enterprise to the "social area" and T_s was the date of our survey, then we compared product per worker for periods T_0-18 months to T_0-6 months and T_s-12 months to T_s.[53] The calculation of the gross value of production for both periods was done with second-period prices. The number of workers was calculated by taking the average number of workers for each 12-month period. Taking the percentage change between the two periods and then dividing by $1 + [(T_s-12) - (T_0-6)]/12$ yielded the average annual rate of change.[54]

The period (T_0-6) to T_0 was not considered because it inaccurately represented the normal presocialization productivity level. It was common for firms during the 6 months prior to socialization to be ridden with labor and economic

[53]Depending on the availability of data, the periods were sometimes moved back a few months. Of our 35 firms, 7 were only in the social area for between 8 and 12 months. In these cases, the periods of comparison were less than a year long. The periods were adjusted to include the same months to control for seasonal fluctuations.

[54]The annual rate of change in productivity was then divided into five categories: Substantial drop (more than 6% per year) equals 0; small drop (between 3% and 6% per year) equals 1; no significant change (between a drop of 3% and an increase of 3%) equals 3; a more than average increase (between 3% and 6% equals 4; and a substantial increase (more than 6% per year) equals 5. The *PROD* variable was categorized because the production data for some firms were incomplete and we had to make estimates. In the cases where data were incomplete, they usually concerned one of several different products produced by a given firm for the presocialization period. By estimating that product's contribution to the total gross value of production in the first period, we could roughly compute the upper and lower bounds of variation in *PROD*, assuming a 10% increase or decrease in the production of the omitted product.

problems.[55] To compare productivity levels and include this period would bias the change upward. As the measure is constructed, there is a slight downward bias in the magnitude of change because the period of deterioration is not considered, but the effects of this period often are. For example, the expropriated capitalist may either have permitted machinery to fall into disrepair or removed some of it. The shorter the time that the enterprise has been in the social area, the more such effects will thwart productivity increases. This assertion is given prima facie support by the positive and significant (at 5%) correlation coefficient between *TIME* and *PROD* ($r = .359$).[56]

The overall productivity performance of the 35 firms in our sample was very positive. Productivity increased or stayed the same in 29 of the 35 firms, and in 14 of the 29 productivity increased at a rate greater than 6% per year. This impressive result must be qualified by the following two conditions: first, Allende's redistributive and expansive economic policy along with other macroconditions set the stage for an overall advance in industrial production;[57] second, as stated earlier in this chapter, there was not a substantial flight of highly skilled workers from the great majority of socialized firms. On the one hand, this meant that technical teams were readily available to advise and make certain decisions. On the other, it was indicative of the fact that the executive hierarchy (organizational chart) in virtually all the socialized firms was kept intact, with the exception of frequent changes at lower supervisory levels. The *normas básicas* provided for worker participation in decision making, not in execution. To the extent that workers participated in execution, it happened gradually and usually was restricted to the more advanced factories. In all probability, the productivity results would have been depressing had there been an attempt to eliminate enterprise hierarchy overnight.[58]

[55]For example, labor strikes or takeovers, raw material shortages, capitalist firings or lockouts, dismantling of equipment, etc.

[56]It is likely that this relationship also reflects other factors such as learning to run an enterprise better with more experience. We shall return to this during our discussion of the Hawthorne effect.

[57]In the industrial manufacturing sector as a whole, using the industrial production figures of the INE (National Institute of Statistics) and the employment changes figures for Santiago and Concepción, productivity increased 6.7% during 1971 and 9.3% during 1972 (yearly averages). The productivity measures for our 35 firms include the first 4 months (and sometimes the fifth and sixth months as well) of 1973. By mid-1972, the favorable macroeconomic conditions which prevailed during Allende's first 2 years (large foreign exchange reserves, material stocks, excess labor, etc.) no longer prevailed, and with January 1973 these conditions were clearly unfavorable to further industrial growth. In comparing the social and private areas of the economy, we should also keep in mind that despite employment increases in both areas, the employment expansion in the social area was probably two or three times as great as that in the private. This resulted from both the government policy to provide full employment and the greater investment in the social area.

[58]Advocates of breaking up enterprise hierarchy immediately should be aware of probable negative production consequences. Our view is that it is desirable to reduce hierarchy as much as possible through the expansion and equalization of educational opportunities and through extensive job rotation and job streamlining. To minimize economic losses, however, this must be done over time.

TABLE 7.8

Productivity, Participation, and Other Variables

Equation number	Dependent variable	Constant	P_F	INFO	TPL_3	VDIF	R^2
(1)	PROD	2.4	.285 (2.86) .350 .446				.199
(2)	PROD	2.0		.033 (2.98) .444 .464			.212
(3)	PROD	1.6			.271 (3.13) .551 .478		.229
(4)	PROD	4.0	.241 (2.48) .296 .377			−.285 (−2.03) .392 .309	.291

Table 7.8 reveals that success in increasing productivity was positively corre-lated to participation in the whole firm (Equation [1]), to the extent and depth of information dissemination (Equation [2]), and to participation in technical and production matters at level 3 (Equation [3]). TPL_3 has a higher t statistic, elastic-ity at the mean, and beta coefficient than either $INFO$ or P_F. We might draw three conclusions from these results. First, P_F is strongly related to productivity, and it is likely that causality runs both ways. Not only does P_F increase productivity, but productivity gains lead to greater worker confidence in and gratification from their participation. Second, participation's impact on productivity is reflected most strongly at the base level. That is, the contribution to productivity seems to come largely from the rank-and-file workers' participation in production prob-lems on the shop floor. Third, the more information and communication that exists within the firm, the more integration and rationalization is achieved, and hence the greater the productivity gains. This suggests an interpretation to Equa-tion (4) where the number of hierarchical levels is shown to be inversely corre-lated with productivity gains controlling for the level of participation.[59] Namely, the more levels, the more difficult are the communication and transmission of suggestions from bottom to top and vice versa. It is probable that the implementa-

[59]Our efforts to test for the interaction effects of productivity on participation with information and vertical differentiation were frustrated by strong multicollinearity which left all coefficients insignifi-cant.

TABLE 7.9

Productivity and Participation, Controlling for Factors of Production and Demand

Equation number	Dependent variable	Constant	P_F	EMPLC	INVEST.	DEF PROD.	$I.MOR_2$	R^2
(1)	PROD	2.0	.258 (2.11)	.013 (.056)	.011 (.845)			.227
(2)	PROD	3.5				.248 (1.78) .046 .295		.088
(3)	PROD	3.4					.039 (1.10)	.035
(4)	PROD	2.4	.276 (2.57)				.009 (.255)	.201

Correlation matrix

	PROD	P_F	EMPLC	INVEST.
PROD	1.00	.446	.179	.333
P_F		1.00	.248	.470
EMPLC			1.00	.458
INVEST.				1.00

tion of suggestions is also slowed down. These two factors thwart productivity gains.

Equation (1) of Table 7.9 controls for two other variables commonly in production functions, employment (*EMPLC*) and investment (*INVEST.*) *EMPLC* is actually a measure of the percentage change per year in the firm's total employment since entering the social area.[60] The correlation between *EMPLC* and *PROD* is insignificant at the 15% level, but their positive relationship is worthy of comment. All other things being equal, an increase in employment lowers the capital–labor ratio and, we would expect, lowers productivity. This is only the case, however, when a factory is producing near or at capacity. It was generally accepted that during the last years of the Frei period Chilean factories were operating at between 60 and 70% capacity.[61] The great spurt in demand produced by Allende's fiscal and monetary policies resulted in a full use of industrial production capacity. It is likely then that the lower capital–labor ratio and the capacity utilization adjustments offset each other and yield the insignificant relation between *EMPLC* and *PROD*. The correlation coefficient between *INVEST*, and *PROD* ($r = .333$) is significant at the 5% level, although its coefficient is insignificant in Equation (1). This latter fact can be explained by the strong tendency for *INVEST.* and *EMPLC* to move together ($r = .458$). *EMPLC* and *INVEST.*, apart from controlling for changes in the factors of production, serve together as a rough proxy for the change in demand that faced particular industries. That is, we can speculate that as demand increased firms tended to increase their capital stock or their employment or both. Thus, when factor changes and demand changes are controlled for, we see from Equation (1) that participation remains significantly correlated with productivity at the 5% level.

A common criticism raised by Allende's opposition in the face of increasing production was that the quality of products was deteriorating. To test this assertion, *PROD* was run on *DEF.PROD*. Equation (2) suggests that defective products not only did not increase when productivity increased but at the 10% level of significance, actually *decreased*. This result is consistent with our earlier statement that Chilean workers in socialized factories experienced a substantial reduction in their alienation from product and process. This reduced alienation, or increased identification, meant more pride in their product, so it is logical that quality improved.

Equations (3) and (4) of Table 7.9 show no significant relation between productivity and the number of strike days in the five years prior to socialization. This counters the possible objection that *PROD* increases not because of P_F, but

---

[60]*EMPLC* is constructed as follows: A decrease in employment greater than 10% equals 1; a decrease between 3 and 10% equals 2; a change between -3 and $+3\%$ equals 3; an increase between 3 and 10% equals 4 and an increase greater than 10% equals 5.

[61]Cf. Ramos (1972, p. 104).

TABLE 7.10

Productivity, Participation, and Technology

Equation number	Dependent variable	Constant	P_F	PRDUM	$P_F \times (PRDUM)$	TINT	$P_F \times (TINT)$	R^2
(1)	PROD	3.6	.192 (2.01)	.829 (2.91)				.367
(2)	PROD	2.9	.335 (2.04)	.163 (.237)	.158 (1.07)			.390
(3)	PROD	2.5	.276 (2.70)			−.002 (−.526)		.206
(4)	PROD	2.8	.196 (1.78)			−.02 (−1.78)	.005 (1.69)	.273

Correlation Matrix

	P_F	PRDUM	$P_F \times (PRDUM)$	TINT	$P_F \times (TINT)$
P_F	1.00	.336	−.281	−.176	.004
PRDUM		1.00	.728	.012	.030
$P_F \times (PRDUM)$			1.00	.060	−.040
TINT				1.00	.919
$P_F \times (TINT)$					1.00

because of the greater number of strikes prior to socialization (which is positively associated with P_F).

Table 7.10 is concerned with technology's direct effect on productivity and its effects on the relationship between P_F and $PROD$. $TTYP$ is the only technology variable with a significant simple correlation with $PROD$ ($r = -.334$). When dummies were used to weight each type with respect to $PROD$, the new variable, $PRDUM$, took on the following values.[62]

Artisan $= -.17$
Machine tending $= -.61$
Assembly $= -2.0$
Assembly line $= -1.6$
Continuous process $= -.86$

That is, artisan technology was the most favorable for productivity gains, while assembly technology was the least favorable. The ordering of the types is the same as that in $TDUM$ (dummies for each type with respect to P_F) with assembly and assembly line interchanged.[63] $PRDUM$ is highly correlated with $PROD$ ($r = .536$).

Equation (1) indicates that $PRDUM$ has a significant (at the 1% level), independent (from P_F) impact on productivity. In Equation (2), both $PRDUM$ and the interaction term have insignificant coefficients because of multicollinearity. $TINT$, the capital–labor ratio, is not significant in Equation (3) but becomes significant at $t_{.10}$ when the interaction term (also significant at the 10% level) is added. In the latter instance, higher capital–labor ratios are associated with lower productivity gains. However, the higher the capital–labor ratio, the stronger is participation's positive effect on productivity (or the less negative is the effect of K/L on productivity as participation rises) controlling for P_F.[64] That is, given that increased capital intensity is associated with lower productivity gains, increased capital intensity also heightens the positive effect of participation on productivity.

[62]The ordering of these values (with the possible exception of continuous process) is consistent with Hirschman's argument on technology and maintenance in underdeveloped countries (1958, pp. 141–151). More complex technologies, he asserts, are more dangerous if not properly maintained. They will be operated with relatively more efficiency and less slack than simple technologies. The least negative coefficient on artisan technology can be interpreted to mean that prior to worker participation there was most slack (or room for improvement) in artisan production. Thus, artisan production is associated with greater productivity gains.

[63]The r between $PRDUM$ and $TDUM$ is .873.

[64]It might be recalled that $TINT$ and $TTYP$ were positively correlated with $INNOV$, while, as we have just seen, they are negatively correlated with $PROD$. This is consistent with the weak correlation between $PROD$ and $INNOV$ ($r = .100$), which in turn can be explained by the fact that a large portion of the innovations we recorded served to replace parts and materials previously imported and now no longer available or difficult to obtain. That is, they raised productivity in a relative (by keeping it from falling) not an absolute sense.

One of the first studies to challenge the Taylor–Weber notions of organizational efficiency was the set of experiments carried out in the late 1920s at the Hawthorne Works of the Western Electric Company in Chicago. The researchers wanted to test the effect of illumination, work breaks, piece rates, length of work day, and other variables on productivity. It happened that productivity increased no matter how they varied these factors. They increased illumination, and producitivity increased; then they decreased illumination, and productivity increased even more. Early writers interpreted this peculiar result to be a function of the unique testing conditions and not the variables themselves. That is, the workers performed better because they were being watched by scientists and because the changing conditions showed that somebody (namely, management) was interested in their welfare.[65] The productivity increase, therefore, was spurious. When the scientists left, productivity would fall to its preexperiment level. Fleeting productivity gains became associated with this experiment and came to be referred to as the *Hawthorne effect*.

The question arises whether or not the gains we are observing in Chile were produced by simple enthusiasm for any change or by the actual nature of the change. An appropriate test, suggested by the interpretations of the Mayo experiment at the Hawthorne Works, is to see whether or not the productivity gains were sustained over time. Above we saw that *TIME* and *PROD* (as well as *TIME* and P_F) were positively correlated. In part, this was attributable to the deterioration of production facilities immediately prior to socialization. We argue that it was caused much more by the substantial and dynamic character of change in socialized Chilean enterprises.

We attempted to look at the interaction of *TIME* and P_F on *PROD*. The functional relationship $PROD = f[TIME, P_F, (TIME) \times (P_F)]$ could not be tested adequately because of the presence of strong multicolinearity. However, a chow test dividing the sample at the mean of *TIME* on the relationship between *PROD* and P_F yielded results consistent with our hypothesis:

$$\text{Below mean:} \quad PROD = 3.4 + .131 \ (P_F)$$
$$(.875)$$

$$\text{Above mean:} \quad PROD = 1.7 + .409 \ (P_F)$$
$$(2.84)$$

Although the hypothesis of no structural shift cannot be rejected at the $F_{.10}$ level, the relationship between *PROD* and P_F is stronger and only significant for firms which have been socialized for at least 17 months. This is consistent with the

[65]Paul Blumberg (1969) has maintained that productivity increased because the workers participated in the decisions on how to vary conditions. This explanation makes more sense than the other from our perspective, but the relative merits of these explanations do not directly concern our present argument.

hypothesis that the relationship between P_F and *PROD* became stronger over time. We conclude that, at least during the 34 months of Allende's presidency, there was no Hawthorne effect operating and, on the contrary, the character of change was dynamic as productivity gains became greater over time.[66]

We discussed how worker-created wage structures are more equal and collective in their orientation than those imposed by capitalists. It is also the case that more equal wage structures and collective incentives are associated with greater productivity gains. After surveying the literature on industrial incentive systems, William F. Whyte (1955) concluded: "In this connection it should be emphasized that the theory of motivation at present generally applied in industry promotes full effort from probably less than 10 per cent of the work force [p. 49]." Whyte explains that piece-rate systems often result in the attempt by workers to hold back production and bargain for higher rates. This finding is corroborated by Opsahl and Dunnette (1973, p. 138) who found that 35% of workers perceived low productivity to help higher earnings in the long run, and by L. Kirsch (1972, p. 42) who finds that Soviet piece-rate workers hold back effort just prior to and during norm review.[67] It is also dubious that high salaries for management stimulate the job efforts put forth by managers. Opsahl and Dunnette cite a study by Lawler where he "recently found that 600 managers perceived their training and experience to be the most important factors in determining their pay—not how well or how poorly they performed their jobs [p. 138]."

In Table 7.11 we find piece rates to be negatively associated with *PROD* in Equations (1) and (2), the elimination of piece-rates to be positively associated with *PROD* (Equations [3] and [4]) and the narrowing of internal wage disparities to be positively associated with *PROD* (Equations [5] and [6]). In addition, each of these wage structure characteristics had a significant impact on *PROD* independent of the impact of P_F (Equations [2], [4], and [6]). Equation (7) shows that, when the presocialization wage disparity (*ORIG.W.DISP.*) is controlled for, the elimination of piece-rates (*CH.P.R.S.*) and the narrowing of wage disparities (*CH.W.DISP.*) both have independent, significant (at 5% and 10%, respectively), and positive impacts on productivity. Together they explain 33% of the variance of *PROD*.

---

[66]Again, since our data collection is cross-sectional, these results, although consistent with this statement, do not directly affirm it. Another interpretation might simply be that the positive correlation between *PROD* and P_F is only significant for firms which had been in the social area at least 17 months at the time of the survey. Even this interpretation would suggest that the Hawthorne effect was not operative.

[67]Kirsch also cites cases where a piece-rate maintenance worker actually perceives his best interest to lie with broken down machinery. Kirsch maintains that most experts feel increased mechanization tend to lower the effectiveness of piece-rate wage systems (1972, p. 42).

TABLE 7.11

Productivity, Participation, and Wage Structure

Equation number	Dependent variable	Constant	P_F	ORIG. P.R.S.	CH.P.R.S.	CH.W. DISP.	ORIG. W.DISP.	R^2
(1)	PROD	4.0		−.801 (−1.80)				.088
(2)	PROD	2.7	.269 (2.77)	−.691 (−1.68)				.264
(3)	PROD	3.6			1.48 (3.00)			.214
(4)	PROD	2.7	.208 (2.09)		1.12 (2.25)			.308
(5)	PROD	2.5				.447 (2.81)		.193
(6)	PROD	1.8	.214 (2.11)			.329 (2.05)		.292
(7)	PROD	2.7			1.20 (2.48)	.312 (1.79)	.003 (.481)	.330

These results contradict the common assertion that the present level of wage differentiation and inequality is necessary to motivate efficient productive behavior. Under the assumption of perfect markets, neoclassical wage determination theory itself suggests this assertion. How, then, can these results be explained? We suggest three possible explanations. First, putting an end to piecerates might curb or eliminate such negative behavior as rate cutting. Second, collective incentives, as have seen, stimulate more investment because ensuing benefits accrue to all workers. Similarly, collective incentives can eliminate rivalries over payoffs for helpful suggestions and thereby stimulate innovation. Third, collective incentives motivate cooperative behavior and there is more concern for alleviating bottlenecks wherever they occur in the plant. This stabilizes production by section and raises overall productivity (Melman 1958). There will be more interaction and a fuller exchange of information, which allows better integration of work tasks and planning.

If collective incentives and equalized wages stimulate higher productivity, why do capitalists not eliminate piece-rates and equalize wages? The answer could lie in our earlier finding that equalized wage structures are associated with worker cohesiveness and solidarity. Too much worker solidarity threatens capitalist control over surplus. According to this interpretation, the wage structure is another device employed by capitalists, along with sex, race, and seniority practices, to divide their work forces. The existing wage structure is not technically efficient. It is only efficient in the sense that it preserves control for and allows accumulation by the capitalist.

It is, perhaps, useful at this point to summarize our discussion in this section by outlining some theoretical considerations for understanding the relationship between participation and productivity. Figure 7.2 attempts, in simplified form, to depict some of the causal mechanisms in this relationship.

Some of these relationsips are discussed in connection with our study and others are taken from different studies. The latter will be explained.

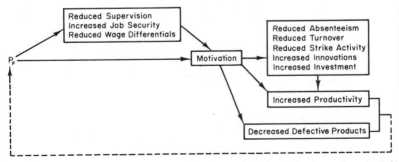

Figure 7.2. Schematic representation of the interaction of participation and productivity.

TABLE 7.12

Intermediate Variables and Variables of Results

Firm	Changes in discipline (1)	Increase in employment (2)	Increase in education and training (3)	Changes in income differential (4)	Thefts and defective products (5)	Absenteeism (6)	Innovations (7)	Strikes (8)	Investments (9)	Changes in productivity (10)	Changes in social services (11)
1	+ 6	5	18.5	4	0	2	4.0	0	30.0	5	27
2	+12	5	24.8	4	3	5	2.0	0	61.0	5	13
3	+ 8	3	45.5	3	2	5	4.0	0	1.8	5	14
4	+12	5	13.2	4	3	5	2.0	0	100.0	5	19
5	+ 4	5	22.0	5	3	5	0.0	0	25.0	5	18
6	0	5	29.8	1	0	4	3.0	0	20.0	4	26
7	0	3	16.5	2	2	2	2.5	0	8.0	2	13
8	− 6	5	2.2	3	0	4	0.0	0	50.0	5	14
9	+ 6	3	9.3	2	2	4	3.0	0	13.0	5	8
10	− 3	5	5.0	3	1	2	0.0	0	4.0	3	12
11	+ 5	4	12.0	4	2	4	2.5	0	30.0	4	18
12	+ 2	4	11.5	3	1	3	1.5	0	10.0	3	12
13	− 3	1	7.7	4	2	2	2.0	0	4.1	3	11

14	+6	5	5.2	3	1	4	4.0	0	30.0	5	8
15	+5	4	1.6	4	2	3	3.0	0	0.0	5	21
16	+6	5	14.5	1	0	4	0.0	2	0.0	5	13
17	-6	3	10.4	2	0	3	0.0	0	0.0	4	8
18	-5	4	21.0	2	0	4	2.0	0	5.0	5	10
19	0	4	7.8	4	2	2	0.0	2	10.0	3	13
20	0	4	14.7	1	0	2	0.0	3	10.0	3	12
21	+4	5	6.4	3	0	3	2.0	0	4.0	3	14
22	0	4	8.6	2	1	1	0.0	0	0.0	1	6
23	0	4	4.2	3	2	3	3.0	0	10.0	3	13
24	+6	3	2.9	4	1	2	0.0	0	0.0	5	20
25	+5	2	40.0	3	-1	4	0.0	0	13.0	3	10
26	0	3	3.1	1	3	2	0.0	2	0.0	2	8
27	-8	5	0.4	3	0	1	1.3	0	25.0	3	22
28	+6	3	4.9	1	-1	4	0.0	0	0.0	4	3
29	+6	5	20.0	0	-4	4	4.0	0	20.0	1	16
30	-6	3	0.0	1	1	2	0.0	3	0.0	5	9
31	0	3	1.9	3	-3	2	0.0	1	19.6	3	10
32	-6	4	5.7	0	0	1	0.0	0	0.0	1	2
33	+3	3	0.0	4	0	3	2.0	1	10.0	3	13
34	-12	5	0.1	4	0	1	0.0	1	20.0	5	7
35	0	4	10.1	2	0	2	3.0	1	8.0	2	16

Participation[68] tends to change the character of or eliminate supervision, reduce alienation, and increase job security. Ley (1966) found that the major factor increasing labor turnover was the extent of authoritarian attitudes among the foremen. Telly, French, and Scott (1972) showed that there was a strong correlation between feelings of inequity in wage earnings and labor turnover.[69] High turnover clearly lowers productivity as it brings adjustment and training costs. For instance, labor turnover was estimated to cost General Motors $79 million in 1972 (Zwerdling 1973). Participation lowers turnover and thereby raises productivity.

In industries where demand is not expanding, the laborer runs the risk of working him- or herself out of a job if he or she increases productivity. In Chile's social area, however, workers were not laid off or fired when the enterprise faced economic problems. If there was a shortage of raw materials, the workers would work fewer hours on typical production. The extra time was usually devoted to the construction of social services. Prior to socialization, job security was low in Chile. The increased job security thus was an important permissive condition for the productivity gains that were experienced.

The remaining causal link explaining productivity increases is motivation. There appears to be widespread agreement that worker motivation is an absolutely crucial factor in determining productivity. Vroom and Deci (1973) have observed:

> If you look at a group of persons who are performing the same job, you will note that some do it better than others. . . . Furthermore, if you have some quantitative measure of their contribution to the organization, you will probably find that the best person in each group is contributing two, five, or perhaps ten times what the poorest is contributing [p. 9].

Vanek (1970) writes that the greatest advantage of the self-managing economy is its ability to produce optimal incentive patterns in governing the effort and quality of labor: "The corresponding gains may reach into hundreds of per cent of national product [pp. 402–403]." Although this estimate appears a bit optimistic, it seems safe to conclude that motivation can potentially account for large variations in national product.

In 1966, H. Leibenstein reviewed the literature which attempted to quantify the addition to "social welfare" provided by efficient resource allocation. He found that in no case had the misallocation of resources brought on a "welfare loss" of more than .1%.[70] Leibenstein concludes that x-efficiency, which in-

---

[68]We refer again to "real" participation, i.e., situations where there has been a transfer of power in the enterprise away from the managers to the workers.

[69]This study and the Ley study are cited in Chris Argyris (1973).

[70]Leibenstein uses gross national product as his measure for social welfare. Accordingly, "welfare loss" is measured as a percentage of gross national product.

cludes enterprise management, organization, and motivation, has a greater effect on "social welfare" than allocative efficiency. Earlier, A. O. Hirschman (1958, Chapter 8) stressed the vital importance of x-efficiency in economic development.

Our discussion in this section has outlined how worker participation operates to increase productivity. The relationship has been documented for the case of Chile, 1970–1973. The results from numerous other studies unanimously support the conclusion that worker participation and worker management either maintain or increase productivity levels. It is an indictment of the economics profession that it has concentrated almost entirely on allocative efficiency. The profession has misallocated its resources.

8

Commentaries and General Conclusions

SOME PRELIMINARY CONSIDERATIONS

In this chapter, we briefly summarize the main results of our study and offer some comments of a more general nature regarding the process of worker participation. Before proceeding with our synthesis, however, it is necessary to recall certain considerations—some of which enhance the significance of our findings, and others which suggest limitations to the validity of the results and to their applicability to other circumstances.

First, as discussed throughout the text and in various footnotes, there are no "optimal" statistical techniques available for our type of analysis. Problems of sample size, multicollinearity, simultaneity and specification bias, and dealing with cross-sectional data engendered certain trade-offs, compromises, and limitations in our interpretation. It must also be recalled that the statistical techniques employed do not permit direct inference of causality, but rather suggest relational patterns which can be interpreted with reference to theoretical propositions. Nevertheless, the causal model we have suggested seems to have responded well by traditional standards to the available techniques.

Second, our survey was conducted in industrial enterprises at the core of the Chilean economy. The social area comprised some 320 establishments in mid-1973 and consequently represented less than 1% of the 35,000-odd industrial establishments existing in Chile at that time. However, some enterprises included in the social area were among the largest in terms of size and productive significance and were in the most dynamic sectors of the Chilean economy. The manufacturing enterprises of the social area thus accounted for upwards of 40% of total industrial production and employed approximately 140,000 persons— over 30% of the industrial labor force. It is similarly important to stress that the workers in social area firms generally had the longest industrial and trade union experience, greatest ability, and highest technical or professional training in the

177

Chilean labor force. Our study therefore stands out in distinct contrast to most studies in the area of worker participation which deal with isolated experiments, usually in firms or producer cooperatives peripheral to the mainstream of productive activity in the economy.

Third, it must be emphasized that the duration of the Chilean experience was quite short. In the longest case, it reached some 32 months and between 20 and 24 months for the majority of the firms. This situation naturally limits the scope of our conclusions, making them valid only for a transitional period. That is, it would not be possible to state that the results obtained are valid in the long run, given the changing nature of a participation process through time. In this regard, it is difficult to indicate precisely how long the transition from a capitalist economy to another with generalized, profound participation will take. Naturally, this will depend upon the speed and intensity of the transformation in each particular case and upon the starting point at which the experience is begun.

Fourth, the societal context in which the Chilean experience with worker participation evolved was unique. It involved profound structural change, political instability, and intense conflict. The struggle over preserving the capitalist system or creating a new socialist system divided the society in half.

Until 1970, economic development in Chile had been characterized by a relatively rigid stratification of social classes, which may also be observed in most Latin American countries. One of Chile's distinctive characteristics had nevertheless been the extraordinary development of its middle class, which enjoyed a greater influence than that stratum enjoyed elsewhere in Latin America, with the possible exceptions of Argentina and Uruguay. This social group constituted a decisive factor in determining the course of social progress or stagnation. In the past, it had frequently formed electoral alliances either with organized groups of workers in the cities or countryside to improve its relative position in economic or political terms, or with groups of entrepreneurs or landowners when more basic issues such as the distribution of power in society were at hand.

After 1970, Salvador Allende's administration proposed a peaceful and democratic trasition to socialism within the institutional framework established by the Constitution and laws of Chile. The new administration held only executive power since it had only a minority position in Congress and little support or control over the rest of the public or semipublic institutions, such as the judiciary, the principal universities, the officer ranks of the armed forces, and a large sector of the civil servants. To be sure, forces in opposition to Allende maintained predominant control over the mass media and accounted for well over half of all media expenditures during the Allende period (cf. Mattelart and Piccini 1973).

In spite of these obstacles, the new administration acted quickly to form a sector of social ownership within the Chilean economy and to redistribute income

and services swiftly. The majority of the most important industrial firms, the big copper and coal mines, the banks, and the *latifundios* were rapidly expropriated or bought. Even though the ideological basis of this program was mainly Marxist in its inspiration, the bulk of the policies and concrete actions put into practice actually represented only a continuation or intensification of reformist programs begun in previous administrations. However, a decisive difference was that the propertied class was convinced the Allende government would fully implement the reforms.

Nevertheless, the options of the Allende government were extremely limited. With a program of socialist change and a government without a clear majority, faced with progressively more violent opposition from economic interests of internal and external origin, toward the beginning of the third year structural changes were brought to an effective halt, and the government was threatened with imminent collapse. Critics have argued either that Allende was too quick in carrying out the UP's socialist program or, on the contrary, that he should have advanced with more celerity and decisiveness, especially in organizing the workers. Many of these arguments, however, like the extensive polemic that has continued on the topic, seem to ignore or at least oversimplify the majority of the problems and concrete realities of the period. Given the national, and especially the international, context of the period, with the U.S. government's and multinational corporations' active opposition and the parties of the Popular Unity coalition increasingly divided over which strategy to follow, the attempt that was initiated resembles in some respects an attempt to achieve the impossible.

There is no doubt that the intensity of social conflict during this period had a sharp and important influence on the participation process—stimulating it in some cases and in others placing obstacles in its path. Because it is to be expected that future movements for social change involving the democratization of economic power will be accompanied by political struggle, the implementation of worker participation must always be considered in light of the broader societal context. To do otherwise is tantamount to treating economic change in a strictly "neutral" and technical manner which, from our perspective, is methodologically deficient and unjustifiable.

On the other hand, because of the inherently political and controversial nature of the Chilean experience with worker participation, it is difficult to analyze this process objectively without appearing to support or criticize the larger process of social change. In this regard, it is important to recall that our methodology permits only a relative evaluation of the enterprises in Chile's social area. Our index of participation does not lend itself to assertions regarding an optimal state of participation or even to the absolute level of worker participation achieved in various firms. Moreover, it is apparent from our results that a wide divergence of experiences existed among the firms of the social area. In some cases, the

development of the system of participation had proceeded quite far, in others it had barely begun. Throughout the study, we underscore the difficulties and recurrent problems encountered in social area enterprises. Finally, it is important to remember that our survey pertains only to the manufacturing sector of the social area and does not consider undertakings in other sectors of the economy such as agriculture, mining, commerce, finance, distribution, and construction.

SPECIFIC CONCLUSIONS

The overall results obtained indicate that participation yielded positive effects not only in economic terms but also in terms of human and social development. Along each of these dimensions, the participatory enterprises of the social area performed better than their earlier incarnations as firms with a traditional capitalist management. In the following paragraphs, we summarize the principal findings of our study.

The Index of Participation

A basic methodological assumption of our study is that worker participation in enterprise management is a measurable process, at least in comparative terms. A cumulative index was constructed which allowed an interfirm comparison of the extent of worker participation in decision making, execution of policies, and control and evaluation of these policies. The index was formed by separately measuring the functioning of the structure of participation (existence of participatory bodies, frequency of meetings, attendance at meetings, etc.) and the content of participation (range of issues covered at meetings, workers influences in forming decisions, etc.) at three different levels within each enterprise. Two principal results of our analysis of the behavior of the components of our index are summarized below.

1. Participation at higher levels within the enterprise (i.e., the administrative council) was always accompanied by active participation at the base or lower levels (i.e., production committees and worker assemblies at the level of the shop floor and general assemblies of the whole enterprise). This finding is consistent with other studies which find that the participatory process only sustains itself and evolves into fuller democracy when it develops from the base. The experience with democratic procedures in a worker's local environment conditions and educates the worker for active participation at higher levels. The mere presence of worker representatives on management boards does not constitute a sufficient condition for rank-and-file interest and involvement in enterprise decision making, as the Western European experience with minority representation and

codetermination has amply demonstrated. Indeed, it appears that higher level worker representation is only effective when accompanied by mobilized and organized support and pressure from below.

2. A related result is the high correlation we found between the structure and the content of participation. The existence of formal participation bodies (structure) does not guarantee that workers will exert effective influence (content) in decision making. In fact, experience elsewhere suggests that without the opportunity to have a real impact on enterprise policies workers lose interest in the formal structure, e.g., they cease to attend meetings, cease to vote for or watch over their representatives, and cease to follow enterprise performance. The content of the participation, then, must not only provide for effective worker input in general, but it must provide for this input in substantive matters. When worker influence is limited to consultation or inconsequential issues, participation will not be dynamic and self-sustaining. When the influence is real and far ranging, however, workers will exert pressure to sustain and deepen the formal structure of participation.

Factors Influencing the Level of Participation

In the following stage of the study, it was hypothesized that the relative level of participation obtained in each firm was a function of the presence in differing degrees of characteristics peculiar to each factory. We considered 29 quantifiable independent variables suggested by previous studies for which information was uniformly available in all sampled enterprises. These variables were grouped into three main categories: technostructure of the enterprise (technology, organizational, and bureaucratic structure); labor force characteristics of the enterprise (level and nature of education, political organization, and ideology); and, intermediate factors (disposition of the administration toward participation, the nature and extent of informational flows). Our principal findings regarding the factors influencing the level of participation can be summarized as follows:

1. One set of variables examined pertained to those characteristics traditionally employed to describe the social and bureaucratic organization of the firm (size, span of control, vertical and horizontal differentiation). None of these variables, alone or together, were found to be significant predictors of the level of participation. Yet other literature on the subject has consistently found one variable in particular, horizontal differentiation, to be positively associated with decentralization of decision making in the firm. We pointed out, however, that this literature refers solely to decentralization to the level of middle management. Since we are measuring participation in decision making by workers and not by management, it is not surprising that we found this variable insignificantly correlated with participation. In fact, it might be argued that as horizontal differentia-

tion increases and the power of middle management grows, middle management becomes increasingly possessive of its new power. This could make it more and more difficult to decentralize decision making beyond the level of middle management to the production workers. This might explain the negative coefficient of horizontal differentiation in relation to participation, although this coefficient does not become significant until the 25% level.

We saw in Chapter 2 that the strengthening of the market mechanism in Yugoslavia with the economic reforms of 1965 stimulated many firms to hire staffs of technical experts to evaluate, plan for, and influence market conditions. In other words, they expanded and increased the power of their middle management staffs (increased horizontal differentiation). In the U.S. economy, Lawrence and Lorsch have demonstrated a positive association between firms facing rapidly changing market conditions and the increase in horizontal differentiation. In both cases, the increased importance of the market is associated with a larger and stronger middle management. This evidence, then, suggests the possibility of a negative correlation between the strength of the market mechanism and worker participation in enterprise decision making.

2. We considered three distinct measurements of technology: complexity (percentage of maintenance workers in the firm's labor force), typology of mechanization (craft, machine tending, assembly, assembly line and continuous process), and intensity (capital–labor ratio). Higher capital–labor ratios and greater mechanization were negatively correlated with participation, while complexity was positively correlated. Although these relationships were statistically significant, they were rather weak, and consequently the relationship between technology and participation was superseded by the stronger relationship between participation and our labor force variables.

3. Our proxies for the level of formal schooling were not significantly correlated with participation. It has been pointed out by several authors that schooling affects not only an individual's cognitive and skill traits but also his or her affective and ideological traits. These two influences may be offsetting with respect to their impact on participation. It is also likely, however, that our proxies were distorted and inadequate measures of educational level. We also considered a variable representing a broader conception of an individual's education suggested by Freire, namely, the degree of labor mobilization and consciousness. The motivating notion here is that labor mobilization and consciousness constitute an active form of education, where the individual learns from mutual interaction with peers based on her or his own life experience. This latter variable, which is also political in nature, was found to be strongly and positively correlated with worker participation.

4. Our two explicitly political variables, (a) ideology and attitude toward participation of union and sectional leaders; and (b) the composition of political party support in each factory, were very significant and complementary ex-

plainers of the level of participation. That is, the more progressive the ideology of worker representatives and the lower the voting support for the Christian Democratic and Communist parties in a factory, the greater was the level of participation observed. Worker participation entails a redistribution of power within the enterprise toward the workers and thus involves a political struggle. The parties and ideological positions that stressed the importance of gaining power for the working class over the state apparatus also were able to generate more effective systems of worker power over the enterprise.

5. The disposition of the enterprise administration toward participation and the nature and extent of informational flows within the enterprise were very powerful explainers of participation. These two variables were classified as intermediate because their own variance was in turn strongly explained by variables of the central labor force characteristics already discussed. That is, the attitude of the factory's administration toward worker involvement in decision making and the extent and accessibility of information provided within the firm appeared to be a direct function of the level of organization, interest, and pressure from the workers. It is almost axiomatic that an effective and dynamic system of participation requires both cooperation from administrators and extensive information dissemination regarding the operation of the enterprise.

6. Finally, it is important to emphasize that our results from multiple regression and factor analysis indicated that the labor force and political variables were of overriding importance. The only technostructure variables significant in explaining the level of worker participation were those describing the firms' technology. However, when the technology variables were considered together with (a) labor mobilization and consciousness, (b) political ideology and attitude toward participation of worker leaders, and (c) political party composition, the former lost all significance. The latter three variables together, on the other hand, explained 65% of the variance of our dependent variable, participation. Finally, when labor mobilization and consciousness, attitude and ideology of union leaders, disposition of the administration toward participation, and the system of internal information were considered together, we explained 83.5% (corrected R^2) of the variance in participation. These results are impressive and suggest that we were able to isolate the most relevant factors which affected the development of worker participation.

The Effect of Participation on Enterprise Performance

In the final part of our study, we analyze the relationship between our index of participation and various indicators of the social and economic performance of the enterprise. Advances derived from participation in the field of human and social development are better known and perhaps more to be expected than those produced in the economic or technical field. This means neither that the latter do

not exist nor that participation has been demonstrated to be antithetical to efficient and improved economic performance. On the contrary, various studies have shown that participation makes a significant contribution to advances in productivity or investment and to decreases in reluctant work, defective products, thefts, labor turnover, and strike activity. Likewise, in this study we found that both the social and economic performance of the enterprise tended to be positively associated with the level of worker participation.

After the changeover of many firms to the social area, the elimination of supervisors, the absence of former bosses, the dissolution, in effect, of the old system of control and disciplinary pressure created an atmosphere of social freedom that occasionally allowed the workers to take advantage of this new situation. However, with the establishment of the new participatory system in the enterprise, these abuses were quickly brought under control, and in most cases improvements beyond previous levels in work discipline and organization were forthcoming. In the following lines, we summarize the major changes observed in enterprise performance.

1. In those firms where a relatively higher level of participation existed, progress and advances in worker discipline were significant, appreciably surpassing former standards. However, in a reduced number of firms where the level of participation was low, discipline deteriorated, weakening internal organization and team spirit. Changes in worker discipline were paralleled by changes in absenteeism, strike activity, and innovative behavior, all which improved with higher levels of participation.

2. An increase in worker education and training courses was strongly associated with higher levels of participation. The opportunity for participation created a demand for more training, and the greater training in turn reinforced the workers' sense of efficacy and interest in participation. Increases in training courses were also clearly correlated with improvements in discipline and decreases in absenteeism. In general, participation put in motion a dynamic which changed the individual's relationship to his or her work by creating an environment of cooperation and contribution.

3. Correspondingly, higher participation levels were associated with a change toward more egalitarian and collective structures of remuneration. Disparities between high and low wages were reduced. The number of wage grades was sharply diminished, and the incentive system was put progressively on a more collective basis, as opposed to individual piece rates. These changes in wage structure connoted a sense of solidarity, team work, high morale, and work spirit which had salutary effects on enterprise performance. Independent from and complementary to the influence of higher levels of participation, the move toward more egalitarian and collective forms of remuneration significantly promoted decreases in thefts and defective products and increases in innovative

behavior, investment, and productivity. The magnitude of these results was superior to that observed in firms in the United States and elsewhere where attempts have been made to improve worker motivation through controlled stimuli and new styles of management.

4. Whereas the annual increase in capital stock in Chilean industry was 3.9% during 1959–1964 and 4.6% during 1965–1970 (Stallings 1975, p. 427), the average annual rate of investment in fixed productive assets in our 35 sample firms was 15.47%.[1] Within our sample, firms with higher levels of participation also tended to have higher investment ratios. These results challenge the assertions of many to the effect that worker-run enterprises will opt for current income rather than future and therefore will invest less than typical capitalist firms. Nor does the rapid growth rate and high investment ratio in Yugoslav industry or in the large worker cooperative in Mondragon, Spain support such assertions. Although workers might resist innovation and investment in a capitalist firm because they are perceived as a threat to their employment, in a worker-run firm job stability is assured and this impediment to innovation and investment is removed.

5. Perhaps the single variable of greatest interest is changes in productivity. In 29 of the 35 sample firms, productivity either increased or stayed the same, and in 14 firms it increased at a rate superior to 6% per year. Given the generalized economic problems of the period and the marked tendency for social area firms to expand employment, these results are impressive. In addition, although it was not the only variable important in explaining increases in productivity, higher levels of participation were clearly correlated with greater increases in productivity.

As indicated previously, collective incentives and narrower earnings differentials were both significantly and positively correlated with productivity, both separately and when the level of participation was controlled for. Also, the positive relationship between productivity and participation remained when we controlled for other variables of the production function and proxies for changes in product demand. It was also found that higher capital–labor ratios strengthened the positive relationship between productivity gains and participation. The positive association between productivity and participation has been found by many authors under widely varying conditions, and no major study has found there to be a negative association between the two.

6. Finally, in the area of social results, without diverting resources from productive uses, socialized factories rapidly expanded the social services available to the worker: plant medical facilities, day-care centers, cafeterias and consumer cooperatives, athletic fields, libraries, and so on. In several factories, cultural departments were also created.

---

[1]Certain qualifications to this high figure and the special circumstances of investment in social area firms are discussed at length in Chapter 7.

Among other interesting aspects, it must be mentioned that the firms in the social area with the most developed worker participation were also pushing hardest for worker participation in sectoral and national planning. That is, the more participant and mobilized sectors of the working class were pressuring hardest to deepen the democratic forms of the state.

MORE GENERAL CONSIDERATIONS AND CONCLUSIONS

In this section, viewing our study as a whole, we conclude with some general remarks on the process and importance of worker participation.

1. In order to derive concrete results from the experience of worker participation, we must necessarily focus specifically on individual enterprises. This methodological imperative, however, should not blind researchers to the fact that enterprises do not exist in isolation from one another or from the rest of society. In our study, the process of worker participation which developed in individual enterprises was a reflection on a microlevel of changes occurring throughout Chilean society.

The new model for society proposed by the Popular Unity, once set in motion, liberated previously latent social forces and became self-reinforcing. The combination of the political vision and will from above provided by the new governing coalition and the growing organization and unrestrained mobilization from below generated a strong dynamic. As new sectors of the population became involved in the process, other sectors were reached through a demonstration effect. In the case of the reform of the industrial structure, once the process of worker mobilization to gain control over the means of production had reached a critical mass, an unrelenting momentum led to successive worker takeovers of new firms and the expansion of the social area considerably beyond the intentions outlined in the Popular Unity program. In a sense, worker participation in social area enterprises was such an attractive alternative to workers in the private sector that worker mobilization and factory takeovers acquired their own momentum, out of the control of the government that had initiated the process.

2. The transition period during which a social sector of the economy is created and a system of worker participation is implanted is characterized by an uneven development across economic sectors. Certain sectors and geographical areas experience rapid socialization, early development of worker control, and immediate economic success, while other sectors lag behind in one or more of these respects. This unevenness can jeopardize the transition. On the one hand, the new system is evaluated by its opponents on the basis of its weakest links. Critics single out laggardly and less successful sectors, and the media claim that they typify the entire economy. Discontent and divisiveness may eventually emerge

within the very social groups supporting the transformation. On the other hand, the old institutions, to the extent that they escape immediate expropriation, will either support the private sector of the economy through trade ties, credits, assistance and training, and boycott or actively sabotage the reformed social sector. These conditions make it advisable, as Oscar Lange pointed out in his 1937 essay on the transition to socialism, for the government to undertake rapid and decisive measures to transform the economy and follow policies that promote a balanced process of change among economic sectors.

3. Although the economic results of the Chilean experience with worker participation were positive, they were in fact a relatively minor aspect of the overall process. Without the consolidation of political power, the entire process of change was abruptly reversed. The social character of the change in participatory enterprises must also be stressed.

One of the most important considerations which can be extracted from the Chilean experience lies in the radical overhaul of purpose and objectives in participatory enterprises. From the unidimensional focus on profit maximization in private firms, social area enterprises were transformed into social communities that pursued the personal and collective development of their members. In addition to concern for efficient and socially useful production, these enterprises sought to stimulate growth in the fields of education, health, and culture and generally radiated these benefits to the surrounding community.

The problem of worker motivation will ineluctably emerge in traditional capitalist firms where objectives are formulated without worker participation and without a link to worker aspirations for self-realization. Even in the most progressive cases, where the human relations school has come to dominate managerial practices and apply methods of job enrichment and work humanization, the motivation and welfare of the workers are still considered only as vehicles for increasing productivity and not as goals in themselves. As we argue in earlier chapters, these efforts rarely go beyond the surface and cannot tap latent sources of worker motivation or creativity. Consequently, they promote neither worker self-realization nor optimal economic performance.

In this regard, it is interesting to note that even traditional development economists are beginning to emphasize the key role played by human, social, and political factors in economic development. Quantitative studies of economic growth have affirmed the importance of an interdisciplinary approach to the subject.[2]

4. Many prominent theorists of political democracy, including Schumpeter, Berelson, Dahl, and Sartori, have emphasized its limited character. This school,

[2]For example, Adelman and Morris (1967) found that variables of a noneconomic nature accounted for a high percentage of the explanation of the variation in growth rates among underdeveloped economies.

which Pateman (1970) has labeled the "modern democractic theorists," argues that democracy is only possible in societies characterized by broad consensus, no intense conflict, slow change, and social and economic stability. They speak of passive democracy through competing elites and removed representatives. In contrast, several classical theorists have argued for a much broader view of democracy. Rousseau, for instance, felt that general equality and an economy of independent producers were necessary for democratic government. Only under these conditions would it be possible to avert a growing imbalance of economic and political power. John Stuart Mill, in *Political Economy,* wrote that "a democratic constitution not supported by democratic institutions in detail, but confined to the central government, not only is not political freedom, but often creates a spirit precisely the reverse."[3] In other writings, Mill argues that universal suffrage and participation in the national government count for little if the individual has not been prepared for this participation at the local level, for at the local level self-government and democratic practices are learned. Consequently, Mill advocated a form of enterprise

> not that which can exist between a capitalist as chief, and workpeople without a voice in the management, but the association of the laborers themselves on terms of equality, collectively owning the capital with which they carry on their operations, and working under managers elected and removable by themselves.[4]

Our results support Mill's position and the findings of other authors (see Chapter 2). That is, we found democracy on the shop floor to be a necessary ingredient of democracy at higher levels within the enterprise. From this perspective, meaningful political democracy must be accompanied by economic and community democracy. The argument for moving beyond limited systems of representational political democracy to deeper, more active forms of economic and political democracy which will reach citizens in their daily lives is a compelling one.

5. The Chilean experience demonstrates once again that the establishment of a broad system of industrial democracy has been held back not by technical considerations of economic performance but by the threat it poses to the power of dominant socioeconomic groups. Arguments opposing participation on the grounds that modern technology precludes an efficient democratic organization of industry or the economy have no basis in scientific research.

Nor do intermediate situations constitute an adequate response to the demand for economic democracy. Where worker restiveness, undiscipline, and pressure increase, proposals for minority or consultative participation appear to be formulas for checking a redistribution of enterprise power and for dissipating

---

[3]Cited in Pateman (1970, p. 30).
[4]From Mill's *Political Economy,* cited in Pateman (1970, p. 34).

worker militance. Experience indicates that worker participation does not arise from the good will or free choice of the owners and managers of industry. Objectively, worker participation presupposes struggle and confrontation between those who wish to gain power and those who already have it.

6. Finally, and related to all these lines of argumentation, true democracy is ultimately incompatible with economic underdevelopment and inequality. Capitalism has meant both underdevelopment and extreme inequality for the overwhelming majority of people in Latin America, Africa, and Asia. It seems to be a question of keeping people sick and oppressed in order to produce a "healthy" economy.

For the submerged humanity, the masses of working men and women in the underdeveloped world, the real threat lies in remaining where they are, at levels close to or below subsistence, while their countries adorn themselves with industrial trappings for the benefit of local minorities and groups tied to multinational concerns.

However, identifying the present situation or structural tendencies of a social system does not signify foreseeing its future. Historical change is a process open to human action and aspirations for freedom, self-determination, and self-realization. In the short run, these aspirations may be repressed. In the long run, they will inexorably reemerge.

Postscript

A recurrent theme in our study is the inherent limitation of "political democracy" without economic democracy. Under capitalism, the drive for profits and the need for control are inextricably bound. Any economic system organized around the private appropriation of socially produced profits cannot surrender economic control to the mass of producers without threatening its very existence.

As long as the wage laborer does not identify with (or is alienated from) the means, process and goals of production, a tension will exist between the laborers' capacity to produce and their actual production. Herein lies the primordial problem governing the nature of management over the labor process. A capitalist manager endeavors to organize production so as to maximize each worker's effort and output. When a worker is hired, his or her capacity to work, not the work itself, is purchased.[1] The workers' ability to control their own labor must be minimized. This is the lesson of Taylorism which advocates the separation of conception from execution in the work process. To the extent that these are separated in the labor process, the workers' ability to withdraw some of their capacity to work is restricted and the distinguishing characteristic of human, as opposed to animal, labor (i.e., thought and conception) is diminished.[2] The human laborer is thus reduced to an appendage of the machine.[3]

[1]The capitalist manager has also attempted to purchase actual work (e.g., the nineteenth-century subcontracting system in steel production, buttying system in coal, piece work, reversion to putting out), but these efforts have, on the whole, proven to be unsatisfactory. They have encountered successful worker opposition in the form of "soldiering," "goldbricking," or simply a backward-bending supply curve of labor.

[2]As a foreman in the machine shop of the Midvale Steel Works, Taylor had "fully recognized that . . . the combined knowledge and skill of the workmen who were under him was certainly ten times as great as his own [Taylor 1947, pp. 48–49]." Thus, Taylor himself did not question the workers' ability in the abstract to direct production. However, given the quest for profits and the consequent problem of worker motivation, it is more "efficient," from a Taylorist perspective, to place the conception of work where the collective knowledge and skill is lowest, i.e., in the hands of management.

[3]Under these conditions, the historical development of technology further promotes the separation of conception and execution by deskilling the character of work and rendering the laborer more and more a replaceable part (cf. Braverman 1974).

In a society where self-employment is becoming extinct, where the prevailing ideology adulates ''democratic'' processes and where the labor force has a high, increasing level of educational attainment, the Taylorist prescription for organizing work becomes progressively contradictory and problematic. In this perspective, the growing cry for and political organization around worker participation in Western Europe and Canada is easily understood. Similarly, the trend in U.S. industry toward ''human resource development'' or ''work humanization'' can be comprehended. The ''work humanization'' movement, however, merely represents an attempt by management to intensify labor and has led, with a possible handful of exceptions, to little more than cosmetic alterations in the work environment (cf. Chapter 2).[4] Genuine worker participation would set in motion a dynamic which would ultimately challenge capitalist control over the production process. Economic democracy is not on capitalism's horizon.

Until recently, capitalism has brought economic growth and rising per capita incomes to the United States, Western Europe, and Japan. However, the growing militance of Third World nationalism, the emerging environmentalist movements, and the rapid depletion of the world's natural resources undermine the basis for continued economic growth. Real average weekly take-home pay for the U.S. worker has stagnated over the last 10 years ($90.86 in 1967, $90.84 in March 1977 in constant 1967 dollars, according to the Bureau of Labor Statistics of the U.S. Department of Labor).[5]

Few would disagree that the capitalist world is confronting an economic crisis. Economic crisis, in turn, portends deepening political crisis. According to a recent major report of the Trilateral Commission, an international policy-planning group founded by David Rockefeller in 1973, whose members dominate the current Carter Administration, it appears that the historical marriage of capitalism and constitutional democracy in the West is being threatened.[6] The report deplores the development of an ''excess of democracy'' due to newly mobilized sectors of the polity. The report states: ''The effective operation of a democratic political system usually requires some measure of apathy and lack of involvement on the part of some individuals and groups.'' The central task is ''to restore the prestige and authority of central government institutions, and to

---

[4]Administrative law Judge Walter H. Maloney, Jr. of the NLRB apparently concurs with this assessment. Responding to a complaint by the grain millers union that the work teams at the Gaines Nutrition Center of the General Foods Corporation were, in essence, management dominated unions, Maloney dismissed the complaint, saying the teams merely were management's view of ''the best way to organize the work force to get the work done (*Wall Street Journal*, January 11, 1977).''

[5]The economic growth ethos in the developed world itself must be questioned. Surveys in the United States and other nations over the last 30 years suggest no clear relationship between higher incomes and self-defined personal well-being (cf. Heilbroner 1977).

[6]The report, *The Crisis of Democracy*, was written by three authors, one from each of the Trilateral Commission's regions (the United States, Western Europe, and Japan). The American author is Samuel Huntington. For more information on this report and the Trilateral Commission see, for one, *Seven Days*, February 14, 1977.

grapple with the immediate economic challenges.'' Higher education must be tied ''to economic and political goals'' and if it is extended to the masses ''a program is necessary to lower the job expectations of those who receive a college education.'' Overall, the solution lies in ''a greater degree of moderation in democracy.''

There are two alternative views of the future of societal organization before us. One advocates that democracy should encourage active citizen participation and mobilization, the other advocates their further restriction; one believes that education should be a creative, useful, and growing experience, the other sees education as an instrument of social control and manipulation; one calls for democracy to be extended to the economic sphere and deepened in the political sphere, the other calls for the further ''moderation'' of existing democracy; one envisions a society which elevates humanity, the other accepts an oppressive social organization as endemic to modern society and rejects the ''idealists'' who believe otherwise.

This study has suggested that the visionaries, in fact, are not utopians. Several years ago, Erich Fromm (1975) wrote:

Only if man masters society and subordinates the economic machine to the purposes of human happiness and only if he actively participates in the social process, can he overcome what now drives him into despair—his aloneness and his feeling of powerlessness. . . . The victory over all kinds of authoritarian systems will be possible only if democracy does not retreat but takes the offensive and proceeds to realize what has been its aim in the minds of those who fought for freedom throughout the last centuries [p. 404].

References

Achtenberg, Ben. "Working Capital." *Working Papers for a New Society* 2 (Winter 1975); pp. 5–8.

Adams, Walter. "Another View of the New Industrial State." *Economics: Readings, Issues and Cases,* edited by E. Mansfield, pp. 273–276. New York: W. W. Norton, 1974.

Adelman, I., and Morris, C. T. *Society, Politics and Economic Development.* Baltimore: Johns Hopkins, 1967.

———. "Analysis of Variance Techniques for the Study of Economic Development." *Journal of Development Studies* (October 1971): 91–106.

Adizes, Ichak. *Industrial Democracy: Yugoslav Style.* New York: The Free Press, 1971.

Albelda, Randy. "Workers' Ownership in the United States." Unpublished paper. Smith College, 1976.

Almond, G. A., and Verba, S. *The Civic Culture.* Boston: Little, Brown, 1965.

Alvarez, José. "Participation in Industry: Workers' Participation in Industrial Firms in Chile." Ph.D. dissertation, University of California, Los Angeles, 1972.

Anderson, Mike. "New Forms of Worker Participation in the Peruvian Economy." Mimeographed. New York: Ford Foundation, 1972.

Anderson, Rigmor. "Towards an Active Society: The Case of Worker Participation in Sweden." Ithaca, N.Y.: Cornell University Program on Participation and Labor-Managed Systems, 1973.

Andors, Stephen, ed. *Workers and Workplaces in Revolutionary China.* White Plains: M. E. Sharpe, 1977a.

———. *China's Industrial Revolution.* New York: Pantheon Books, 1977b.

Angell, Alan. *Politics and The Labor Movement in Chile.* Oxford: At the University Press, 1972.

Aranda, S., and Martínez, A. "Estructura económica: Algunas características fundamentales." In *Chile, hoy* edited by Victor Brodersohn, pp. 55–72. Santiago: Editorial Universitaria, 1970.

Argyle M.; Gardner, G.; and Cioffi, F. "Supervisory Methods Related to Productivity, Absenteeism and Labor Turnover." In *Management and Motivation,* edited by Victor H. Vroom and E. Deci, pp. 170–191. Balimore: Penguin Books, 1973.

Argyris, Chris. "Personality and Organization Theory Revisited." *Administrative Science Quarterly* 18 (June 1973): 141–167.

Aronowitz, Stanley. *False Promises.* New York: McGraw-Hill, 1973.

Arroyo, Victor. "Participación: Teoría y práctica en Chile." Mimeographed. Stanford, Cal.: Portola Institute, Stanford University, 1974.

Babeau, André. *Los consejos obreros en Polonia.* Barcelona: Editorial Nova Terra, 1968.

Bacha, Edmar. "Comparación entre la productividad industrial de México y los Estados Unidos." *El Trimestre Económico* 33 (October–December 1966): 657–673.

195

Ball, Robert. "The Hard Hats in Europe's Boardrooms." *Fortune* 93 (June 1976): 180–190.
Barkin, David. "Popular Participation and The Dialectics of Cuban Development." *Latin American Perspectives* 2 (1975): 42–59.
Barkin, Solomon, ed. *Worker Militancy and Its Consequences, 1965–75.* New York: Praeger, 1975.
Barraclough, S., and Fernández, J. A. *Diagnóstico de la reforma agraria chilena.* México City: Siglo Veintiuno Editores, 1974.
Barrera, Manuel. "Perspectiva histórica de la huelga obrera en Chile," *Cuadernos de la Realidad Nacional* (September 1971a): 119–155.
———. *El sindicato industrial como instrumento de lucha de la clase obrera chilena.* Santiago: Instituto de Economía, 1971b.
———. *El conflicto obrero en el enclave cuprífero.* Santiago: Instituto de Economía, 1973.
Barrera, Manuel; Aranda G.; and Diaz, J. *El cambio social en una empresa del APS.* Santiago: Instituto de Economía, 1973.
Barría, Jorge. *Breve historia del sindicalismo chileno.* Santiago: Instituto de Organización y Administración, 1967.
———. *El movimiento obrero en Chile.* Santiago: Ediciones Prensa Latinoamericana, 1970.
———. *Historia de la CUT.* Santiago: Ediciones Prensa Latinoamericana, 1971.
Bates, F. L. "Power Behavior and Decentralization." In *Power in Organizations,* edited by Mayer N. Zald, pp. 175–177. Nashville: Vanderbilt University Press, 1970.
Becker, Gary. *Human Capital.* New York: National Bureau of Economic Research, 1964.
Bellas, Carl J. *Industrial Democracy and the Worker-Owned Firm: A Study of Twenty-One Plywood Companies in the Pacific Northwest.* New York: Praeger, 1972.
Berg, Ivar. *Education and Jobs: The Great Training Robbery.* New York: Praeger, 1970.
Berliner, Joseph. *Factory and Manager in the USSR.* Cambridge: Harvard University Press, 1957.
Berman, Katrina. *Worker-Owned Plywood Companies.* Pullman: Washington State University Press, 1967.
Bernstein, Paul. "An Overlooked Alternative: The Czechoslovak Experience and Its Lessons for Humanizing American Society." Ph.D. dissertation, Stanford University, 1973.
———. "Run Your Own Business," *Working Papers For a New Society* 2 (Summer 1974): 24–34.
Bettelheim, Charles. *Cultural Revolution and Industrial Organization in China: Changes in Management and the Division of Labor.* New York: Monthly Review Press, 1974.
Bitar, Sergio. "Foreign Investment in Chilean Industry." Mimeographed. Cambridge: Harvard University, 1971. Reprinted as "La inversión extranjera en la industria chilena." *El Trimestre Económico* 33 (October–December 1971): 995–1009.
Bitar, Sergio, and MacKenna, A. "Impacto de las areas de propiedad social y mixta en la industria chilena." Departamento de Industrias, University of Chile, 1973.
Blalock, H. M., Jr., ed. *Causal Models in The Social Sciences.* Chicago: Aldine-Atherton, 1971.
Blau, Peter M. "Decentralization in Bureaucracies." In *Power in Organizations,* edited by Mayer N. Zald, pp. 150–174. Nashville: Vanderbilt University Press, 1970.
Blau, Peter M. and W. Richard Scott. *Formal Organization.* San Francisco: Chandler Publishing, 1962.
Blauner, Robert. *Alienation and Freedom.* Chicago: University of Chicago Press, 1964.
Blumberg, Paul. *Industrial Democracy: The Sociology of Participation.* New York: Schocken Books, 1969.
Boorstein, Edward. *Allende's Chile: An Inside View.* New York: International Publishers, 1977.
Bosquet, Michel. "The Prison Factory." *New Left Review* (May–June 1972): 23–34.
Bowles, Samuel. "Schooling and Inequality from Generation to Generation." *Journal of Political Economy* 80 (May–June 1972): 219–255.
Bowles, Samuel, and Gintis, Herbert. "IQ in the U.S. Class Structure." *Social Policy* 3 (January–February 1973): 65–96.

———. "Class Power and Alienated Labor." *Monthly Review* 26 (March 1975): 9–25.

———. *Schooling in Capitalist America.* New York: Basic Books, 1976.

Boyer, Richard, and Morais, H. *Labor's Untold Story.* New York: United Electrical, Radio and Machine Workers, 1973.

Braverman, Harry. *Labor and Monopoly Capital.* New York: Monthly Review Press, 1974.

Brecher, Jeremy. *Strike!* San Francisco: Straight Arrow Books, 1972.

Brinton, Maurice. *The Bolsheviks and Workers' Control, 1917 to 1921.* Detroit: Black and Red, 1972.

Brown, Emily. *Soviet Trade Unions and Labor Relations.* Cambridge: Harvard University Press, 1966.

Brugger, William. *Democracy and Organization in The Chinese Industrial Enterprise, 1948–1953.* Cambridge: At the University Press, 1976.

Burt, W. J. "La participación de los trabajadores en la gestión empresarial en Yugoslavia." *Boletín del Instituto Internacional de Estudios Laborales* 9 (November 1972): 146–194.

Cahiers de Mai. "The Lip Watch Strike." *Radical America* 7 (November–December 1973): 1–18.

Campero, Guillermo, and Jaramillo, Silvestre. "Consciencias de clase, economicismo y acción obrera," *Cuadernos de la Realidad Nacional* (June 1971): 24–42.

Cantoni, Wilson. "Poder popular en el agro chileno." *Cuadernos de la Realidad Nacional* (January 1972): 80–103.

Caputo, Orlando, and Pizarro, Roberto. "Dependencia e inversión extranjera." In *Chile, hoy,* edited by Victor Brodersohn, pp. 173–212. Santiago: Editorial Universitaria, 1970.

Carnoy, M., and Levin, H. "Workers' Triumph: The Meriden Experiment." *Working Papers for a New Society* 3 (Winter 1976): 47–58.

Carr, E. H. *The Bolshevik Revolution, 1917–1923.* 2 vols. London: Pelican Books, 1966.

Carrasco, Osvaldo. *El Nuevo Sindicato del Area Social.* Santiago: Sánchez y Cia., 1972.

Castillo, F.; Echeverría, R.; and Larrain, J. "Las masas, el estado y el problema del poder en Chile." *Cuadernos de la Realidad Nacional* (April 1973): 3–70.

Castillo, F., and Larraín, J. "Poder obrero-campesino y transición al socialismo en chile." *Cuadernos de la Realidad Nacional* (December 1971): 161–198.

Castillo, Leonardo. "Capitalismo e industrialización: Su incidencia sobre los grupos obreros en Chile." *Cuadernos de la Realidad Nacional* (June 1971): 5–23.

Castillo, Leonardo; Saez, Arturo; and Rogers, Patricio "Notas para un estudio de la historia del movimiento obrero en Chile." *Cuadernos de la Realidad Nacional* (June 1970): 3–30.

Chile, Comité Ejecutivo Nacional CUT-Gobierno de Participación. "Informe sobre el comité." Mimeographed. Santiago, 1972a.

———. "Informe sobre la situación de la participación en las empresas del area social y mixta." Mimeographed. Santiago, 1972b.

Chile, CORFO. *Obreros industriales chilenos.* Publicación No. 12-A/70, Santiago: 1970.

Chile, CUT. *Las normas básicas de participación.* Santiago, 1971.

———. "Encuentro de trabajadores y organismos de gobierno del sector textil." Mimeographed. Santiago, July, 1972.

———. *El proyecto de complementación de las normas básicas.* Santiago, 1973.

Chile, Instituto Nacional de Estadísticas. *XIV censo nacional de población y III de vivienda.* Santiago, 1971.

Chile, ODEPLAN. *Cuentas nacionales de Chile, 1960–1969.* Santiago, 1970.

———. *Plan anual de 1971.* Santiago, 1971a.

———. *Antecedentes sobre el desarrollo chileno 1960–1970. Plan de la economía nacional 1971–1976.* Serie 1, no. 1, Santiago, 1971b.

———. "La participación popular." Santiago, 1972.

———. "El area social." Santiago, 1972.

Chile, Dirección Nacional de Estadística y Censos. *Encuesta suplementaria sobre niveles de instrucción y calificación.* Santiago, 1966.

Chile, Popular Unity Government. *Proyecto de ley sobre participación de los trabajadores en las empresas del area social y mixta.* Bill presented to Chilean Congress, June 1972a.

————. *Proyecto de ley que crea un sistema nacional de autogestión.* Bill presented to Chilean Congress, June 1972b.

Chile Hoy, June 23–29, 1972 and August 3–9, 1973.

Clegg, Ian. *Workers' Self-Management in Algeria.* New York: Monthly Review Press, 1971.

Cohn-Bendit, Daniel, and Cohn-Bendit, Gabriel. "Attempts to Institute Workers' Control." In *Participatory Democracy,* edited by T. Cook and P. Morgan, New York: Harper & Row, 1971.

Cortés, Gemima, and Vivanco, A. "La participación en empresa X." Mimeographed. Santiago: University of Chile, 1973.

Crozier, Michel. *The Bureaucratic Phenomenon.* Chicago: University of Chicago Press, 1971.

Davis, T., and Ballesteros, M. "The Growth of Output and Employment in Basic Sectors of the Chilean Economy." *Economic Development and Cultural Change* (January 1963): 152–176.

de Castro, Cecilio. *Política de participación.* Buenos Aires: Editorial Universitaria de Buenos Aires, 1969.

de la Fuente, Pedro. "La participación obrera en la gestión de empresa Y." Mimeographed. Santiago: University of Chile, 1973.

Deleyne, Jan. *The Chinese Economy.* New York: Harper and Row, 1974.

de Tocqueville, Alexis. *Democracy in America.* New York: Random House, Vintage Books.

Deutscher, Isaac. *Soviet Trade Unions.* London: Royal Institute of International Affairs, 1950.

"Devuelve Pinochet 28 milliones de acciones al sector privado." *Excelsior* Mexico City, June 13, 1974.

Diaz-Alejandro, Carlos. "Industrialization and Labor Productivity." *Review of Economics and Statistics* 47 (May 1965): 207–214.

Dickson, Paul. *The Future of The Workplace.* New York: Weybright and Talley, 1975.

Dolgoff, Sam. *The Anarchist Collectives.* New York: Free Life Editions, 1974.

Dreyer, Ann. "Industrial Co-Determination in West Germany." *Challenge* 19 (March–April 1976): 54–56.

Durbin, R.; Homans, G.; Mann, F.; and Miller, D. *Leadership and Productivity: Some Facts of Industrial Life.* San Francisco: Chandler Publishing, 1965.

Edwards, Richard. "Alienation and Inequality: Capitalist Relations of Production in Bureaucratic Enterprises." Ph.D. dissertation, Harvard University, 1972.

Emery, F., and Thorsrud, E. *Democracy at Work.* Leiden: Martinus Nijhoff, 1976.

Espinosa, Juan Guillermo. "Los trabajadores, la participación y la propiedad sobre los medios de producción." *El Trimestre Económico* 40 (Abril–Junio 1973): 393–409.

————. "The Experience of Worker Participation in The Management of Industrial Firms (The Case of The Social Ownership Area in Chile: 1970–73)." Ph.D. dissertation, Cornell University, 1975.

Experiencias de masas. Santiago: Pastoral Popular, 1972.

Ferri, Franco. "El problema del control obrero." In *Consejos obreros y democracia socialista,* edited by V. Gerratana, pp. 75–94. *et al.* Córdoba, Argentina: Ediciones Pasado y Presente, 1972.

Fine, Keitha. "Worker Participation in Israel." In *Workers' Control,* edited by Gerry Hunnius, G. Garson, and J. Case, pp. 226–267. New York: Random House, Vintage Books, 1973.

Flanders, A.; Pomeranz, R.; and Woodward, J. *Experiment in Industrial Democracy.* London: Faber & Faber, 1968.

Foa, Lisa. "Los Soviets y octubre." In *Consejos obreros y democracia socialista,* edited by Gerrantana, pp. 99–124. Córdoba, Argentina: Ediciones Pasado y Presente, 1972.

"Foro sobre participación," *Panorama Económico* (September 1972): 16–32.

Frank, André Gunder. *Capitalism and Underdevelopment in Latin America.* New York: Monthly Review Press, 1969.

Freire, Paolo. *Pedagogy of the Oppressed.* New York: Seabury Press, 1973.

French, J.R.P.; Israel, J.; and Aas, D. "An Experiment in Participation in a Norwegian Factory." *Human Relations* 13 (1960): 3–19.

Fromm, Erich. "Escape from Freedom." In *Self-Governing Socialism,* edited by Branko Horvat, M. Marković, and R. Supek, pp. 396–404. White Plains, N.Y.: International Arts and Sciences Press, 1975.

Garcés, Joán. *1970: La pugna política por la presidencia en Chile.* Santiago: Editorial Universitaria, 1971.

―――. "The Popular Unity Government's Workers' Participation Model: Some Conditioning Factors." In *The Chilean Road to Socialism,* edited by Ann Zammit, pp. 181–186. Sussex: Institute of Development Studies at the University of Sussex, 1973.

Garretón, Oscar, and Cisternas, Jaime. "Algunas características de proceso de toma de decisiones en la gran empresa: La dinámica de concentración." Mimeographed. Santiago: University of Chile, 1970.

Garson, G. David. "Recent Developments in Workers' Participation in Europe." In *Self-Management,* edited by J. Vanek, pp. 161–186. Baltimore: Penguin, 1975.

Gil, Federico. *The Political System of Chile.* Boston: Houghton Mifflin, 1966.

Gintis, Herbert. "Education, Attitudes and Worker Productivity." *American Economic Review* 61 (May 1971): 266–279.

―――. "Alienation in Capitalist Society." In *The Capitalist System,* edited by Richard Edwards, M. Reich and T. Weisskopf, pp. 274–286. Englewood Cliffs: Prentice-Hall, 1972.

Goldthorpe, John H. "Industrial Relations in Great Britain: A Critique of Reformism." *Politics and Society* 4 (1974): 419–452.

Goldthorpe, John H.; Lockwood, D.; Bechhofer, F.; and Platt, J. *The Affluent Worker: Industrial Attitudes and Behavior.* Cambridge: At the University Press, 1968.

Goldwasser, J., and Dowty, S. *Huan-Ying: Workers' China.* New York: Monthly Review Press, 1975.

Gooding, Judson. "It Pays to Wake Up the Blue-Collar Worker." *Fortune* 82 (September 1970): 133–168.

Gooding, Judson. *The Job Revolution.* New York: Macmillan 1972.

Gordon, D.; Reich, M.; and Edwards, R. "Labor Market Segmentation in American Capitalism." Mimeographed. Cambridge: Harvard University, 1974.

Gorz, André. "Domestic Contradictions of Advanced Capitalism." In *The Capitalist System,* edited by Edwards *et al.,* pp. 478–491. Englewood Cliffs: Prentice-Hall, 1972.

―――. *Strategy for Labor.* Boston: Beacon Press, 1964.

Gouldner, Alvin. *Patterns of Industrial Bureaucracy: A Case Study of Modern Factory Administration.* New York: The Free Press, 1964.

Gramsci, Antonio. "Los consejos de fábrica en Italia." In E. Mandel, pp. 74–103. *Control obrero, consejos obreros y autogestión,* edited by Santiago: Ediciones Carlos Mariátegui, 1973.

Granick, David. *El hombre de empresa soviético.* Madrid: Ediciones de la Revista de Occidente, 1966.

Griffin, Keith. *Underdevelopment in Spanish America.* Cambridge: MIT Press, 1969.

Gurvitch, Georges. *Les cadres sociaux de la connaissance.* Paris: Presses Universitaires de France, 1966.

Habakkuk, H. J. *Technological Change in the Machine Tool Industry.* New York: Asia Publishing House, 1967.

Hampden-Turner, Charles. *Radical Man: The Process of Psycho-Social Development.* Cambridge, Mass.: Schenkman Publishing Co., 1970.

Harnecker, Marta. *Cuba: Dictadura o democracia?* Mexico City: Siglo Veintiuno, 1975.

Harper, Paul. "Workers' Participation in Management in Communist China." Paper presented at Sixtieth Annual Meeting of the American Political Science Association, September 1970, Los Angeles.

Heilbroner, Robert. "The False Promise of Growth." *New York Review of Books* 24 (March 3, 1977): 10–12.

Herman, Peter. "Workers, Watches and Self-Management." *Working Papers for a New Society* (Winter 1974):

Herzberg, Frederick. *Work and the Nature of Man.* London: Staples Press, 1968.

Hinkelammert, Franz, and Villela, R. "Autogestión, participación y democracia socialista." *Mensaje* (June 1971).

Hinton, William. "Reflections on China." *Monthly Review* 25 (June 1973): 30–43.

Hirschman, A. O. *The Strategy of Economic Development.* New Haven: Yale University Press, 1958.

Hoffmann, Charles. *The Chinese Worker.* Albany: State University of New York Press, 1975.

Holter, H. "Attitudes towards Employee Participation in Company Decision-Making Processes." *Human Relations* 18 (1965): 297–321.

Holubenko, M. "The Soviet Working Class: Discontent and Opposition." *Critique* 1 (Spring 1975): 5–26.

Horvat, Branko. "A New Social System in The Making: Historical Origins and Development of Self-Governing Socialism." In *Self-Governing Socialism,* vol. I, edited by Branko Horvat, M. Marković and R. Supek, pp. 3–66. White Plains, N.Y.: International Arts and Sciences Press, 1975.

——— *The Yugoslav Economic System: The First Labor-Managed Economy in the Making.* White Plains, N.Y.: International Arts and Sciences Press, 1976.

Howe, Christopher. "Labor Organization and Incentives in Industry, before and after the Cultural Revolution." In *Authority, Participation and Cultural Change in China,* edited by S. Schram. pp. 233–256. Cambridge: At the University Press, 1973.

Huerta, Pedro, and Jamis, Ricardo. "Evaluación de sistemas de participación organizacional: Informe sobre Ardigas-Sotramet E.T.A., Cootralaco and CRAV." Santiago: University of Chile, School of Economics, 1972.

Hunnius, Gerry. "Workers' Self-Management in Yugoslavia." In *Workers' Control,* edited by Gerry Hunrius, G. Garson and J. Case, pp. 268–322. New York: Random House, Vintage Books, 1973.

Hyatt, James. "Workers' Capitalism: Free Distribution of Stock to Employees Are Spurred by a New Tax Law Provision." *Wall Street Journal,* April 29, 1975.

Instituto de Economía y Planificación. *La economía chilena en 1972.* Santiago: Instituto de Economía y Planificación, 1973.

International Labor Organization (I.L.O. or O.I.T.). *Participation of Workers in Decisions within Undertakings.* Geneva: Labor-Management Relations Series no. 33 and no. 48, 1969 and 1975.

James, Richard, "Employees' Suggestion Erupts in Legal Fight for United Airlines." *Wall Street Journal,* February 23, 1976.

Jenkins, David. *Job Power: Blue and White Collar Democracy.* Garden City, N.Y.: Doubleday, 1973.

————. "Democracy in The Workplace: The Human Factories." *The Nation* 218 (January 12, 1974): 45–48.

Jones, Derek C. "Economic Aspects of British Producer Cooperatives: Preliminary Results." Paper presented at the First Annual Conference of People for Self-Management, January 12–13, 1974, Cambridge, Mass.

Jović, Borisav. *Economic Development of Yugoslavia.* Belgrade: Federal Committee for Information, 1975.

Kannappan, Subbiah. "Workers' Participation in Management: A Review of Indian Experience." *International Institute for Labour Studies Bulletin* 3 (November 1968): 138–220.

Karl, Terry. "Work Incentives in Cuba." *Latin American Perspectives* 2 (1975): 21–41.

Karlsson, Lars. "Industrial Democracy in Sweden." In *Workers' Control,* edited by Gerry Hunnius, G. Garson and J. Case, pp. 176–193. New York: Random House, Vintage Books, 1973a.

————. "Experiences in Employee Participation in Sweden: 1969–1972," Ithaca, N.Y.: Cornell University, Program on Participation and Labor-Managed Systems, 1973b.

Katz, Daniel, and Kahn, Robert. *The Social Psychology of Organizations.* New York: John Wiley & Sons, 1966.

Kaus, Robert Michael. "Job Enrichment and Capitalist Hierarchy." B.A. honors thesis in social studies, Harvard College, 1973.

Khitrov, L. "The Role of Management and Workers in Raising the Efficiency of Soviet Industry." *International Labor Review* 3 (June 1975): 507–526.

Kirsch, Leonard. *Soviet Wages: Changes in Structure and Administration since 1956.* Cambridge: MIT Press, 1972.

Knight, Peter. "New Forms of Economic Organization in Peru: Toward Workers' Self-Management." In *The Peruvian Experiment,* edited by A. F. Lowenthal, pp. 350–401. Princeton: Princeton University Press, 1975a.

————. "Social Property in Peru: The Political Economy of Predominance." Mimeographed. Ithaca, N.Y.: Cornell University, Department of Economics, September 1975b.

Kolaya, Jiri. "Workers' Participation in the Management of a Polish Textile Factory." *Human Organization* 19 (1960): 13–16.

————. "A Yugoslav Workers' Council," *Human Organization* 20 (1961): 27–31.

Kollontai, Aleksandra. "The Workers' Opposition in Russia." In *Self-Governing Socialism,* vol. I edited by Branko Horvat, M. Marković and R. Supek, pp. 163–172. White Plains, N.Y.: International Arts and Sciences Press, 1975.

Kovanda, Karel. "The Works Councils in Czechoslovakia, 1945–47", *Soviet Studies* 29 (1977): 255–269.

Kuznets, Simon. *Modern Economic Growth.* New Haven: Yale University Press, 1966.

Lange, Oscar. "On the Economic Theory of Socialism." *Review of Economic Studies* 4 (October 1936 and February 1937): 53–71; 123–142.

Lardy, Nicholas R. "Economic Planning in the People's Republic of China: Central-Provincial Fiscal Relations." In *China: A Reassessment of the Economy,* U.S., Congress, Joint Economic Committee. Washington, D.C.: U.S. Government Printing Office, 1975.

Lauterbach, Albert. "Executive Training and Productivity: Managerial Views in Latin America." *Industrial and Labor Relations Review* 17 (April 1964): 357–379.

Lawrence, Paul, and Lorsch, Jay. *Organization and Environment.* Cambridge: Harvard University Press, 1967.

Leavitt, Harold J. "Applied Organization Change in Industry: Structural, Technical and Human Approaches." In *Management and Motivation,* edited by Victor H. Vroom and E. Deci, pp. 363–376. Baltimore: Penguin Books, 1973.

Lee, Rensselaer W. "The Hsia Fang System: Marxism and Modernization." *China Quarterly* 7 (October–December 1966): 40–62.

Lehmann, David. "Worker Participation in the Soviet Union." In *The Chilean Road to Socialism*, edited by Ann Zammit, pp. 192–211. Brighton: University of Sussex, Institute of Development Studies, 1973.

Leibenstein, Harvey. "Technical Progress, the Production Function and Development." In *The Economics of Take-Off*, by W. W. Rostow, pp. 185–200. New York: St. Martin's Press, 1966a.

———. "Allocative Efficiency vs. X-Efficiency." *American Economic Review* 56 (June 1966b): 392–415.

Lenin, V. I. "The Immediate Tasks of the Soviet Government." In *Selected Works*, vol. 2, part 1, by V. I. Lenin, pp. 448–491. London: Lawrence and Wishart, 1953.

Lesieur, Frederick. *The Scanlon Plan.* Cambridge: MIT Press, 1958.

Ley, Ronald. "Labor Turnover as a Function of Worker-Differences, Work Environment, and Authoritarianism of Foremen." *Journal of Applied Psychology* 50 (1966): 497–500.

Likert, Rensis. *The Human Organizations.* New York: McGraw-Hill, 1967.

Lipset, Seymour M.; Trow, Martin; and Coleman, James. *Union Democracy.* Garden City, N.Y.: Doubleday, Anchor Books, 1956.

MacEwan, Arthur. "Incentives, Equality and Power in Revolutionary Cuba." *Socialist Revolution* 4 (Fall 1974): 87–108.

Machlup, Fritz. *The Production and Distribution of Knowledge in the United States.* Princeton: Princeton University Press, 1962.

Mandel, Ernest, ed. *Control obrero, consejos obreros y autogestión.* Santiago: Ediciones Carlos Mariátegui, 1972.

Mandel, William. *Russian Re-examined: The Land, The People and How They Live.* New York: Hill and Wang, 1964.

Manns, Patricio. *El movimiento obrero.* Santiago: Quimantú, 1972.

Marchetti, Peter, and Maffei, Eugenio. "Estructura agraria y consejos comunales campesinos: situación actual, análisis y estrategia." *Cuadernos de la Realidad Nacional* 14 (October 1972): 81–104.

Marglin, Stephen. *Economic and Social Rights in the Advanced Capitalist World.* Report to the Division of Human Rights, United Nations, January 1973.

———. "What Do Bosses Do? The Origins and Functions of Hierarchy in Capitalist Production." *Review of Radical Political Economics* 6 (Summer 1974): 60–112.

Mamalakis, Markos, "Historical Statistics of Chile, 1840–1965." Mimeographed. Economic Growth Center, Yale University, 1968.

Marotta, Mercedes, and Urzúa, Pedro. "Evaluación de la participación en la empresa A." Mimeographed. Santiago: University of Chile, School of Economics, 1973.

Marx, Karl. *Capital.* New York: International Publishers, 1967.

———. *Economic and Philosophic Manuscripts of 1844.* New York: International Publishers, 1971.

Marx, Karl and Engels, Frederick. "Germany: Revolution and Counter-Revolution." In *Selected Works*, vol. 2, by Karl Marx, pp. 39–153. London: Lawrence and Wishart, 1942.

Maslow, A. H. "A Theory of Human Motivation." In *Management and Motivation*, edited by Victor H. Vroom and E. Deci, pp. 27–41. Baltimore: Penguin Books, 1973.

Mattelart, Michele, and Piccini, M. "La prensa burguesa: No será más que un tigre de papel?" *Cuadernos de la Realidad Nacional* (April 1973): 250–263.

Mayoría, February 16, 1972.

McGregor, Douglas. *The Human Side of Enterprise.* New York: McGraw-Hill, 1960.

Meissner, Mitch. "The Shenyang Transformer Factory—A Profile." *The China Quarterly* 52 (1972): 717–737.

Melman, Seymour. *Dynamic Factors in Industrial Productivity.* New York: John Wiley & Sons, 1956.

————. *Decision-Making and Productivity.* Oxford: Basil Blackwell, 1958.

————. "Industrial Efficiency under Managerial vs. Cooperative Decision-Making." *The Review of Radical Political Economics* 2 (Spring 1970): 10–31.

Mills, Ted. "Human Resources—Why the New Concern?" *Harvard Business Review* 53 (March–April 1975): 120–134.

Molina, Sergio. *El proceso de cambio en Chile.* Santiago: Editorial Universitaria, 1972.

Morris, David. *We Must Make Haste—Slowly.* New York: Random House, Vintage Books, 1973.

Mulcahy, Susan. "Blue-Collar Women: Patterns of Work and Commitment in a Factory." M. A. dissertation, University of Massachusetts, Amherst, 1976.

Myrdal, Jan. *Report from a Chinese Village.* New York: Pantheon, 1965.

North American Congress on Latin America. "Facing the Blockade." *NACLA's Latin America and Empire Report,* 7 (January 1973a): 1–32.

————. "Chile: The Story Behind the Coup." *NACLA's Latin America and Empire Report* 7 (October 1973b): 1–32.

————. "U.S. Counter-Revolutionary Apparatus: The Chilean Offensive." *NACLA's Latin America and Empire Report* 8 (July–August 1974): 1–39.

Narkiewicz, Olga A. *The Making of The Soviet State Apparatus.* Manchester: Manchester University Press, 1970.

Nazar, Víctor. "El autoritarismo en la clase obrera chilena y el proceso de cambios en las relaciones sociales de producción." *Cuadernos de la Realidad Nacional* (July 1972): 222–234.

Noe, Marcela. "La central única de trabajadores: Orientaciones de su acción histórica." *Cuadernos de la Realidad Nacional* (June 1971): 43–53.

Northrup, Bowen. "Working Happier: More Swedish Firms Attempt to Enrich Production-Line Jobs." *Wall Street Journal,* October 25, 1974.

Núñez, Osvaldo. "La participación: Antecedentes y dificultades de un desarrollo formidable." *Revista Laboral,* Minister of Labor, Santiago, 1972.

Oakeshott, R. "Mondragon: Spain's Oasis of Democracy." In *Self-Management,* edited by J. Vanek, pp. 290–298. Baltimore: Penguin Books, 1975.

Obradovic, Josep. "Distribution of Participation in the Process of Decision Making on Problems Related to the Economic Activity of the Company." In *Participation and Self-Management,* Vol. 2, edited by Eugen Pusić and Rudi Supek, pp. 137–164. Zagreb: Council of the Federation of Trade Unions of Yugoslavia, 1972.

Organización Internacional del Trabajo (O.I.T. or I.L.O.). *La participación de los trabajadores en las decisiones que se adoptan en las empresas.* Geneva: Oficina Internacional del Trabajo, 1969.

Opsahl, Robert, and Dunnette, Marvin. "The Role of Financial Compensation in Industrial Motivation." In *Management and Motivation,* edited by Victor H. Vroom and E. Deci, pp. 127–159. Baltimore: Penguin Books, 1973.

Pásara, L., and Santistevan, J. "Industrial Communities and Trade Unions in Peru." *International Labour Review* 108 (August 1973): 127–142.

Pateman, Carole. *Participation and Democratic Theory.* Cambridge: At the University Press, 1970.

Pearson, Donald W. "The *Comunidad Industrial:* Peru's Experiment in Worker Management." *Inter-American Economic Affairs* 27 (Summer 1973): 15–29.

Pelikan, Jiri. "Workers' Councils in Czechoslovakia." *Critique* 1 (Spring 1973): 7–19.

Peppe, Pat. "Working-Class Politics in Chile." Ph.D. dissertation, Columbia University, 1971.

Perrow, Charles. "A Framework for the Comparative Analysis of Organizations." *American Sociological Review* 32 (1967): 194–208.

Petras, James. "Regionalism and Working Class Politics in Argentina," *Liberation* 17 (August 1972a): 60–68.

————. "Chile: Nacionalización, cambio socio-económico y participación popular." *Cuadernos de la Realidad Nacional* (January 1972b): 3–24.

Petras, James, and Morley, M. *The United States and Chile: Imperialism and the Overthrow of the Allende Government.* New York: Monthly Review Press, 1975.

Pinto, Aníbal. *Chile: Un caso de desarrollo frustrado.* Santiago: Editorial Universitaria, 1962.

Prankratova, A. "Los comités de fábrica en Rusia en el período de la revolución." In *Control obrero, consejos obreros y autogestión,* edited by Ernest Mandel. Santiago: Ediciones Carlos Mariátegui, 1972.

Pugh, D. S.; Hickson, D. J.; Hinings, C. R.; and Turner, C. "Dimensions of Organizational Structure." *Administrative Science Quarterly* 13 (1968): 65–105.

————. "The Content of Organizational Structures." *Administrative Science Quarterly* 14 (1969): 91–114.

Quijano, Aníbal. *Nationalism and Capitalism in Peru: A Study in Neo-Imperialism.* New York: Monthly Review Press, 1972.

Ramírez, Hernan Necochea. *Historia del movimiento obrero en Chile, siglo XIX.* Santiago: Editorial Austral, 1956.

Ramos, Sergio. *Chile: Una economía de transición?* Santiago: Editorial Prensa Latinoamericana, 1972.

Reich, Michael. "The Evolution of the United States Labor Force." In *The Capitalist System,* edited by Richard Edwards, M. Reich, and T. Weisskopf, pp. 174–183. Englewood Cliffs: Prentice-Hall, 1972.

Revista Agraria of Chile Hoy, January 1973, February 1973, April 1973, May 1973.

Ribeiro, Lucia, and DeBarbierre, Teresita. "La mujer obrera chilena: Una aproximación a su estudio." *Cuadernos de la Realidad Nacional* (April 1973): 167–202.

Rice, A. K. *The Enterprise and Its Environment.* London: Tavistock, 1963.

Richman, Barry. *Industrial Society in Communist China.* New York: Random House, 1969.

Riquelme, Hernán, and Gonzales, Aliro. "Trabajo práctico de participación en fábrica B." Mimeographed. Santiago: University of Chile, School of Economics, 1973.

Riskin, Carl. "Incentive Systems and Work Motivation: The Experience of China." *Working Papers for a New Society* 1 (Winter 1974): 27–89.

Rivero, Juan Lamas. *Estructura de la empresa y participación obrera.* Barcelona: Ediciones Ariel, 1969.

Robinson, Joan. *Economic Management in China.* London: Anglo-Chinese Educational Institute, 1973.

Rogers, Everett. *Diffusion of Innovations.* New York: Free Press, 1962.

Rosner, Menachem. "Principles, Types and Problems of Direct Democracy in the Kibbutz." In *The Kibbutz as a Way of Life in Modern Society,* Southfield, Mich.: College of Jewish Studies, 1970.

Saez, Arturo; Rogers, Patricio; and Castillo, Leonardo. "Notas para un estudio de la historia del movimiento obrero en chile." *Cuadernos de la Realidad Nacional* (June 1970): 3–30.

Salvadori, Massimo. "Orígines y crisis del sovietismo." In *Consejos Obreros y Democracia Socialista,* edited by V. Gerratana *et al.* pp. 39–56. Córdoba: Ediciones Pasado y Presente, 1972.

Schauer, Helmut. "Critique of Co-Determination." In *Workers' Control,* edited by Gerry Hunnius, G. Garson and J. Case, pp. 210–225. New York: Random House, Vintage Books, 1973.

Schell, Orville. *In the People's Republic: An American's Firsthand View of Living and Working in China.* New York: Random House, 1977.

Schurmann, Franz. *Ideology and Organization in Communist China.* Berkeley and Los Angeles: University of California Press, 1968.

Schwarz, Solomon. *Labor in the Soviet Union.* New York: Praeger, 1951.

Selden, Mark. *The Yenan Way in Revolutionary China.* Cambridge: Harvard University Press, 1971.

Seven Days, February 14, 1977.

Shearer, Derek. "Social Democracy in British Columbia." *Ramparts* 12 (February 1974): 21–26.

Sheppard, Harold. "Task Enrichment and Wage Levels as Elements in Worker Attitudes." Paper presented at the Industrial Relations Research Association meetings, December 1973, New York.

"The Silent Crisis in R and D." *Business Week* (March 8, 1976): 90–92.

Smith, Adam. *The Wealth of Nations.* New York: Random House, 1937.

Smith, G.A.E. "Political Economy of the Soviet Reforms." *Critique* 1 (Spring 1975): 27–42.

Snow, Edgar. *Red Star Over China.* New York: Grove Press, 1968.

Stallings, Barbara. "Economic Development and Class Conflict in Chile, 1958–73." Ph.D. dissertation, Stanford University, 1975.

Stallings, Barbara, and Zimbalist, Andrew. "The Political Economy of the *Unidad Popular,*" *Latin American Perspectives* 2 (Spring 1975): 69–88.

Stone, Katherine. "The Origins of Job Structures in the Steel Industry." *The Review of Radical Political Economics* 6 (Summer 1974): 113–173.

"Stonewalling Plant Democracy," *Business Week* (March 28, 1977): 78–82.

Strassman, Paul. *Technological Change and Economic Development.* Ithaca, N.Y.: Cornell University Press, 1968.

Sturmthal, Adolf. *Workers' Councils.* Cambridge: Harvard University Press, 1964.

Sweden, Labor Legislation Committee. "Proposals for an Industrial Democracy Act." Vällingby: Swedish Ministry of Labor, 1975.

"Sweden Outdates Modern Times." *The Economist* (November 9, 1974).

"Sweden: Worker Participation Becomes the Law." *Business Week* (June 21, 1976).

Tabb, J. Y., and A. Goldfarb, *Workers' Participation in Management: Expectations and Experience.* Oxford: Pergamon Press, 1970.

Taylor, Frederick Winslow. *Scientific Management.* New York: Harper & Row, 1947.

Teillac, J. *Autogestion en Algerie.* Paris: Peyronnet, 1965.

Telly, Charles; French, Wendell; and Scott, William. "The Relationship of Inequity to Turnover among Hourly Workers." *Administrative Science Quarterly* 16 (June 1971): 164–172.

Thiesenhusen, William. "Agrarian Reform: Chile." In *Land Reform in Latin America,* edited by P. Dorner, pp. 103–126. Madison: Land Economics, 1971.

Thomas, Jack Ray. "The Socialist Republic of Chile." *Journal of Inter-American Studies* 6 (April 1964): 203–221.

Touraine, Alain. *Workers' Attitudes to Technical Change.* Paris: O.E.C.D., 1965.

Trist, E. L., and Bamforth, K. W. "Technicism: Some Effects of Material Technology on Managerial Methods and on Work Situation and Relationships." In *Industrial Man,* edited by Tom Burns, pp. 331–358. Baltimore: Penguin Books, 1969.

Trist, E. L.; Higgin, G. W.; Murray, H.; and Pollock, A. B. *Organizational Choice.* London: Tavistock, 1963.

Trotsky, Leon. *The Revolution Betrayed.* New York: Pathfinder Press, 1972.

———. "Programa de transición de la IV internacional (1938)." In *Control obrero, consejos obreros y autogestión,* edited by Ernest Mandel, pp. 144–170. Santiago: Ediciones Carlos Mariátegui, 1972.

Turner, Steve. "Caution: Working May Be Dangerous," *The Valley Advocate* (March 2, 1977): 5–8.

U.S., Congress, Senate, Foreign Relations Committee. *Covert Action in Chile, 1963–73.* Washington, D.C.: U.S. Government Printing Office, 1975.

U.S., Department of Commerce. *Statistical Abstract of the United States.* Washington, D.C.: U.S. Government Printing Office, various years.

U.S., Department of Health, Education and Welfare. *Work in America.* Cambridge: MIT Press, 1972.

U.S., Department of Labor, Bureau of Labor Statistics. *Monthly Labor Review,* January 1972, July 1973, August 1975, October 1975.

Valencia, Luis. "La participación del trabajador en la administración de la empresa: El caso chileno." Thesis for degree of commercial engineer, University of Chile, 1968.

Valenzuela, Julio S. "The Chilean Labor Movement: The Institutionalization of Conflict." In *Chile: Politics and Society,* edited by Arturo Valenzuela and J. Samuel Valenzuela, pp. 135–172. New Brunswick, New Jersey: Transaction Books, 1976.

Vanek, Jaroslav. *The General Theory of Labor-Managed Economies.* Ithaca, N.Y.: Cornell University Press, 1970.

———. *The Participatory Economy.* Ithaca, N.Y.: Cornell University Press, 1971.

Vanek, Jaroslav, and Espinosa, Juan G. "General Program for Peru as a Participatory Economy." Report to the Peruvian Government, September 1971.

———. "The Subsistence Income Effort and Development Potential of Labor Management and Other Economic Systems." *Economic Journal* 82 (September 1972): 1000–1013.

Vroom, Victor H. "Industrial Social Psychology." In *The Handbook of Social Psychology,* edited by G. Lindsey and E. Aaronsen, pp. 196–268. Reading, Mass.: Addison-Wesley, 1969.

———. "The Nature of the Relationship between Motivation and Performance." In *Management and Motivation,* edited by Victor H. Vroom and E. Deci, pp. 229–236. Baltimore: Penguin Books, 1973.

Vroom, Victor H. and E. Deci (eds.) *Management and Motivation.* Baltimore: Penguin Books, 1973.

Wachtel, Howard. *Workers' Management and Workers' Wages in Yugoslavia.* Ithaca, N.Y.: Cornell University Press, 1973.

Walker, Kenneth, and de Bellecombe, L. G. "Participación de los trabajadores en la gestión empresarial." *Boletín No. 2 del Instituto Internacional de Estudios Laborales* (February 1967).

Ward, Benjamin. *The Socialist Economy. A Study of Organizational Alternatives.* New York: Random House, 1967.

Weber, Max. *The Theory of Social and Economic Organization.* New York: Oxford University Press, 1947.

Wheelwright, E. L., and McFarlane, Bruce. *The Chinese Road to Socialism.* New York: Monthly Review Press, 1970.

Whisler, Thomas, and Leavitt, Harold "Management in the 1980's." *Harvard Business Review* 36 (1958): 41–48.

Whyte, William F. *Money and Motivation.* New York: Harper & Row, 1955.

Winn, Peter. "Workers into Managers: Worker Participation in The Chilean Textile Industry." Paper presented at the Sixtieth International Congress of Ethnology and Anthropology, September 1973, Chicago.

Woodward, Joan. *Industrial Organization: Theory and Practice.* Oxford: At the University Press, 1965.

Zammit, Ann, ed. *The Chilean Road to Socialism.* Brighton: University of Sussex, Institute of Development Studies, 1973.

Zapata, Francisco. "The Chilean Labor Movement and Problems of the Transition to Socialism." *Latin American Perspectives* 3 (Winter 1976): 85–97.

Zapp, Kenny. "Summary Conclusions on Yugoslav Workers' Self-Management." Mimeographed. Allendale, Mich.: William James College,1973.

Zeitlin, Maurice. *Revolutionary Politics and the Cuban Working Class.* New York: Harper & Row, 1970.

Zimbalist, Andrew. "La expansión de la educación primaria y el desarrollo capitalista: El caso de Chile." *Revista del Centro de Estudios Educativos* (Mexico) 3 (1973): 51–72.

———. "Worker Participation in the Management of Socialized Industry: An Empirical Study of the Chilean Experience under Allende." Ph.D. dissertation, Harvard University, 1974.

————. "The Dynamic of Worker Participation: An Interpretive Essay on the Chilean and Other Experiences." *Administration and Society* 7 (May 1975a): 43–54.

————. "Worker Participation in Cuba." *Challenge, The Magazine of Economic Affairs* 18 (November–December 1975b): 45–54.

————. "The Limits of Work Humanization." *Review of Radical Political Economics* 7 (1975c): 50–60.

————. "Worker Management of Industry." *Journal of Economic Issues* 10 (June 1976): 476–489.

Zimbalist, Andrew, and Stallings, Barbara. "Showdown in Chile." *Monthly Review* 25 (October 1973): 1–24.

Zupanov, J., and Tannenbaum, A. S. "The Distribution of Control in Some Yugoslav Industrial Organizations as Perceived by Members." In *Control in Organizations,* edited by A. S. Tannenbaum, pp. 91–109. New York: McGraw-Hill, 1968.

Zwerdling, Daniel. "Beyond Boredom—A Look at What's New on the Assembly Line." *The Washington Monthly* 5 (July–August 1973): 80–92.

————. "Managing Workers." *Working Papers for a New Society* 2 (Fall 1974): 11–15.

Index

A

Absenteeism, changes in, 143–146, 172–173, 184

Administrative staff, effect on P_F, 88, 93–95

Age, effect on P_F, 96

Agrarian reform (Chile), 31, 8n

Alessandri, Arturo, 36

Allende, Salvador, 34, 37, 42, 43, 48–50, 134–135, 146–147, 156, 162, 165, 178–179

Argentina, 3

Arroyo, Victor, 41, 42

C

Canada, 192

Chilean labor movement
  history of, 35–38
  unionization by sector, 31
  labor code, 36, 52n

China, 25, 27–28, 114, 139, 149n, 161

Christian Democratic party of Chile, 39–43, 45, 48, 51, 77, 100, 104, 106, 148, 157, 183

Communist party of Chile, 77, 100, 104–106, 148, 183

CORFO (Chilean Development Corporation), 46, 54, 56, 70n, 133, 135

Cuba, 25, 139, 143, 161

CUT (Chilean Central Trade Union Federation), 37, 51, 53, 56, 70n, 77, 99, 132
  May 1972 elections, 100 ff.

Czechoslovakia, 106

D

Denmark, 5

deTocqueville, Alexis, 14

Discipline, changes in, 141–143, 172–173, 184

Disposition of the administration, effect on P_F, 114–117, 183

Distribution system, changes in 135–136

E

Education, effect on P_F, 96–104, 182

England, 4, 6, 22, 88, 139, 160

F

Figueroa, Luis, 105

France, 3, 89n

Frei, Eduardo (government of), 29–30, 39–43, 45, 153

Freire, Paolo, 98, 102, 104, 133, 182

H

Hawthorne experiments, 159, 168–169

Horizontal differentiation, effect on P_F, 86, 93–95, 181–182

Hungary, 106

I

I.L.O. (International Labor Organization), 1, 3–6, 58

Income distribution (Chile), 31–32

India, 4, 160

Industrial structure (Chile), 33–34

Information, system of, effect on P_F, 114–117, 183

Innovations, 148–151, 172–173

Investment, 152–157, 172–173, 185

Israel, 6, 139, 161

L

Labor force variables, effect on P_F, 95–113, 119, 181–183
Labor mobilization, effect on P_F, 102–104, 182
Lenin, V. I., 2, 106

M

Marx, Karl, 14–15, 88, 139n
Mayo, Elton, *see* Hawthorne experiments
Mexico, 3, 158
Mill, John Stuart, 188

N

Normas básicas de participación, 51–56
Norway, 160

P

Peru, 3
P_F, index of worker participation *see* Worker participation, index of
Poland, 106, 128, 139, 160
Political democracy, 19, 86, 186–189, 191–193
Political organization, effect on P_F, 104–113, 182–183
Political parties, effect on P_F, 105–108, 113, 182–183
Popular Unity Government (UP), 45–51, 186
Product line, changes in, 134–135
Productivity, and P_F, 20, 157–175, 185

R

Rousseau, Jean Jacques, 188

S

Scanlon Plan, 4, 20, 139, 149n
Scientific management, 15, 16, 19, 85, 100, *see also* Taylor, F. W.
Sex, effect on P_F, 96
Size of enterprise, effect on P_F, 88, 93–95
Smith, Adam, 14, 134
Social services, provision of, 131–132, 172–173, 184
Soviet Union, 25, 27–28, 106, 139n, 141n, 149n, 161, 169
Spain, 3, 6, 88, 139, 160, 185
Span of control, effect on P_F, 88, 93–95

Strike activity, changes in, 146–147, 172–173, 184
Sweden, 3, 4, 18, 24, 160

T

Taylor, F. W., 15–16, 19, 106, 134, 142, 168, 191–192
Technology, 85–95, 113, 119, 151, 166–167, 181–182, 185,
    effect on P_F, 85–94, 113, 119, 182, 185
    effect on innovations, 151
    effect on productivity, 166–167
Technostructure, and P_F, 85–95, 119, 181
Thefts and defective products, changes in, 147–148, 164–165, 172–173, 184
Tomic, Rodomiro, 34, 43, 45
Training courses, 101, 132–134, 145

U

Unions, effect on P_F, 108–113, 182–183
United States
    absenteeism, 20
    evolution of labor force, 17
    industrial accidents, 19
    labor turnover, 20
    quit rate, 20

V

Vertical differentiation, effect on P_F, 87, 93–95
Vogel, Ernesto, 105

W

Wage structure, changes in, 138–141, 169–171, 184–185
    wage inequality and work effort, 138–139
    wage equalization and P_F, 140–141
    collective wages and P_F, 140–141
    piece-rates and P_F, 140–141
    wage structure and productivity, 169–171
Weberian theory of bureaucracy, 85–88, 168
West Germany, 5, 6
Work humanization, 20–24, 158, 160, 187, 192
    experiments
        General Foods Corporation, 23, 192n
        Polaroid Corporation, 22
        Rushton Coal Mine, 23n

Work organization, changes in
  job rotation, 136–138
  job enlargement, 136–138
  working conditions, 136–138
  elimination of supervisors, 136–138
Worker participation index, P_F
  characteristics of, 67–70

  construction of, 57–63, 74–82, 180–181
  reliability of, 63–66

Y

Yugoslavia, 5, 26–27, 139, 158–159, 182, 185

A
B
C 8
D 9
E 0
F 1
G 2
H 3
I 4
J 5

STUDIES IN SOCIAL DISCONTINUITY

Under the Consulting Editorship of:

CHARLES TILLY
University of Michigan

EDWARD SHORTER
University of Toronto

William A. Christian, Jr. Person and God in a Spanish Valley

Joel Samaha. Law and Order in Historical Perspective: The Case of Elizabethan Essex

John W. Cole and Eric R. Wolf. The Hidden Frontier: Ecology and Ethnicity in an Alpine Valley

Immanuel Wallerstein. The Modern World-System: Capitalist Agriculture and the Origins of the European World-Economy in the Sixteenth Century

John R. Gillis. Youth and History: Tradition and Change in European Age Relations 1770 – Present

D. E. H. Russell. Rebellion, Revolution, and Armed Force: A Comparative Study of Fifteen Countries with Special Emphasis on Cuba and South Africa

Kristian Hvidt. Flight to America: The Social Background of 300,000 Danish Emigrants

James Lang. Conquest and Commerce: Spain and England in the Americas

Stanley H. Brandes. Migration, Kinship, and Community: Tradition and Transition in a Spanish Village

Daniel Chirot. Social Change in a Peripheral Society: The Creation of a Balkan Colony

Jane Schneider and Peter Schneider. Culture and Political Economy in Western Sicily

Michael Schwartz. Radical Protest and Social Structure: The Southern Farmers' Alliance and Cotton Tenancy, 1880-1890

Ronald Demos Lee (Ed.). Population Patterns in the Past

David Levine. Family Formations in an Age of Nascent Capitalism

Dirk Hoerder. Crowd Action in Revolutionary Massachusetts, 1765-1780

Charles P. Cell. Revolution at Work: Mobilization Campaigns in China

Frederic L. Pryor. The Origins of the Economy: A Comparative Study of Distribution in Primitive and Peasant Economies

Harry W. Pearson. The Livelihood of Man by Karl Polanyi

Richard Maxwell Brown and Don E. Fehrenbacher (Eds.). Tradition, Conflict, and Modernization: Perspectives on the American Revolution

Juan G. Espinosa and Andrew S. Zimbalist. Economic Democracy: Workers' Participation in Chilean Industry 1970-1973

In preparation

Randolph Trumbach. The Rise of the Egalitarian Family: Aristocratic Kinship and Domestic Relations in Eighteenth-Century England

Arthur L. Stinchcombe. Theoretical Methods in Social History

H. A. Gemery and J. S. Hogendorn (Eds.). The Uncommon Market: Essays in the Economic History of the Atlantic Slave Trade

This is a volume in

STUDIES IN SOCIAL DISCONTINUITY

A complete list of titles in this series appears at the end of this volume.

Economic Democracy

Workers' Participation in Chilean Industry
1970–1973